100 THINGS VIRGINIA TECH FANS SHOULD KNOW & DO BEFORE THEY DIE

100 THINGS VIRGINIA TECH FANS SHOULD KNOW & DO BEFORE THEY DIE

Andy Bitter

Library of Congress Cataloging-in-Publication Data available upon request

This book is available in quantity at special discounts for your group or organization. For further information, contact:

Triumph Books LLC
814 North Franklin Street
Chicago, Illinois 60610
(312) 337-0747
www.triumphbooks.com

Printed in U.S.A.
ISBN: 978-1-62937-699-8
Design by Patricia Frey

To my two favorite girls, Annie and Emily

Contents

Acknowledgments

When Triumph Books first approached me about writing a book about Virginia Tech, I thought, "That sounds like a great experience—for the off-season."

The timing couldn't quite wait until January for me to start, so juggling a great new job at The Athletic, a book project, and a two-year-old daughter became life for the better part of 5½ months.

What made it possible was the substantial support from my family and the wealth of articles written by numerous sources about Hokies athletics that served as reference material for this book.

First, this all isn't possible without my wonderful wife, Annie McCallum, who not only offered words of encouragement throughout but also weathered the frequent complaints I'm sure all first-time book writers have. Also, thanks to my shining star of a daughter, Emily, for generally going to bed at a reasonable hour, allowing dad to get cracking on some chapters.

Writing this was not possible without the support, even from a distance, from family members. Mark and Judy McCallum offered that throughout the project. Jim and Rose Bitter have offered that my entire life, especially when a college kid at Wisconsin tried writing for the student paper one semester and kinda, sorta thought it might make for a neat career path.

I've been covering Virginia Tech athletics full-time since 2011, though my familiarity with the athletic department began when I got my first professional sportswriting job in Danville in 2002. You'll notice that many of the events chronicled in this book took place long before that, which required me to lean on the volumes of reporting done by numerous writers for decades.

Let's just say I'm fortunate to cover a school that's been so well chronicled over the years.

I was a newspaperman for the longest time, and writers at the *Roanoke Times*, *Richmond Times-Dispatch*, *Daily Press*, *Virginian-Pilot*, *Washington Post*, *Lynchburg News & Advance*, (Fredericksburg) *Free Lance-Star*, and others did a tremendous job of telling the story of the Hokies' history over the years. The *Daily Press*, in particular, should be lauded for successfully maintaining a functioning digital archive of its paper for what seems like at least 30 years back.

But the papers didn't produce those articles. The writers did. And to David Teel, Nathan Warters, Aaron McFarling, Norm Wood, Mike Barber, Mark Giannotto, Kyle Tucker, Darryl Slater, Randy King, Robert Anderson, Doug Doughty, Dave Fairbank, Dave Johnson, Ed Miller, Harry Minium, Mike Harris, Nate Crossman, Chris Lang, Adam Kilgore, Ava Wallace, Gene Wang, Mike Niziolek, Hank Kurz, and, yes, even Mark Berman, I owe a debt of gratitude.

That's not to ignore the contribution of online sites. The folks at TechSideline.com were particularly helpful, with Will Stewart and Chris Coleman offering their wealth of knowledge of Hokies history and passion as fans of the program to help me refine my list.

Chris Colston straddles the print and online world and was perhaps as important as anyone, helping me fill some gaps of forgotten players who starred before Virginia Tech was a household name. In publishing his series "Go Tech Go: The Inside Story about the Rise of Virginia Tech Football" on TechSideline, he provided as detailed of a timeline as there is of every significant Hokies football event from the '70s to Virginia Tech's admittance to the ACC. The autobiographies Colston and Jeff Snook each wrote with Frank Beamer were especially helpful.

Virginia Tech's media relations has been accommodating ever since I got on the Hokies beat, with Dave Smith and Bryan Johnston welcoming me here when I started and Pete Moris and

Peter Long putting up with my requests nowadays. Damian Salas and Jimmy Robertson should be commended for all the information available on the Hokies' website. To that end, the people I've interviewed at Virginia Tech over the years deserve thanks, too. Yes, Frank Beamer really is that nice. And people like Bill Roth, Dwight Vick, and Shane Beamer have graciously provided me their time and knowledge as go-to interviews over the years.

Steve Hemphill and Colleen McDaniel hired me to cover Tech back in 2011 and I'm grateful that they did.

The Athletic has been as good of an organization as I've ever worked for, and the support of my bosses, Dan Uthman, Stewart Mandel, and Mike Huguenin, and others in my first year on the job has been amazing. That they signed off on this project was particularly reassuring about their belief in my ability to juggle two fairly monumental tasks—covering a beat in a different way for a new company and writing a book for the first time.

Also, thanks to Triumph Books for even considering me for this undertaking.

This was an illuminating project, one that gave me a far deeper knowledge and understanding of Virginia Tech's athletics history than I ever thought I'd have. It wasn't easy to narrow this list to 100 topics, and though I've tried to include every significant contributor to Hokies football and a few other sports, inevitably there's someone that got short shrift.

This book is not meant to be the final say on Virginia Tech athletics history, but rather a starting point for a discussion. Chapters will undoubtedly move up and down the list if future editions of this book exist. Some might get dropped altogether for bigger, better stories that pop up in Blacksburg. Things change with time, after all. Who knows? Maybe the Hokies' briefly used Foghorn Leghorn–like helmet logo will look better 10 years from now (ehh, probably not).

Regardless, read the book and enjoy it for what it is: a look back at some of the most memorable games, people, eras, and experiences in Virginia Tech history. It was an honor to put it together.

1 Frank Beamer

After 29 years as Virginia Tech's head coach, Frank Beamer begrudgingly said goodbye, announcing in November 2015 that he'd retire at the end of the season. It was a tough decision, an emotional one, and tears welled in his eyes as his wife, Cheryl, stood by his side at the podium in front of a room full of family members, coaches, and players, when he called himself the most fortunate guy in the world.

As the Q&A session with the media began, Beamer was asked how he'd like to be remembered at Virginia Tech. He didn't mention his 238 victories, seven conference titles, national championship game appearance, or national Coach of the Year award, any of which would have been a worthy answer.

Instead, he hoped people would remember him as a person.

"He is who he is," Beamer said. "Honest, caring and respectful."

It's not just that Beamer helped Virginia Tech's football program reach new heights and established a consistent national presence in his nearly three decades as the team's head coach, guiding the Hokies from a football independent that was on NCAA probation to one attractive enough to be pursued by two conferences, win numerous league titles, and play in several major bowl games.

It's how he did it that puts him No. 1 in Hokies fans' hearts and minds; a caring and loyal mentor in a profession littered with coaches who aren't and an avuncular ambassador for Virginia Tech who's as recognizable as anyone in the university's history.

"I know he wanted to win a national championship," Cheryl said, mentioning the one missing piece in his impressive résumé.

"I've told him, 'You've already won one.' I said, 'Your national championship is the type of man you were and that legacy of how you treated people and the way these kids loved you.' I said, 'That's your national championship.' And those kids won't forget him."

To even get to coach at Virginia Tech was a storybook tale in itself. Beamer was born in Mount Airy, North Carolina, in 1946 and grew up in Fancy Gap, Virginia, in the southwest corner of the state, not far from Blacksburg.

He had a humble upbringing that gave him plenty of perspective in life. At age seven, he'd used a push broom to keep a pile of burning trash in place. A spark ignited a nearby can of gasoline, exploding in front of him and leaving him with burns on his shoulders, chest, and the right side of his neck. His brother, Barnett, saved his life by rolling him on the ground. After Beamer's hospital stay, his mother, Herma, wouldn't let him allow the scarring to hold him back in life.

"Mom would always tell me, 'Concentrate on what you have and be thankful for it. Don't waste any time feeling sorry for what you don't have or for what happened to you in the past,'" Beamer wrote in his autobiography *Let Me Be Frank* in 2013. "It taught me a lesson; something like, hey, take what you have, build on it, but it is what it is. Take the situation and ask, 'What can I do to make it better?'"

It became a guiding principle in his life and coaching career. Beamer played three sports at Hillsville High before coming to Virginia Tech, where he played defensive back. Wearing No. 25, he was a starting cornerback for three years under Jerry Claiborne, playing on teams that went to the Liberty Bowl in 1966 and '68.

He eventually got his college coaching start as a graduate assistant at age 25 for Claiborne at the University of Maryland in 1972, though it was a humble beginning. His first task was sitting on top of the visitors' locker room behind the end zone with a pair of binoculars, relaying through a headset to the Terps coaches what

Frank Beamer celebrates the Hokies' 20–7 win over Cincinnati in the 2009 Orange Bowl. (Lynne Sladky / AP Photo)

technique North Carolina's defensive tackle was playing. He did it dutifully for about 10 plays, getting no response. He soon figured out that nobody could hear him on the other end.

"I told Cheryl after we went back home, I said, 'Cheryl, I don't think I'm going to do this very long,'" Beamer said with a laugh.

Needless to say, it got better. He got a job as the defensive line coach on Bobby Ross' staff at The Citadel in 1973 and was promoted to defensive coordinator in 1977. He got the Murray State defensive coordinator job in 1979, first pairing up with a hard-hitting safety and outside linebacker named Bud Foster, and later got his first head coaching job there in 1981. After going 42–23–2 in six seasons, winning the Ohio Valley Conference in 1986 and making the I-AA playoffs, he was hired as the Hokies' head coach late in 1986.

He wasn't a sexy hire. Ross' name had been briefly mentioned as a possibility to replace the outgoing Bill Dooley, though he ended up going to Georgia Tech instead. When Beamer was hired, famously prickly *Roanoke Times* columnist Bill Brill wrote that Beamer's hire was like a kid on Christmas morning expecting to get a toy, only to open the box and see a sweater. Beamer's response? "Maybe Virginia Tech needed a sweater?"

The lack of enthusiasm from some didn't stop Beamer from dreaming big.

"I really think that someday we can play for national championships here," he declared in his introductory press conference, a statement as audacious as it was ambitious, given Tech's football history.

Had he known what he was getting into, he might not have been so bold. Unbeknownst to Beamer when athletic director Dutch Baughman hired him, the NCAA was about to hit Virginia Tech for violations committed by Dooley. When the hammer came down in 1987, with the football team losing 20 scholarships and placed on a two-year probation, it was yet another hurdle for a school that was a football nomad at the time, not tied to any conference.

Beamer's early teams struggled against a tough schedule. Though he came close to getting over the hump a couple times, a 2–8–1 season in 1992 seemed like it might be the end. He was 24–40–2 in six seasons with the Hokies at that point, a record that would get you fired at any school today.

When Virginia Tech lost a heartbreaker at Louisville early that year, a disgruntled fan called the Beamers' listed phone number and, when the coach's then 11-year-old daughter, Casey, picked up the phone, let loose with a string of insults about her dad, leaving her in tears. Beamer didn't let it get him or his family down.

"Part of that is he did such a good job of not bringing it home and not letting it affect my sister and me when I was at home," said his son, Shane, who'd later play as a long snapper at Tech and get into the coaching business himself, including with the Hokies from 2011 to '15. "He was Dad."

Fortunately, Beamer had athletic director Dave Braine on his side. Braine, who took over after Baughman resigned in anger six months into the job for not being told about the NCAA investigation into the basketball program, did his homework to make sure Beamer was the right coach for the job. He sat in on coaches meetings, famously bringing Carol Lee Donuts to Sunday film sessions and asking questions about why Beamer made decisions that he did in that woeful '92 campaign.

"And he never lost his patience," Braine said. "Answered the questions well. And I had a great deal of respect for him. He was a great coach."

Beamer made some staffing changes before the '93 season, most importantly bringing on combative defensive coordinator Phil Elmassian to shake things up, and things finally turned around.

With a run-based offense that had some added firepower from quarterback Maurice DeShazo and receiver Antonio Freeman, a defense that welcomed star recruit and fearsome pass-rusher Cornell Brown, and strong special teams that would be foundation of "Beamer Ball," the Hokies went 9–3, capping the season with their first bowl appearance under Beamer, a 45–20 win against Indiana in the Independence Bowl.

Through it all, Beamer was a steadying presence in the locker room, one of his best traits as a coach.

"I pride myself on it today," said John Ballein, his longtime right-hand man as director of operations. "When there's turmoil, I want to be at my very best. I take pride in that, me professionally. And I think I learned that…I don't think—I know I learned that from him. When things are at their very worst, then you need to be in control of the situation."

Virginia Tech had an upward trajectory after that initial bowl breakthrough. The Hokies were in the Big East at that point and won back-to-back league titles in '95 and '96, the former season punctuated by a 28–10 Sugar Bowl victory against Texas that put the program on the map and gave Tech its first Top 10 finish at No. 10.

The program reached new heights a few years later when quarterback Michael Vick burst on the scene, an amazing athlete who was as good of a runner as he was a passer. With Vick electrifying the offense as a redshirt freshman and Foster's famed Lunch Pail Defense paced by fearsome All-American defensive end Corey Moore, the Hokies breezed through an undefeated regular season in 1999, getting to the BCS title game in January 2000 against No. 1 Florida State. Though the Hokies lost to the Seminoles in the Sugar Bowl, they held their own, actually leading FSU 29–28 after three quarters.

Though Beamer thought about leaving for the North Carolina job, actually accepting it after the 2000 season, he changed his mind after flying back to Blacksburg.

All-Time Virginia Tech Football Coaching Victories

1. Frank Beamer, 238–121–2 (1987–2015)
2. Bill Dooley, 64–37–1 (1978–86)
3. Jerry Claiborne, 61–39–2 (1961–70)
4. Frank Moseley, 54–42–4 (1951–60)
5. H.B. Redd, 43–37–8 (1932–40)
6. Branch Bocock, 34–14–2 (1909–10, 1912–15)
7. B.C. Cubbage, 30–12–6 (1921–25)
8. Justin Fuente, 25–15 (2016–present)
9. Andy Gustafson, 22–13–1 (1926–29)
10. Jimmy Sharpe, 21–22–1 (1974–77)

"I knew we could win there," Beamer wrote in his autobiography about UNC. "What was most important to my decision-making process was the fact that those football facilities were built on somebody else's blood and sweat. They weren't built from my work. What we had at Virginia Tech at that time, on the other hand, and what we have built for the future, were built largely because of the success we had since 1993."

He stayed at Virginia Tech and helped guide the Hokies through their transition to the ACC in 2004, winning the league in their very first season, a surprising champion that was picked to finish sixth in the preseason.

That 2004 team that went to the Sugar Bowl started an impressive streak of consistency that saw the Hokies win 10 or more games for eight straight seasons. Tech went 84–24 from 2004 to 2011, winning four ACC championships in the Hokies' first seven years in the league.

Beamer won two ACC Coach of the Year awards to go with the three he'd won in the Big East. He guided Tech to five BCS bowls in a span of eight years, which gave him eight major bowl appearances in his time as the Hokies' coach. He dominated the in-state rivalry with Virginia like no one ever before, winning 12 straight to finish his career and 16 of the last 17 matchups with the Cavaliers.

Coaches loved to work for him. Beamer generally stayed hands off and let his assistants do their jobs. He didn't demand around-the-clock hours and wasn't someone who jumped on them at every opportunity. It's why support staff and assistants like Ballein (29 years), Foster (29 years), Bryan Stinespring (26 years), Billy Hite (24 years), and Charley Wiles (20 years) joined his staff and never left.

But Beamer had a far greater impact than that on campus, particularly in the wake of the tragic shooting on April 16, 2007, which claimed 32 lives, the deadliest shooting in U.S. history at that time. Afterward, Beamer met with the parents of some of the victims, trying to offer whatever comfort he could at such a sad time, a small but important piece in helping the campus heal.

"When you walked in and you looked back and you saw the hurt and the pain and the grief in the eyes…I'll never forget seeing those eyes," Beamer said.

"I went to a Richmond race right after that and somebody said, 'Well, you're probably always going to be remembered for the tragedy that happened at Virginia Tech.' And I said, 'No, I think what we're going to be remembered for is how Virginia Tech reacted to that tragedy and how they came together and got close, cared about each other.' I think that's what we'll really remember about that deal, and that's kind of Virginia Tech right there."

Like all coaches, time caught up to Beamer, whose post–2012 teams struggled to stay above .500, despite occasional stunners like the 35–21 upset of eventual national champion Ohio State at the Horseshoe in 2014.

That team finished the regular season 6–6, however. Beamer had a health scare that year, undergoing throat surgery right after the UVa game for what he'd later reveal was cancer. It prevented him from participating directly in the lead-up to the Military Bowl against Cincinnati. He watched from the press box and—after the Hokies beat the Bearcats 33–17 with Shane Beamer serving as acting coach—danced with his players in the locker room afterward.

In 2015, when Frank Beamer announced his eventual retirement midway through what was shaping up to be another mediocre season, he did it with Virginia Tech in mind.

"I didn't want to let Hokies down," Beamer said. "And that's the hardest part about being average here for the last few years. That's another thing I'm proud of: at one time average was not so bad, but now average is unacceptable, really. And that's a good thing. I'm proud of that. But that's the thing that Tech fans deserve better than—we've been average too long."

The Hokies won two of three down the stretch to get him to his 23rd consecutive bowl game. He finished off the last of his record 238 victories at Virginia Tech with a wild 55–52 win against Tulsa back where it all began at the Independence Bowl.

Since then, he has been a popular figure at Tech in retirement: a daily walker around campus with Ballein. He has been an ambassador for the athletic department, a face of the school's Drive for 25 donor initiative, and a resource for Justin Fuente in the coaching transition.

In January 2018, he was selected for the College Football Hall of Fame, inducted at a ceremony in New York the following December. He was as gracious as always about his inclusion with the sport's greats and was thankful for the opportunity to have coached his alma mater for so long.

"To have stayed at one place, a place I love, for 29 years," Beamer said, "I couldn't be more lucky."

2 Michael Vick

Frank Beamer used to chuckle about it later in his career, recalling just how many high school coaches he'd encountered who came to him with the same claim: "We've got the next Michael Vick for you."

As polite as he was, Beamer probably heard them out, knowing full well the truth about Vick: he was a comet who came through Blacksburg, unseen before or since, a flash who changed the way the college game was played and forever altered the perception of Virginia Tech on the national scene. Replicating him was going to be hard, if not impossible.

"He was just a different guy, and I was fortunate to coach him," Beamer said. "He was such a pleasant guy to coach. All that came his way and he never changed. Everybody on our team loved him. He'd do anything you asked him from a coaching standpoint. Never a problem, never in my office for an issue. I can't say enough good things about Michael Vick."

The full story of Vick's life is far more complicated, Shakespearean almost, with his rapid rise from the Newport News projects to college and NFL stardom, his precipitous fall from grace and prison term stemming from dog-fighting charges, and his reconciliation in a post-incarceration life spent making amends for those past misdeeds.

He might not be the most successful player in Virginia Tech history—it's hard to top defensive end Bruce Smith's body of work as a two-time first-team All-American, national award winner, and pro football Hall of Famer—but Vick is without a doubt the Hokies' most recognizable player, having reached a level of fame greater than Smith and influencing a generation of quarterbacks who run it as well as they throw it.

Vick grew up in a rough part of Newport News, a soft-spoken kid who tried to stay away from trouble. He learned the game from his second cousin, Aaron Brooks, who was four years older and would go on to star at Virginia. Soon, Vick was a standout for Tommy Reamon at Warwick High.

Though Ronald Curry was the bigger quarterback star out of the 757 in Vick's high school class, the Hokies were focused on the speedy left-hander from the start, given a heads-up by assistant coach Jim Cavanaugh. Beamer said all the convincing he needed was a quick glance at Vick's game film.

"I needed only three plays to tell that Michael Vick was the most different player that I had ever seen," Beamer wrote in his autobiography. "How quickly he got rid of the ball was amazing. How much zip he put on the ball for his size was amazing. How he ran around and the speed and quickness he had: it was even more amazing. He would run around, and nobody would be able to tackle him."

Virginia Tech ended up getting his services over Syracuse, which wanted to make him the next Donovan McNabb. He'd do a pretty good impersonation of McNabb for the Hokies...once they let him play.

Beamer stuck to a promise he made to Reamon to redshirt Vick, not to put him out on the field until he was ready for the big stage. That was tough in the short term. Tech's QB situation was dire in 1998 because of injuries and the intriguing freshman was tearing things up on the scout team. Beamer stuck to his promise, however, and Vick didn't debut until 1999.

When he did, Virginia Tech football would never be the same. Vick exploded on the scene in '99, playing the quarterback position with an athleticism and a playmaking ability rarely seen. He flipped into the Hokies' consciousness, literally going head over heels on a quarterback run for a touchdown against James Madison in his debut.

Though his stats that year seem modest by today's standards (1,840 passing yards and 12 TDs in the regular season, with 585 rushing yards and eight more scores), he left defensive coordinators with many sleepless nights based on everything he could do on a football field. A perfect example was the West Virginia game that year, when Vick engineered a two-minute drill, almost effortlessly darting up the right sideline past the defense for a 26-yard gain on a scramble to set up Shayne Graham's game-winning field goal at the gun.

Vick, who was among the leaders in passing efficiency that year, helped Tech finish an undefeated season. He got an invitation to the Heisman Trophy ceremony in an era when freshmen were rarely considered for the award. Vick finished third in the voting behind the winner, Wisconsin running back Ron Dayne, and runner-up, Georgia Tech quarterback Joe Hamilton.

Had the voting taken place after the BCS title game against Florida State, the voters might have felt differently. Though the Hokies lost that game to the Seminoles 46–29, there might not have been a better athlete on the field than Vick, who looked like he had a different gear than anyone on FSU's star-studded defense. He threw for 225 yards and a touchdown and ran for 97 more yards (145 in gains, though he was sacked seven times).

"There ain't a darn thing you can do about this guy," FSU coach Bobby Bowden said afterward. "You put four or five guys on him, and he runs 50 yards. Boy, is he something. Better than I thought. I knew he was good. I didn't know he was this darn good."

Vick followed up his breakout '99 season with another strong year in 2000. Though again his stats weren't gaudy (1,234 passing yards, eight TDs, 617 rushing yards, eight TDs), his effect was profound. The Hokies averaged 41.1 and 40.3 points per game in Vick's two seasons, tops in school history.

An ankle injury limited Vick later in the year, and he barely played in a 41–21 loss to No. 3 Miami that ended the Hokies' national title hopes. Tech still finished the year 11–1 and stomped Clemson in the Gator Bowl 41–20, with Vick winning game MVP honors.

It'd be Vick's last college game. He entered the NFL Draft and, after wowing at his Pro Day by running a 4.33-second 40-yard

Michael Vick eludes Clemson's Keith Adams in the first quarter of the Gator Bowl. (Steve Helber / AP Photo)

dash, was taken first overall by the Atlanta Falcons, who traded up to get him. He became the first black quarterback to be selected with the top overall pick and didn't disappoint early in his time in Atlanta.

He was a Pro Bowl pick in three of his first five seasons, bringing an athleticism to the quarterback position never seen in the NFL. One of his early highlights came against the Vikings in 2002 when he ran for 173 yards, a single-game quarterback record in the NFL. He punctuated it by running through the Minnesota defense for a 46-yard touchdown in overtime, with two Vikings defenders who underestimated his speed running into each other in his wake while trying to make a tackle. Later that season, he led the Falcons to a playoff upset of the Packers and Brett Favre in Lambeau Field.

He signed an NFL record 10-year, $130 million extension with Atlanta in 2004 to become the face of the franchise after leading the Falcons to a division title and the NFC title game. In 2006, he became the first NFL quarterback to ever rush for more than 1,000 yards in a season.

It made his downfall all the more shocking. In April 2007, allegations arose that he funded and participated in an illegal dogfighting ring in Surry County, Virginia, injuring and killing dozens of dogs in heinous ways at a place dubbed Bad Newz Kennels, then lying about it to authorities.

In July 2007, Vick and three others were indicted on federal and state felony charges related to dog fighting. By August, he'd pleaded guilty and in December was sentenced to 23 months in federal prison, which he served at Leavenworth in Kansas. The NFL suspended him indefinitely for conduct that commissioner Roger Goodell called "cruel and reprehensible." Atlanta owner Arthur Blanks sought to recoup $20 million of Vick's $37 million signing bonus.

Vick was released from federal penitentiary after 19 months of incarceration in May 2009 and, after two months of home confinement, was released from federal custody that July. He was reinstated conditionally in the NFL later that month and eventually signed a one-year contract with coach Andy Reid and the Philadelphia Eagles as McNabb's backup.

After McNabb was traded to the Redskins in 2010, Vick ended up starting 12 games for the Eagles, throwing for 3,108 yards and a career-high 21 touchdowns to go with 676 rushing yards and nine more scores. He earned the NFL Comeback Player of the Year Award and made his fourth Pro Bowl.

Vick started 2½ more years for the Eagles before losing his job to Nick Foles when he suffered multiple leg injuries in 2013 after Chip Kelly came on as coach. He ended up playing seasons with the Jets and Steelers before retiring in February 2017 after a full year out of the league.

In a 13-year NFL career interrupted by a two-year prison stretch in his prime, Vick threw for 22,464 and 133 touchdowns and ran for 6,109 yards, the most in a career by an NFL quarterback, and 36 more scores.

While Vick was trying to make a comeback on the field, he went about trying to make amends off it. He's taken responsibility for his actions and has worked with the Humane Society to promote animal welfare, testifying before Congress in support of the Animal Fighting Spectator Prohibition Act and speaking in front of Pennsylvania lawmakers in 2015 about a bill that would allow police officers to rescue dogs and cats in cars with unsafe temperatures.

His past crimes will be hard for some people to overlook or ever forgive, as evident from the protests by animal rights activists when he was inducted into the Virginia Tech Sports Hall of Fame in 2017. But Vick, who still makes trips to Blacksburg and whose name still graces the hallway to the Hokies' meeting rooms in the Merryman Athletic Center, has made considerable efforts to try to prevent others from making the same mistakes he did.

"I just try to make it right after going through what I went through, after what transpired," Vick told ESPN in 2015. "The best thing to do was make amends for what I did. I can't take it back. The only thing I can do is influence the masses of kids from going down the same road I went down. That's why I work with the Humane Society, affecting a lot of kids' lives and saving a lot of animals.

"We've had a lot of progress. We've been able to change some laws and do some great things that I'm very proud of. I never thought I'd be doing that."

3 Bud Foster

Virginia Tech just completed a 33–17 win against Cincinnati in the 2014 Military Bowl when the emotions of the previous month all converged at once for longtime Hokies defensive coordinator Bud Foster.

After having discussions about joining Texas A&M, Foster eventually finalized a five-year extension to stay with the Hokies, a moment made even more tender by the fact that Frank Beamer, the man who'd brought him to Blacksburg 27 years earlier, returned to the team to watch the bowl game from the press box after having throat surgery a month prior.

Foster choked up when explaining how Beamer danced with the team in the locker room after the victory, tears welling in his eyes. He hugged radio color analyst Mike Burnop, who brought up Foster's well-deserved contract extension.

"For me," Foster managed to get out in a hoarse voice, "this is home."

For more than three decades, the last 24 years as Virginia Tech's defensive coordinator, Blacksburg has been exactly that for Foster, who's one of the premier defensive minds in college football history and was as big a part of Beamer's success as anyone.

With a jawline from central casting, an unmatched intensity, and facial hair that was ever-evolving—from mustache to goatee to beard—Foster's been an institution at Virginia Tech. He's a loyal assistant coach who's a rarity in the sport, having anchored himself in one place for nearly his entire career and maintained a high level of performance throughout most of his tenure.

"In Bud We Trust" is a common philosophy around campus and an apt one considering how long Foster's defenses have thrived and on how many occasions they saved the day when the offense wasn't up to muster.

"I think he's the best in the business," Beamer has said many times. "I don't think there's any question."

It's hard to envision Virginia Tech football history without the Beamer-Foster pairing. The two go all the way back to 1979, when a 32-year-old Beamer was hired at Murray State to be Mike Gottfried's defensive coordinator. Back then, Foster was a 19-year-old, hard-hitting strong safety and outside linebacker.

The two helped the Racers reach the I-AA semifinals that year and it was the start of a special pairing that would last 35 years on the football field. Foster finished up his eligibility after the 1980 season and joined the Racers' staff as a graduate assistant when Beamer became head coach in 1981. Foster was later promoted to outside linebackers coach and added special teams to his duties in 1986.

When Beamer took the head coaching job at Virginia Tech in 1987, Foster came with, a 27-year-old put in charge of the Hokies' inside linebackers. Foster's groups helped Beamer finally turn things around in Blacksburg. When defensive coordinator Phil Elmassian bolted for another job after the 1994 season, Beamer promoted Foster to co-coordinator, pairing him with the slightly more seasoned Rod Sharpless.

That '95 defense was loaded, with defensive linemen Cornell Brown, J.C. Price, and Jim Baron; linebackers George DelRicco, Myron Newsome, and Brandon Semones; and defensive backs Antonio Banks, Torrian Gray, and William Yarborough. The Hokies had the nation's No. 1 rushing defense (77.4 ypg) and No. 10 overall defense (285.9 ypg), helping Tech break through on the national stage with a Sugar Bowl victory over Texas to complete a 10–2 season.

To symbolize the group's blue-collar ways, Foster and Sharpless procured an actual lunch pail, and *voila*, a symbol that has lasted decades was born.

Sharpless was off to Rutgers the following year, making it Foster's show. He went on to produce more than two decades of rock-solid groups. Perhaps none was finer than his 1999 squad, one headlined by national Defensive Player of the Year and fearsome defensive end Corey Moore, a group that led the nation in points allowed (10.5 ppg) and got within a quarter of winning the national championship.

That was the first of four times Foster was a finalist for the Broyles Award, which is given annually to the nation's top assistant coach. He finally won it 2006, the second straight season his group led the country in total defense.

Foster's defenses have led the nation in a major statistical category nine times and have placed in the Top 5 on 44 different occasions. The Hokies have finished first or second nationally in scoring defense five different times during his watch, finishing in the Top 10 every year from 2004 to '09, Tech's first six seasons in the ACC.

His defenses have been known for the pressure they put on opposing offenses, forcing them into mistakes. Since he became the sole coordinator in 1996, the Hokies lead all FBS programs in sacks

(837) and interceptions (380). Tech has not only forced turnovers but also capitalized on them, with 53 different players scoring a total of 81 defensive touchdowns in that time.

The Hokies have been particularly strong in the defensive backfield, where they've claimed the moniker "DBU" for their consistency in the last two decades. Virginia Tech has had 27 defensive backs drafted in the last 23 years, with three (DeAngelo Hall, Kyle Fuller, and Terrell Edmunds) going in the first round.

Since 1996, 45 of his defensive players have been drafted, including 11 in the first or second round. Linebacker Tremaine Edmunds was his other first-rounder. He's had 22 different players earn All-America honors in the last 24 seasons.

When Beamer retired, the Hokies made a major effort to retain Foster, who'd been passed over as the internal hire in favor of Memphis' Justin Fuente. Before Tech finalized its deal with Fuente, however, it secretly flew Foster to meet with the young coach to see if they could make things work going forward. So clandestine was the meeting that Foster didn't know where he was flying or with whom he was meeting until mid-flight.

The two met in Memphis, talked some ball, and hit it off. When Fuente became a done deal at Tech, Foster remained in the fold as his defensive coordinator.

"One of the beautiful draws about this opportunity was I believed that hopefully it potentially came with the best defensive coordinator in all of America," Fuente said at his introductory press conference. "And I'm awfully happy that he's agreed to stay on with us and help us continue what Coach Beamer started."

"Once I had a chance to visit with him, it was an easy decision," Foster said. "I'm excited about the next chapter here. Obviously, we put a lot of time and effort into this thing.... What's kept me here and continues to keep me here is that I think we can win at the highest level."

Fuente was under no directive to hire Foster. Athletic director Whit Babcock made it clear that Fuente was free to hire whomever he wanted, though he did share the opinion of nearly every Hokies fan at the time who'd watched Foster's defenses tear up the Big East and ACC over the years.

"If it's not Bud, you better have a darn good one you bring in here."

4 Bruce Smith

Even in retirement, he's tough to miss on the sideline. Bruce Smith is a 6-foot-4, 280-pound presence wherever he is, and even among a group of college football players, he's easy to spot.

And if you can't locate him, just follow the telltale sound of the Virginia Tech crowd calling him by name in unison—"Bruuuuuuuuuuce!"

Smith wasn't the Hokies' first star and he might not even be the one who achieved the most fame in college (Michael Vick's tough to top in that regard), but this line on his résumé is undeniable: no Virginia Tech player in history went on to have a better NFL career than the 11-time Pro Bowl, 10-time All-Pro, Hall of Fame defensive end, who's the league's all-time leader in sacks.

Smith's an in-state star from Norfolk who played at Booker T. Washington High School. He came to Virginia Tech to play for Bill Dooley in 1981 and went on to have one of the best careers in Hokies history.

"Coach Bill left a lasting impression on me," Smith said at his Pro Football Hall of Fame induction decades later. "He said, 'If you

Pete Rozelle holds up a jersey for Bruce Smith after Smith was drafted by the Buffalo Bills in New York on April 30, 1985. (Dave Pickoff / AP Photo)

come to Tech, you will receive an excellent education. And if you can play, they will find you.'"

Smith could and they did. The defensive tackle had 46 sacks for 402 yards in his four years, which was believed to be an NCAA record at the time (sack stats weren't kept as thoroughly as offensive numbers back then). He had a school-record 71 tackles for a loss. In his junior year alone, he had 31 tackles for a loss, including what remains a school record 22 sacks.

He was twice named a first-team All-American, honored as a junior and senior, the latter as a consensus choice. He won the Outland Trophy as the nation's top interior lineman in 1984, only the second Hokie in history to win a national award. His No. 78 was retired by Virginia Tech years later.

"No ifs, ands, or buts about it," Dooley said as Smith headed to the NFL Draft. "I've said all along that Bruce is the best college lineman I've ever coached and the best I've ever seen in 18 years as a head coach. He's got the strength and explosiveness of a running back. And he's determined. Very determined. Often times they put two or more people to him, but he never gives up. He keeps fighting and he enjoys it."

For as good as Smith was in college, he was even better as a pro, a No. 1 overall pick who actually lived up to the hype. The Bills selected him in 1985 and Smith became one of the pillars of the Buffalo teams that would make four straight Super Bowls in the early '90s.

After not being in the best of shape his rookie season, Smith slimmed down to a lean, mean, 265-pound tackling machine, one dedicated to tremendous conditioning.

"I'm afraid of not playing well," Smith said. "If I'm not at the top of my game each week, I will get my ass kicked by someone trying to make a name for himself, and I won't let that happen."

"Bruce likes to do things quietly, when he doesn't think people see him, like working out every week on his day off," Bills coach Marv Levy said. "I guess he feels if people think he has stayed so good for so long on natural talent alone, so be it."

Though Smith was a well-rounded defensive player who'd make over 1,000 tackles in his career, he stood out above the crowd in one particular category—sacks. He had 200 of them in his 279-game career, eclipsing former Eagles and Packers star Reggie White by two and earning the nickname "The Sack King." In his 19 NFL seasons, he had 10 or more sacks 13 times and was a rare combination of size and speed.

"He is so strong that he can bulldoze over you," Hall of Fame quarterback Warren Moon said once.

He made his first NFL All-Pro team in 1987 and had a career-high 19 sacks in 1990, helping lead the Bills to their first Super Bowl appearance against the Giants. Smith played well in Super Bowl XXV, sacking New York quarterback Jeff Hostetler for a safety to give the Bills an early 12–3 lead, but they'd lose 20–19 in heartbreaking fashion when Scott Norwood's 47-yard field goal attempt in the final seconds went wide right. Smith and the Bills made it back to the Super Bowl the next three years, though they'd never win the big one.

Smith, however, continued to enjoy great individual success. On two occasions ('90 and '96) he was named NFL Defensive Player of the Year, and he earned AFC Defensive Player of the Year honors four times ('87, '88, '90 and '96).

After 15 years with the Bills, he went to play for the Redskins, adding 29 more sacks in his final four seasons to claim the NFL record, setting the mark when he took down Giants quarterback Jesse Palmer in a December game in 2003 just before his retirement. Smith's longevity was so great that he made the NFL's All-Decade Team in the 1980s and '90s.

He's made numerous halls of fame, including Virginia Tech's (1995), college football's (2006) and pro football's (2009), becoming Virginia Tech's first (and only, so far) member of the Pro Football Hall of Fame. The Bills retired his No. 78 jersey in 2016, a ceremony commemorating the perfect pairing of player and city.

"What fit so well for me going to Buffalo was I was a blue-collar player that played for a blue-collar town on a blue-collar team," Smith said. "They're very passionate and they love their players. They embraced me and they loved me. And I wanted to provide a great deal of entertainment for them because I could see the smiles on their faces, the joy in their heart, the energy they brought to the stadium.

"My desire to give them a great performance every time I walked out on that field—that's what it was all about for me."

5 The 2000 BCS Title Game

Frank Beamer may have gotten out over his skis at his debut press conference at Virginia Tech in 1987 when he said, "I really think that someday we can play for national championships here."

The thought was laughable for a program of Virginia Tech's stature at the time, but Beamer, an eternal optimist, believed it was true, nevertheless. And he was eventually proven correct.

The Hokies qualified for the 2000 Bowl Championship Series title game after going 11–0 in the 1999 season and finishing No. 2 in the final BCS standings behind No. 1 Florida State. They'd meet in the Sugar Bowl for the national title on January 4, 2000, and the Hokies came much closer to taking home the title than most remember.

Those '99 Hokies were led by the brilliance and sheer athleticism of quarterback Michael Vick, who burst on the scene as a redshirt freshman, aided by a lockdown defense in the Lunch Pail mold, headlined by intense and relentless pass-rusher Corey Moore.

Moore famously cursed at reporters during a terse media day session in the leadup to the game, playing into his unnerving reputation, though he later told some in the program that he did it to take some of the media blitz off Vick. The blowup came in response to a question Moore had heard a thousand times in the month before the game: Did Virginia Tech belong?

It didn't look like it early on. The Hokies were particularly un-Hokie-like in the first 20 minutes, falling behind 28–7.

Rather than kick a field goal on the opening drive, Tech went for it on fourth-and-1 from the 4-yard line, with Vick losing yards and fumbling into the end zone for a touchback, one of three lost fumbles for the Hokies on the night. The usually conservative

Beamer called for a fake field goal and a fake punt, plus a pair of two-point conversions on the night, all of which failed.

"I kick myself on that one," Beamer said. "All those years that we played them, and I knew how good they were and how talented they were, and it kind of got in my head a little bit, I think. I felt like we were going to need to do something special to beat them.

"And so, we faked a punt. Didn't make it. We faked a field goal. Didn't make it. Now, if we had made them, it would have been good coaching. But we didn't make it. And then you lost field position with each of those. And when I look back at it, I really think we had a good enough team to just play them straight up and win the game. It was going to be close.... I think I let the past games and their talent level kind of influence my thinking a little bit as far as what was right for that particular game."

Worse yet, Tech's fabled special teams deserted it in the biggest game in program history. FSU blocked a punt and returned it for a touchdown. Early in the second quarter, Peter Warrick returned a punt 59 yards for a touchdown to make it 28–7.

"I haven't gotten over it," said Shane Beamer, a long snapper on that team who made a futile dive at Warrick's legs as he broke away. "I think about it probably every day. And it sticks with you. That was a special season. But it just leaves a bitter taste in your mouth because you got so close and you just couldn't close the deal."

To Tech's credit, however, it stormed back. A 3-yard Vick touchdown run just before halftime made it 28–14. Vick threw for 225 yards and a touchdown and ran for 97 more yards, stealing the show for much of the night. He made an FSU defense full of future NFLers look slow at times.

The Hokies kept up their run in the third quarter, getting a field goal from Shayne Graham and two Andre Kendrick touchdown runs to take a 29–28 lead into the fourth quarter, a fact many people forget.

It was all Florida State in the fourth, however, with the Hokies running out of gas. Chris Weinke threw touchdown passes to Ron Dugans and Warrick to pull away in a 46–29 win for Bobby Bowden's second and final national championship.

"It was right there on our plate for us and we didn't capitalize," defensive coordinator Bud Foster said. "We got back in it, but we didn't finish it, and that was kind of disappointing because that's one thing we were known for that season, is finishing the games and taking over the fourth quarter."

The final stats were misleading, though they showed Virginia Tech wasn't blown off the field. The Hokies outgained the Seminoles 503–359 and outrushed FSU 278–30. Still, the turnovers, special teams breakdowns, and failed gambles kept Tech on the losing end.

The national championship ended up being the one thing that eluded Beamer during his Hall of Fame career, though it wasn't because of inattention. For years, Tech had an empty trophy case in the lobby overlooking the practice field. In a glass case was a sign that read: "This area is reserved for the National Championship Trophy. GO HOKIES!"

Although Beamer won 238 games in his coaching career with the Hokies, went to 23 bowl games, and won seven conference titles, he'll always lament the fact that he never quite got Virginia Tech to the mountaintop in college football.

"My biggest disappointment here was not getting back to the national championship," Beamer said. "That's the one regret I have."

6 "Beamer Ball"

During his 29 years at Virginia Tech, Frank Beamer's teams had a certain style, capable of scoring no matter what unit was on the field—offense, defense or special teams. The term came to be known as "Beamer Ball," and it's ingrained in the program even after Beamer's retirement.

Beamer was a defensive-minded coach, having worked up the ranks as a coordinator at both The Citadel and Murray State before being promoted to the Racers' head coaching job and later getting hired by Virginia Tech. So, contributions on defense were going to be a given.

Although he emphasized special teams at Murray State, it really took off when he got to the Hokies, with Beamer stealing an idea from the best team and coach he knew in the late '80s and early '90s: Florida State and Bobby Bowden.

"It seemed like it was the first place I remember when you were getting ready to punt, the crowd was on their feet and screaming and hollering," Beamer said. "Because what was happening was they were either getting ready to block a kick, because they had those good athletes. And they had a lot of good athletes right there rushing the punt. And then they had Deion Sanders back there getting ready to return it. So that was an exciting play. So that's where I kind of got the idea of, hey, get your good players back there on special teams."

Soon, special teams play and non-offensive touchdowns became synonymous with Virginia Tech. The coach didn't pass off coaching special teams to his assistants either. They all had specific units that they'd coach, but Tech never had a special teams coordinator in Beamer's time. That's because the head coach himself took on those duties, with a very hands-on approach.

That attention to detail showed, with players—even the best on the team—wanting to be part of Tech's special teams. It wasn't an afterthought. The Hokies named their punt team "Pride" and their punt block unit "Pride and Joy."

Beamer's groups turned the tide in plenty of games and made up for occasionally sluggish offensive performances by scoring all sorts of non-offensive touchdowns, 143 in all during his three-decade run in Blacksburg.

That included 89 defensive scores (58 off interceptions and 31 off fumbles) and 54 in every way imaginable on special teams. Kicking against the Hokies was a white-knuckle situation, especially when Lane Stadium was rocking. Tech blocked 136 kicks during Beamer's tenure—67 punts, 41 field goals, and 28 extra points.

Fittingly, the Hokies had a special teams score in Beamer's very first game as Virginia Tech's coach, with Jon Jeffries taking back a kickoff 92 yards for a touchdown against Clemson in 1987.

The Hokies' much-touted bowl streak began in 1993 with a game that turned in what would become quintessential "Beamer Ball" fashion. Tech turned a tight contest against Indiana in the Independence Bowl into a rout when Lawrence Lewis returned a fumble for a touchdown and Antonio Banks returned a blocked field goal for a score, all in the final 35 seconds of the first half.

When Virginia Tech scored on defense or special teams, it'd become almost unbeatable, winning 75 percent of its games when scoring a non-offensive touchdown under Beamer.

Blocking kicks became so synonymous with the school's style of play that even when the Hokies get one today, it's still usually met with shouts of "Beamer Ball!"

Tech peaked with 12 blocked kicks in 12 games in 1998, including two in a 38–7 Music City Bowl rout of Alabama. The

Most Non-Offensive Touchdowns Under Beamer at Virginia Tech

1. DeAngelo Hall—7 (5 PR, 1 FR, 1 INT)
2. Macho Harris—5 (4 INT, 1 KR)
3. André Davis—4 (4 PR)
4. Xavier Adibi—3 (2 INT, 1 FR)
   Ike Charlton—3 (2 INT, 1 FR)
   Ricky Hall—3 (1 PR, 1 blocked punt, 1 recovered blocked punt)
   Jason Lallis—3 (2 FR, 1 INT)
   Andrew Motuapuaka—3 (1 INT, 2 FR)
   Eddie Royal—3 (3 PR)

most prolific kick blockers under Beamer were Bernard Basham, a 6-foot-7 defensive end whose height helped him get seven blocks in his career. Safety Keion Carpenter blocked six.

Some of the most memorable plays from Virginia Tech's heyday came in "Beamer Ball" fashion. Reserve running back Wayne Ward's jaw-rattling block sprung André Davis for a punt return touchdown against West Virginia in 2000. When the Hokies knocked off No. 2 Miami in 2003, it started with a 28-yard strip and score by cornerback DeAngelo Hall. In a 41–23 win against Clemson in 2007, the Hokies had only 219 yards of offense, but they scored touchdowns on an interception (D.J. Parker), a punt (Eddie Royal), and a kickoff (Victor "Macho" Harris).

Virginia Tech became a resource for programs across the country seeking to improve their special teams, holding clinics and welcoming coaching staffs on pilgrimages to Blacksburg to learn Beamer's methods.

So revered was Beamer's special teams work that when the new College Football Hall of Fame opened in Atlanta in 2014, he was honored in an exhibit championing the sport's innovators. Next to displays saluting Pop Warner for popularizing the single wing, Bud

Wilkinson for the 5–2–4 defense, Emory Bellard for the wishbone, and five others was one for Beamer, whose special teams contributions changed the way the game was played in the 1990s and 2000s.

"It can be a momentum play," Beamer wrote in one of his autobiographies. "It can be a scoring play. And it can be a momentum and scoring play. Basically, if we out-play the other team in special teams, we give ourselves a great chance to win the game."

Beamer's special teams tradition is a strong one, naturally being passed on to his son, Shane. As an assistant at Georgia in 2017, Shane's special teams helped the Bulldogs nearly win the national title. In the national semifinal in the Rose Bowl against Oklahoma, Georgia made numerous tide-turning special teams plays, including a gamechanger in overtime, when Lorenzo Carter blocked a field goal attempt.

Frank was at the game and sought out Shane on the field in the celebration afterward to congratulate him. His first words to his son was a phrase he repeated often over the years about the impact of special teams: "Quickest way to win a football game."

7 Jump to "Enter Sandman"

When it comes to pregame traditions established in the modern age of college football, you'd be hard-pressed to find a more iconic one than Virginia Tech's entrance to the head-banging sounds of Metallica's "Enter Sandman."

It's such a staple at football games, basketball games, and, yes, commencement ceremonies, that your Virginia Tech experience won't be complete without jumping in unison with your fellow Hokies to the opening of Metallica's most famous metal song.

The tradition started in 2000 when the Hokies added a new scoreboard to Lane Stadium, with the marketing team wanting an entrance video and song to go with it. The team also considered "Welcome to the Jungle" by Guns N' Roses, "Thunderstruck" by AC/DC, and "Sirius" by the Alan Parsons Project (also known as the Chicago Bulls' intro song during the Michael Jordan years), but opted for the Metallica hit released in 1991.

"For me, it was great because of the rhythm of it," Roger Springfield, the producer of the Hokies' original "Enter Sandman" video, told the *Washington Post* in 2009. "The beats in it, the rhythm—for editing purposes, it lent itself well to what we were talking about doing".

It was first played as the Hokies ran out of the tunnel before a scheduled contest against Georgia Tech on August 27, 2000, though the game was canceled after a torrential rainfall and a too-close-for-comfort lightning strike that hit ESPN *College GameDay* analyst Lee Corso's rental car.

Fans didn't jump right away, but before a frigid home game in 2001, members of the Virginia Tech marching band began jumping up and down to keep warm before the team's entrance. Just like that, a tradition was born.

Now, the entire stadium gets in on the action, with Virginia Tech's Regimental Band (also known as the Highty-Tighties) and cheerleaders lining up on the field in two columns to welcome the team into the stadium. The anticipation grows on the football team's walk from its locker room in the Jamerson Athletic Center to get lined up in the tunnel in the north end zone.

Call and response chants of "Let's go" and "Hokies" fill the stadium as everyone waits for the opening guitar riff to kick in. When it does, it's pandemonium, quite a sight to see, with close to 65,000 people jumping in unison to the 1991 hit off Metallica's "Black Album."

Virginia Tech's 11 Conference Championships

1909 South Atlantic: 6–1, coach Branch Bocock
1916 South Atlantic: 7–2, coach Jack Ingersoll
1918 South Atlantic: 7–0, coach Charles Bernier
1963 Southern: 8–2, coach Jerry Claiborne
1995 Big East: 10–2, coach Frank Beamer
1996 Big East: 10–2, coach Frank Beamer
1999 Big East: 11–1, coach Frank Beamer
2004 ACC: 10–3, coach Frank Beamer
2007 ACC: 11–3, coach Frank Beamer
2008 ACC: 10–4, coach Frank Beamer
2010 ACC: 11–3, coach Frank Beamer

Led by their head coach and players serving as flag bearers, the Hokies spill onto the field as a team right as the main guitar riff hits with a crescendo of drums about a minute in. Players sprint to the opposite end of the stadium and, in a new tradition, jump up into the front row of the stands by the Corps of Cadets.

Though the song fades before the chorus kicks in, fans have recently started singing it in unison after the music stops, capping it with the line: "Exit light / Enter night / Take my hand / We're off to never-never land."

The team has embraced every aspect of the song, which has become ingrained in Virginia Tech's football culture. "Start jumping" is a favorite phrase of every Hokie. Coach Justin Fuente has taken to using as a "bat signal" on Twitter whenever Virginia Tech gets a commitment from a recruit. (The team's used both #ExitLight and #EnterNight as hashtags for signing classes.)

The song's used anywhere at any time too, with smaller versions of the jumping intro used at neutral sites and bowl games. Tech will break it out in key moments of games, too, as it did before a final fourth-down play at the end of a 38–35 win against Miami in 2011.

"These people are losing their minds!" play-by-play man Mike Patrick remarked after seeing the stadium go crazy.

How loud does it get? The Hokies' much-hyped intro and the crowd's reaction routinely registers on seismographs.

On a couple of occasions, Metallica has pre-recorded special messages that have played on the videoboard before the song kicks in, first in 2011 prior to that Miami game and later as a farewell tribute ahead of Frank Beamer's final home game in 2015.

The band has never appeared live in Blacksburg to play the song before a game, though the rumor seems to pop up every year on the message boards, with someone's friend's cousin's brother's uncle always swearing he saw the band's tour buses in Roanoke or knowing of a hotel listing in Blacksburg that has four rooms reserved with names that are aliases for the band's members. (Pro-tip for debunking this one: in the unlikely event that Metallica ever came to Blacksburg, the band and its crew would require far more than four hotel rooms.)

Still, the recording of the song rocks enough to be worth the experience. Just be ready and in your seat so you can get out of it when Virginia Tech is ready to enter the stadium. When the guitar kicks in, you'll know when it's time to get up and start jumping.

8 The 1995 Sugar Bowl: Virginia Tech Belongs

Virginia Tech's path to national respect never got a bigger bump than it did when the Hokies earned their first trip to a major bowl game in the 1995 Sugar Bowl. A 28–10 New Year's Eve win against No. 9 Texas, the Southwest Conference champion coached by John Mackovic, legitimized their credentials on the national scene and set the path for the team's eventual run to the national title game appearance four years later.

"That game did wonders for our program," head coach Frank Beamer said. "Because we played a big-name opponent in the Sugar Bowl and won. And so that kind of said, 'Hey, you're at a different level. You can achieve different things.' So, after that, that kind of got us rolling."

It's hard to believe now it wasn't even a slam dunk the Hokies would be picked for the game. Tech finished the year at No. 13 in the AP poll and in a first-place tie with Miami atop the Big East standings. Though the Hokies beat the Hurricanes head-to-head, the Big East had no tiebreaker at the time, and the Bowl Alliance could take either of the league's co-champions. That was bad news for Virginia Tech, which didn't have the national cachet that "The U" did.

Things were hairy until the NCAA ruled on a sanctions case for Miami sooner than expected, stripping the 'Canes of 24 football scholarships and banning them from a bowl game in 1995. It opened up a spot for Virginia Tech, which was just three years removed from a 2–8–1 season.

"We wanted to have our own recognition," said All-America defensive end Cornell Brown, who'd end up coaching in a Sugar Bowl at his alma mater, too. "I don't think anybody gave us respect or thought we really belonged, because we were the type of team in transition. We were improving, getting better year in and year out."

With excitement at an all-time high, Hokies fans descended on New Orleans in bunches, selling out the school's ticket allotment of 15,000 in four days and sending an estimated 25,000 fans to the Big Easy. They ended up getting a good show.

Eventually.

Things started out poorly for Virginia Tech, which fell behind 10–0 early in the second quarter.

Frank Beamer winces after being doused with water near the end of the Hokies' 28–10 win over Texas in the Sugar Bowl at the Louisiana Superdome on Sunday, December 31, 1995. (AP Photo)

It was all Hokies from there, though. In true "Beamer Ball" fashion, it started with a special teams play, with Bryan Still taking back a punt 60 yards for a touchdown, bursting up the middle past tacklers before breaking free up the right sideline.

"When I found out we were going to the Sugar Bowl, I had dreams about making big plays," Still said after the game. "And today they came true. All that talk 'we didn't belong,' I think today we showed we belong with the big names in college football."

That jump-started the Hokies, who dominated in the second half. Marcus Parker scored on a 2-yard touchdown run in the third quarter to give Tech its first lead of the night at 14–10.

Still, who'd earn game MVP honors, got in the end zone a second time when quarterback Jim Druckenmiller hit him for a wide open 54-yard touchdown early in the fourth quarter to make it 21–10. Still had 119 receiving yards in the game and Druckenmiller threw for 266.

Tech's defense, in its first year with Bud Foster as a coordinator, took it from there. Led by Cornell Brown, who had three sacks and four tackles for a loss, the Hokies harassed Texas quarterback and Southwest Conference Player of the Year James Brown all night. They sacked him five times total and forced three interceptions, two by All-Big East safety Torrian Gray.

The ballyhooed Texas rushing trio of James Brown, Shon Mitchell, and future Heisman Trophy–winner Ricky Williams finished with only 78 yards rushing—129 below their season average—against Tech's rushing defense, which was No. 1 in the nation. With all the sack yards, Brown finished with minus–43 rushing yards. The Longhorns had only 226 total yards as a team.

The last of Cornell Brown's three sacks put a fitting exclamation mark on the game, knocking loose the ball from James Brown. Defensive tackle Jim Baron picked it up for the Hokies and returned it for a 20-yard touchdown, Tech's seventh defensive touchdown in the final six games, giving Virginia Tech an offensive, defensive, and special teams touchdown in the game.

The win checked off a couple of postseason boxes for the Hokies, who'd won 10 straight games to finish the season. They never finished in the Top 10 of a final poll or played in a major bowl. Nor had they beaten a Top 10 team in the postseason.

Tech did all those things by topping No. 9 Texas, finishing the season ranked No. 10.

More than the ranking, though, was the respect the program garnered for winning on such a big stage, the first of eight major postseason appearances under Beamer that included four Orange Bowls and three more trips to the Sugar Bowl.

"We've been working to get this program to the top of the college football world," Beamer said after the game. "I think we took another step tonight. I think this is the greatest win in Tech history. We've got our eye on some more here in the future, too."

Little did he know the pinnacle of the program would come on that same Superdome field four years later.

9 Attend a Game at Lane Stadium

Tailgate beforehand, jump to "Enter Sandman," chow down on a turkey leg, and show them what it's all about by doing the Hokie Pokie. If you're coming to visit Blacksburg, no experience is complete without doing all those things and more by visiting the town's signature venue and attending a game at Lane Stadium.

The Hokies usually come close to filling the 66,233-seat stadium each home Saturday (or Thursday or, more and more lately, Friday), making it one of the premier venues in the country to watch a college football game in the fall.

Sports on Earth ranked it the 15th best college football stadium in the country in 2017, with Matt Brown writing: "LSU and Penn State are typically mentioned as among the best night-game atmospheres in college football. Lane Stadium isn't as big, but it's right there with them. The venue grew right along with the Frank Beamer era as it was transformed from national afterthought to consistent success. The addition of the trademark Virginia Tech stone in the end zones is a nice touch."

It's hard to believe that from humble beginnings, the stadium's grown into one of the nation's best.

In 1963, Virginia Tech sought to upgrade its football home from the 17,000-seat Miles Stadium where it had played since 1926. Construction began on Lane just south of Cassell Coliseum in 1964, with the Gobblers making their debut in the still-being-built venue on October 2, 1965, a 9–7 win over William & Mary.

It looked far different back then. Only the west stands and center section of the east side were in place, with open end zones on both ends and a capacity of just 35,000. By the summer of 1968, it was officially completed at a total cost of $3.5 million.

Lane Stadium—which was named for Edward Hudson Lane Sr., a student in the early 1900s who co-founded a company that would be the world's largest producer of cedar chests and later a member of the board of visitors—has since undergone several renovations to make it the third-largest on-campus stadium in the ACC. An addition to the east stands in 1980 raised the capacity to 52,500. A modern lighting system was added in 1982, allowing the Hokies to play their first night game that year, a 21–14 win over Virginia on Thanksgiving Day.

In 1999 and 2000, 5,100 seats were installed as permanent bleachers in the north end zone. Ahead of the 2002 season, Tech enclosed the south end of the stadium with a section of 11,120 more seats, 15 luxury suites, and a new visitors locker room at a cost of $37 million.

A major 2006 renovation to the west side that cost $52.5 million gave the stadium the look it has today. That upgrade included a new press box, luxury suites, president's area, private club seating, ticket office, athletic fund offices, memorabilia area, and student-athlete academic services. A video board nearly five times as large as the one it replaced was installed ahead of the 2013 season.

If you're coming during the week, be sure to hit Virginia Tech's Hall of Fame museum, which isn't open on weekends or gamedays. It's on the west side of the stadium and has galleries,

Lane Stadium Facts

Capacity: 66,233
Seasons: 55th in 2019
Inaugural Season: 1965
Construction Began: 1964
New Press Box/West Side Completed: 2006
South End Zone Expansion Completed: 2002
All-Time Tech Games: 315 as of 2018
Tech's Record: 223–86–6 (.708)
Longest Tech Win Streak: 16 games (September 4, 1999 to October 13, 2001)
Elevation Above Sea Level: 2,057 feet

display cases, and interactive screens to get you up to speed on Tech's football history.

On gamedays, there's plenty to do. Every good visit to Lane actually starts outside the stadium. Be sure to take advantage of the school's ample tailgating scene, whether it's setting up shop and grilling some meat or, not for the faint of heart, dropping by Center Street, just behind the Stadium Woods and not far from Lane, where there's a wall-to-wall mass of students before games, most of whom surely partake in some pregame spirits.

Line Beamer Way just outside of the stadium for the Hokie Walk to greet the team as it arrives on buses from Roanoke about 2½ hours before kickoff. Kids will want to hit up Hokie Village, a family-friendly area with inflatables, tailgating games, concessions, music, and more on the turf soccer/lacrosse practice field across the street from Lane. Before coming inside, be sure to snap a picture next to Frank Beamer's statue in Moody Plaza outside the southwest corner of the stadium.

Once inside, the maroon and orange–clad Hokies fans will show you the ropes. Get there in time to start jumping for the famed "Enter Sandman" entrance not long before kickoff. Clap along as The Marching Virginians play "Tech Triumph" and "The VPI Victory March" throughout the day. Cheer loudly on third downs when a familiar turkey gobble plays over the stadium's speakers. And whenever Virginia Tech scores, be sure to cover your ears when the Corps of Cadets fires the country's largest game cannon, "Skipper," to commemorate the occasion, a tradition since 1963.

The stadium's been friendly confines for most of Virginia Tech's history. At the conclusion of 2018, the Hokies are 223–86–6 in 315 games there all-time, with their longest home winning streak being 16 games from 1999–2001.

Still on the fence? Leave it to a football expert like ESPN analyst Kirk Herbstreit to give the Lane Stadium experience a glowing review: "Blacksburg is a place that has an absolute love affair with its football program. It's a 100 percent crazy, loud stadium environment. You can go to places with 100,000 people and Tech's stadium is just as loud or louder, especially for night games."

10 The UVa Rivalry

Virginia Tech has some football rivalries that engender more white-hot rage (West Virginia), some that are more competition-based than anything (Miami and Georgia Tech), some that are recruiting based (North Carolina), some that are forced by the schedule (Boston College), and some that have simply faded with time (Virginia Military Institute).

But through its history, one rival stands out that hits most of those categories: that school to the northeast in Charlottesville.

Ask Virginia Tech fans which team they'd like to beat the most in a given year and the answer is simple: the Virginia Cavaliers. And there's not really a close second.

"I've been gone 11 years. Your feelings toward UVa don't change in those 11 years," former Tech running backs coach Shane Beamer said when he came back to be on his dad's staff in 2011. "It's exciting to be back and a part of this rivalry. I've been a part of Tennessee–Florida. I've been a part of Ole Miss–Mississippi State. I've been a part of Georgia Tech–Georgia. I've been a part of South Carolina–Clemson. And this one is as heated as any of them."

It's been like that from the start, with the schools founded in very different ways and representing people of vastly different backgrounds, reputations that, fair or not, persist today. As Roland Lazenby and Doug Doughty begin their book, *Hoos 'N' Hokies, the Rivalry*:

> From the start, it was more than just Wahoos vs. Hokies. It was class warfare, Virginia style. A clash of backgrounds and pedigrees. The sons of bankers vs. the sons of farmers. Haughty fraternity boys vs. stone-faced cadets. It was blue-bloods vs. bumpkins.
>
> The bumpkin part of the equation would be Virginia Tech, known back in the old days as Virginia Agricultural and Mechanical College (VAMC). Heck, the Hokies were so country they used a plow to mark off their first playing field. And when opponents wanted to tweak 'em, they'd bring out signs that read, "Kill the Farmers!"
>
> Actually, the Wahoos were just happy to ignore them.
>
> After all, the "University" had its reputation to uphold. It was Mr. Jefferson's intellectual village, a place of statues and colonnades, a symbol of that old Virginia aristocracy, a center of law, medicine and—well, snobbery.

The rivalry was born in 1895, driven to new heights in its first 10 years by the obsession of the first Virginia Polytechnic Institute (VPI) great Hunter Carpenter to beat the Cavaliers. Carpenter, who lost his first four games to University of Virginia (UVa) while with the Gobblers, went so far as to transfer to North Carolina to try to do it. Failing there in 1904, he eventually came back to Tech in 1905 for his sixth season and finally beat the Wahoos 11–0.

UVa's contention that Carpenter was a professional and the controversy that ensued put the series on ice for 18 years. By the time the schools eventually began playing again, nobody was quite sure why they'd stopped in the first place. All they knew is that they were supposed to dislike each other.

The series resumed in 1923, alternating between Charlottesville and Blacksburg, but it eventually moved to other locales. Norfolk hosted the game from 1940 to 1942 before a break because of World War II. Roanoke's Victory Stadium became home of the game for much of the next two decades before it returned to alternating campus sites once Lane Stadium opened in 1965.

After Tech won 12 of 14 games between 1953 and '66, the series halted for a few years, then resumed in 1970. The schools have played every year since, with the matchup settling in on the Friday or Saturday after Thanksgiving nearly every year since 2000.

Tech coach Bill Dooley won six of his last seven against UVa in the '80s before George Welsh and the Cavaliers reversed that trend in the early Frank Beamer years, winning five out of six between 1987 and 1992.

The heyday of the rivalry happened from 1993 to 1999, with future Hall of Famers Welsh and Beamer both having their programs humming. UVa and Tech met six times as ranked foes during that stretch and produced some of the most memorable games of the rivalry.

That included Tech's fourth-quarter comeback for a 36–29 win in Charlottesville in 1995, when Jim Druckenmiller hit

Virginia Series by the Numbers

Series Started: 1895
Games Played: 100
Overall Record: Virginia Tech leads 58–37–5
Tech's Home Record: 24–9–1
Tech's Away Record: 23–17–3
Tech's Neutral Record: 11–11–1
Tech's Record vs. UVA as ACC Opponent: 15–0
Longest Winning Streak: 15 games by the Hokies (2004–18)

Jermaine Holmes for a late touchdown and Antonio Banks sealed it with a walk-off pick six, dodging a half-hearted trip attempt on the sideline by UVa trainer Joe Gieck.

The Cavaliers pulled off their own comeback in Blacksburg in 1998, winning 36–32 on a pair of fourth-quarter touchdown passes from Aaron Brooks, the second a 47-yarder to Ahmad Hawkins to put a dagger in the Hokies.

After that, it's been almost all Virginia Tech. Beamer not only turned around the rivalry; he ground it into dust. Starting with the 1999 victory, the Hokies have won 19 of the last 20 games against the Cavaliers, including 15 straight as of 2018. It gives Tech a 58–37–5 all-time advantage in the series.

Despite the recent lopsidedness, it still gets heated. Sometimes that dislike boils over onto the field. The teams had a pregame jawing session at midfield in 2014, more bark than bite, but entertaining nonetheless.

Sometimes, it's just harmless tweaking. In 2005, some Tech fans snuck into Scott Stadium before the game and painted an orange "T" next to the giant "V" in the Cavaliers' crossed-swords logo at midfield. The Hokies won that game 52–14, so maybe they really did have ownership of the field.

The players get in on the action sometimes too. Hokies defensive end James Gayle was particularly fond of talking a little trash during his career from 2010 to '13. When informed that UVa had a countdown clock to the matchup with Tech ahead of the 2013 game, Gayle reminded the 'Hoos of which school had been in possession of the Commonwealth Cup for nearly a decade at that point.

"We don't have a clock," Gayle said. "We have a Cup."

Though that general dislike between the programs exists, it's not malicious. In fact, when it gets down to it, there's a general level of respect, even if occasionally begrudging, between the Commonwealth's two Power 5 football schools.

"I wouldn't use the words 'not like,'" Frank Beamer said. "I would probably use the word respect. I think it's two programs that have done it right over the years in the same state, and I don't think everyone does that."

11 Cornell Brown

If there's a single recruit that signified a turning point for the direction of the Virginia Tech football program under Frank Beamer, it was defensive end Cornell Brown.

Though born in Englewood, New Jersey, Brown attended E.C. Glass High in Lynchburg, Virginia, helping lead the Hilltoppers to the state championship game as a junior and senior in 1991–92.

He had plenty of college options, ranked by the *Roanoke Times* as the No. 2 player in the state behind James Farrior, who'd sign with UVa. The Cavaliers had plenty of momentum recruiting the state in those years. Brown's older brother Ruben was at Pitt. So, things didn't necessarily look promising when Cornell narrowed his choices to Tech, UVa, Maryland, and Pittsburgh.

The Hokies won out, however, with Brown making Tech fans' hearts jump out of their chests at a press conference when he announced, "I'm going to the University of Virginia...Tech."

For a program coming off a 2–8–1 season and Beamer, a coach who was perilously hanging onto his job, it was just what the doctor ordered.

"I didn't feel like at Virginia Tech they were putting on a show for that weekend necessarily to entice me," Brown said of his recruitment. "I felt like the people there were just being who they are and what they are. And it's been proven."

Beamer was confident he had Virginia Tech going in the right direction. He just needed a player like Brown to reinforce that thinking.

"When he comes to visit our place, if our players are moaning and groaning and telling him what lousy coaches we are and they don't treat the players right, then Cornell Brown's not going to come to that school," Beamer said. "He can go wherever he wants to go. But he came to Virginia Tech. So, it's kind of a symbol that the foundation's right. We were doing things right. We were close to being okay. We just needed a little more time to get over the hump."

He fit in right away, one of the missing pieces that helped the Hokies go from losing close games in every way conceivable in 1992 to earning their first bowl bid under Beamer in '93 after a 9–3 season earned them an invitation to the Independence Bowl, in which they beat Indiana.

Brown's career took off. As a four-year starter, he'd finish with 36 sacks, the second-most all-time at Tech behind former No. 1 pick Bruce Smith. He twice earned All-America honors—a consensus first-teamer in 1995 when he had 14 sacks and 25 tackles for a loss in the regular season as the Hokies went 10–2 and earned a Sugar Bowl berth against Texas. Brown led Tech in a program-defining 28–10 win, finishing with four tackles for a loss, including three sacks and a forced fumble.

He was named the Big East Defensive Player of the Year for his efforts and *Football News* named him National Defensive Player of the Year.

Knee surgery limited him to eight games in his senior year in 1996, though he still earned a first-team All-America selection by the Walter Camp Football Foundation after finishing with eight sacks. Virginia Tech went 37–11 in Brown's four seasons, making four straight bowl games and winning the Big East twice.

Cornell Brown (right) and Kerwin Hairston celebrate during the Orange Bowl against the Cornhuskers. (Andy Lyons / Getty Images)

He went in the sixth round of the 1997 NFL Draft to the Baltimore Ravens and played seven professional seasons at outside linebacker, earning a Super Bowl ring when the Ravens and their famed defense beat the Giants in 2001.

"The biggest highlight for me was just simply being able to year in, year out get with a bunch of guys that I created a bond with and enjoy a game as simple as football," Brown said. "Going and competing against other guys and basically saying, 'Who's the best?'"

Brown had his jersey retired by Virginia Tech in 2002, one of only nine football players to earn that honor, and was inducted into the Virginia Tech Sports Hall of Fame in 2007.

He also found his way back to Blacksburg. After getting into coaching, starting in NFL Europe, he served as a graduate student on Beamer's staff. In 2011, Beamer hired him as a full-time assistant, slotting Brown as the whip linebackers coach in an effort to get younger on the coaching staff and reinvigorate the team's recruiting.

Brown spent five years on Beamer's coaching staff, and though he wasn't retained when new coach Justin Fuente succeeded Beamer, he spent a year as Norfolk State's defensive coordinator before getting back to an FBS job at Marshall in 2017.

In 2018, he returned to Lane Stadium on the opposite sideline when the Thundering Herd played the Hokies late in the year, joined by fellow Marshall assistant J.C. Price, who was an All-American defensive tackle on those same ferocious Hokies fronts in the '90s.

"Those guys J.C. Price and Cornell Brown are special guys to me," said defensive coordinator Bud Foster, who coached them both. "They are two of my favorite players of all-time here.... Obviously, they were great football players, but I love them as people. I love them how they've grown and grown up as men."

12 Corey Moore

The first thing you remember is his eyes. Corey Moore's stare could cut through steel. And the defensive end sliced through offensive lines with just about as much ease during his Virginia Tech career from 1996 to '99, headlining a Bud Foster defense that helped key the Hokies' run to the national title game in 2000.

Moore bucked plenty of conventions in his college career. Originally destined for Ole Miss, the prospect out of Haywood High in Brownsville, Tennessee, had his scholarship withdrawn in 1995 when the Rebels were hit with major NCAA sanctions and had their scholarship allotment slashed. He ended up at Holmes Community College in Mississippi before reconnecting with Virginia Tech defensive line coach Charley Wiles, who'd recruited him at Murray State.

Wiles had to sell head coach Frank Beamer on a defensive end who stood just 6 feet tall and weighed a little over 200 pounds when he arrived, a frame that added some size in Mike Gentry's strength program.

"He just got better and better," Wiles said. "He always had that me-against-the-world mentality, being a smaller, undersized defensive lineman. He's very, very smart, very good football IQ, very coachable, but he kind of willed himself into the player that he got to be."

Even if he wasn't 6-foot-4, 250 pounds, Moore was everything you'd want in a defensive end. He ran the 40-yard dash in 4.38 seconds and, on the occasions he didn't simply run past opposing linemen, had a powerful burst that could that could knock them on their backside.

"You don't see many 6-footers around that can change the game the way Corey can," Beamer told *Sports Illustrated* in a 1999 profile of Moore. "In his anticipation of the snap he gains a half step, and then there's no one fast enough to catch him. If you use one guy on him, you can't block him. I don't know if it makes any difference if it's a pro guy or a college guy. I don't think there's an offensive tackle anywhere who can block him on a consistent basis."

In 1998, as a junior, Moore finished with 13½ sacks and 18½ tackles for a loss, was named the Big East Defensive Player of the Year for his efforts, and nabbed several All-America honors, including a first-team nod by the American Football Coaches Association.

His senior year was even better, a historic defensive performance in a dream Virginia Tech season that ended with the Hokies playing for the national title. Moore set a Big East record with 17 sacks and finished with 28 tackles for a loss, repeating as the league's top defender.

Known as one of the best trash talkers in the game, he welcomed Clemson to "The Terror Dome" in a Thursday night game in September, doing everything a defender could to harass the Tigers at Lane Stadium. He finished with five tackles, four tackles for a loss and two sacks, punctuating Tech's win by forcing a fumble on a blindside rush, picking up the loose ball and running 32 yards for a touchdown in the Hokies' 31–11 victory.

"I'll use my opponents' names or call them Fat Ass, and I'll tell them, 'Fat Ass, I'll be coming at you all day,'" Moore told *Sports Illustrated*. "A lot of them get intimidated. A lot of them change their technique. They get all out of whack looking for me, and they start jumping out of their stance. That makes it easier for me because they have no leverage. Fat guys are leaners anyway. Lungers. They try to get physical, but they're off balance, and I can run by them, and they fall on their face. They hear about that from me, too."

Virginia Tech's National Award Winners

Sammy Baugh Trophy (top quarterback): Don Strock, 1972
Outland Trophy (interior lineman): Bruce Smith, 1984
Bronko Nagurski Trophy (defensive POY): Corey Moore, 1999
Lombardi Award (lineman or linebacker): Corey Moore, 1999
Rimington Trophy (top center): Jake Grove, 2003

Moore was a unanimous All-American in 1999 and won a pair of national awards—the Bronko Nagurski Trophy as the nation's top defensive player and Lombardi Award as a national Player of the Year. (Rather than take the Nagurski Trophy back on a plane, Moore entrusted *Roanoke Times* scribe Randy King to drive it back from New York to Virginia, though the trophy riding shotgun became an interesting topic of conversation with a state trooper after King was pulled over for speeding.)

The nation got a taste of Moore's intense nature ahead of the 2000 BCS title game against Florida State. A ticked off Moore cussed at reporters on media day,

"[Bleep] you guys," he said. "You guys aren't going to win for us. Who cares? You guys can write your little stories you like to write. Write stuff. Write what I'm saying right now."

It was a ploy of his to take some of the media attention and pressure off the Hokies' young quarterback Michael Vick. (A give-away might have been him stopping in the middle of his rant to say to an arriving King, "How you doin', Randy?"—a moment that lives on in YouTube glory.) It worked, though Moore offered an apology the following day for snapping at the press.

He had a tackle for a loss and a forced fumble in the game, though Virginia Tech lost to Florida State 46–29, the closest it has ever come to a national title.

Moore was a third-round pick by the Bills the following spring, though his build—too small to play defensive end in the pros and too much of a down lineman to be an effective linebacker—led to a short career that lasted only a couple seasons.

He largely eschewed the spotlight after football, only popping up in public on rare occasions at Virginia Tech, like when he was inducted into the school's hall of fame and had his jersey retired in 2010. If that sounds like a long time to finally retire the numbers of one of the school's all-time greats, it's because it was. Tech tried several times to get him to come back to Blacksburg to retire his number, with no success.

Finally, it happened, though, a fitting honor for one of the best defensive players in college football history, someone who in recent years has appeared on the ballot for the College Football Hall of Fame.

"I was shocked," Moore said of his jersey retirement. "It's a great honor, I guess. I'm not trying to downplay it. But you know me. I never made a fuss over all that individual stuff."

13 Getting into the Big East

For the longest time Virginia Tech football was a nomad, a football independent for 26 years until its inclusion in the newly-created Big East football conference in 1991, a watershed moment for a program that would go on to grow into a national power.

That wasn't an obvious outcome at the time. The Hokies had moments but were nothing special after they left the Southern Conference before the 1965 season, and efforts to gain admittance to the ACC failed on a number of occasions, including most recently in 1977.

But when Dave Braine was hired as the Hokies' athletic director in 1988, one of his goals was to get Virginia Tech into a major conference in football.

The Big East, which was founded on its Northeast basketball roots back in 1979, was looking to sponsor football as a conference for the first time. Penn State agreed to join the Big Ten in 1989, with Arkansas and South Carolina doing the same with the SEC and Florida State the ACC in 1990. Conference expansion was in the air and football was driving it.

Mike Tranghese, who succeeded Dave Gavitt as the Big East's commissioner in June 1990, wanted to make his league more viable. He recognized football as the biggest money-maker in college sports and worried the football independents in the league (Boston College, Syracuse, Pitt) would have wandering eyes.

Shortly after Tranghese became commissioner, the league went after a big fish, extending an invitation to football powerhouse Miami, an independent which had won national championships in 1983, '87, and '89.

Virginia Tech got a call soon after, with Tranghese contacting Braine to inquire about the Hokies' interest in the league. Boy, were they interested.

In December of that year, the league officially extended the invitation, with the Hokies joining the league on a football-only basis on February 5, 1991. The Big East added Rutgers, Temple, and West Virginia as football-only members as well, pairing them with Boston College, Syracuse, Pitt, and Miami.

"I wanted to celebrate, just knowing this was the piece of the puzzle Virginia Tech had lacked all those years," Frank Beamer wrote in his autobiography *Let Me Be Frank* more than two decades later. "Having a conference affiliation, especially with a powerhouse program like Miami joining too, would now give us a recruiting advantage we never had as an independent. The potential of the program had suddenly increased dramatically in one day."

Big East Award Winners

Coach of the Year: Frank Beamer, 1995, 1996, 1999

Offensive Player of the Year: QB Jim Druckenmiller, Co- 1996; QB Michael Vick, 1999; RB Lee Suggs, Co- 2000

Defensive Player of the Year: DE Cornell Brown 1995; DE Corey Moore, 1998, 1999

Special Teams Player of the Year: PK Shayne Graham, 1999; PR DeAngelo Hall, Co- 2003)

Rookie of the Year: QB Michael Vick, 1999; RB Kevin Jones, 2001

With the Northeast presence of the league, the Hokies' recruiting made inroads in Pennsylvania, New Jersey, and New York. The team undoubtedly benefited from its Big East membership, winning the league in 1995 and '96 and garnering Alliance Bowl bids thanks to the conference's access. They played in the Sugar Bowl and Orange Bowl those two seasons.

It would be a while until the Hokies' other sports programs would join the football team in the Big East. They were denied full membership in 1994 and, with the Metro Conference falling apart, had to house their non-football sports in the Atlantic 10.

"We're not going to be the trigger,"' athletic director Jim Weaver told the *Daily Press* in 1997. "But we need to be a player. We're too good an institution and have too good an athletics department not to be a player."

Eventually, they got full access to the Big East. Tech announced late in 1999 that they would move all their sports (other than wrestling) to the league as a full-fledged member in the 2000–01 academic year.

Though the Big East was a tremendous boost for Virginia Tech, the league was held together tenuously, unwieldy in size and with friction between the football and non-football playing schools. When the expansion craze of the early 2000s began, the Big East was a prime target.

The ACC, the league the Hokies long coveted, came calling in 2003, offering Tech full membership along with Miami, and Boston College in 2005. Tech played one last lame-duck year in the Big East in 2003 before joining the ACC in the 2004–05 academic year.

Though the Hokies jumped at the opportunity to move, they were still well served by their time in the Big East and vice versa. The football team won three Big East titles and represented the league in the second Bowl Championship Series title game in 2000 against Florida State. The Hokies and Hurricanes were the only two Big East schools to qualify for the championship game.

"Getting in the Big East back then was huge," Beamer said. "It gave us an avenue to bowl games. It got us on TV, and that helps recruiting. We got to the national championship game through the Big East. Getting in there really helped us get things going in the right direction."

14 Tyrod Taylor

When Tyrod Taylor was a five-star recruit tearing up the football fields at Hampton, where he went 34–4 as a starter, scored 100 total touchdowns, and won a Division 5 state championship, Virginia Tech came with an all-out blitz to secure the dual threat's services.

He was a gamechanger in the Michael Vick mold, and the Hokies—who languished on offense in 2006 two years after Bryan Randall graduated and the year after Marcus Vick got booted from school—knew they would need a difference-maker at quarterback for the future.

Running back Darren Evans (32) lifts Tyrod Taylor (5) as they celebrate Evans' touchdown run in the fourth quarter against Cincinnati in the 2009 Orange Bowl. (Wilfredo Lee / AP Photo)

Nerves were high when Taylor was about to make his decision on TV in Hampton. After explaining why he narrowed down his choices to Virginia Tech and Florida, the future ACC Player of the Year and NFL starter announced his decision, saying he was bound for the "University of Virginia Tech."

Let's just say Hokies fans have forgiven him for the verbal gaffe.

Outside of Michael Vick, there's not a quarterback at Virginia Tech who had a greater impact than Taylor, who went 34–8 as a starter, blowing by Randall's 26 victories to be the winningest quarterback in Hokies history.

It's no accident that Tech won 42 games in Taylor's four years, with three ACC titles and a Top 16 finish in the final *Associated Press* poll every season.

"I think Tyrod is a true winner," Hokies head coach Frank Beamer said. "It's a very deserving accomplishment to be the all-time winningest quarterback. But what he's meant to this

Notable Virginia Tech Passing Records

Pass attempts in a game: Michael Brewer, 56, (against East Carolina in 2014)

Pass attempts in a season: Michael Brewer, 441 (2014)

Pass attempts in a career: Logan Thomas, 1,248 (2010–13)

Completions in a game: Don Strock, 34 (against Houston in 1972)

Completions in a season: Jerod Evans, 268 (2016)

Completions in a career: Logan Thomas, 693 (2010–13)

Yards gained in a game: Don Strock, 527 (against Houston in 1972)

Yards gained in a season: Jerod Evans, 3,546 (2016)

Yards gained in a career: Logan Thomas, 9,003 (2010–13)

Touchdown passes in a game: Bryan Randall, 5 (at Syracuse in 2002), Jerod Evans, 5 (against Boston College in 2016), Josh Jackson, 5 (at East Carolina in 2017)

Touchdown passes in a season: Jerod Evans, 29 (2016)

Touchdown passes in a career: Logan Thomas, 53 (2010–13)

program—who he is, what he is, and how he is—he just couldn't be better. I appreciate a lot of things about Tyrod Taylor."

It wasn't a straight-line path to success at Tech. The Hokies wanted to redshirt him initially in 2007, though a 48–7 destruction by LSU in Week 2 and a shaky offensive line made them scrap those plans.

Taylor shuttled in and out of the lineup with Sean Glennon, serving as more of a rushing threat (429 yards, 6 TD), though he came up big in a 40–21 win against Florida State, Beamer's first against Bobby Bowden, when he accounted for 296 yards and three touchdowns. That was also the game he converted a third-and–31 on a quarterback draw, the birth of his Blacksburg legend.

The Hokies tried to redshirt him again in 2008, though a 27–22 loss to East Carolina in the opener changed those plans again. He ended up starting 10 games on a team that repeated as ACC champions, though Taylor's stats (2 TD, 7 INT, and 7 rushing TD) left something to be desired.

It all started to come together in 2009, when Taylor threw for 2,311 yards and 13 touchdowns, with another five scores on the ground in his first year as the full-time starter. That season included Tech's 16–15 come-from-behind win against Nebraska, when Taylor hit Danny Coale for an 81-yard pass, then scrambled to buy time before hitting Dyrell Roberts for the game-winning touchdown with 21 seconds left. It prompted Bill Roth to exclaim to his radio partner Mike Burnop that "Tyrod did it, Mikey!" The Hokies went 10–3 but came up short of the ACC title game.

Taylor remedied that with a big-time senior season, when he finally put it all together. He threw for 2,743 yards and 24 touchdowns against only five interceptions, adding 659 yards and five touchdowns on the ground to become Tech's second ACC Player of the Year.

The Hokies' national title hopes were dashed with a season-opening heartbreaker of a loss to Boise State and a head-scratching letdown against James Madison just five days later. Then Tech rebounded to win its final 10 games of the regular season, with Taylor leading the way. The Hokies beat Florida State in the ACC title game 44–33, with Taylor throwing for 263 yards and three touchdowns, adding another score on the ground to earn game MVP honors.

"He was awesome," Coale said afterward. "He came here as a great athlete and you know he's leaving here as a great quarterback. He's a tremendous runner and a tremendous passer and I think everybody here saw that tonight."

Though many of his marks have since been eclipsed, by the time he was finished at Tech, he held career school records in total offense (9,213 yards), passing yards (7,017), rushing yards by a quarterback (2,196), rushing touchdowns by a quarterback (23), and touchdown passes in a season (24). Nobody's come close, or might ever come close, to his wins record.

"He gives you a chance to win every Saturday," Beamer said. "We were fortunate to have Michael Vick at Virginia Tech. We were fortunate to have Tyrod Taylor. You get that feeling on the sideline like the next play could be a big play."

Taylor wasn't as hot of an NFL prospect as the No. 1 overall pick Vick, taken in the sixth round of the 2011 Draft by Baltimore. He won a Super Bowl ring with the Ravens as a backup to Joe Flacco before getting his shot as a starter, first in Buffalo, where he helped get the Bills back to the playoffs in 2018 for the first time in 17 years, and later briefly in Cleveland before No. 1 pick Baker Mayfield took over. He signed with San Diego ahead of the 2019 season.

In eight NFL seasons, Taylor's thrown for 9,529 yards and 53 touchdowns, adding another 16 scores on the ground.

Virginia Tech fans just want to see Taylor get his chance to quarterback a team for an extended period of time. They've seen what he can do from his four years in Blacksburg.

"I'd hope that he would be remembered as one of the best to ever play here, right up there with Michael Vick," Coale said. "The amount of winning he's done, the numbers he's put up, the leadership he's provided—it's the best you can get. He's made everybody around him better, made this team better. He's been a tremendous leader for us throughout his career here."

15 Visit the April 16 Memorial

Blacksburg and the Virginia Tech community were forever changed on April 16, 2007, though the spirit of those taken in the shooting tragedy on campus has been forever immortalized in the university's April 16 Memorial.

Thirty-two students and faculty members were tragically killed that day in what was at the time the deadliest mass shooting in U.S. history. The university and community have spent the ensuing decade-plus trying to heal from the senseless act.

Through that healing process, Hokies have vowed to never forget the events of that day or those who were lost, and nowhere is that more apparent than the April 16 Memorial at the center of campus.

It sits near the school's Drillfield reviewing stand, across the street from Burrus Hall, and not far from Norris Hall, where the majority of victims were slain.

In the immediate aftermath of the tragedy, the student-driven volunteer organization Hokies United took 32 Hokie Stones from construction sites on campus and placed them on the Drillfield in a semi-circle in an impromptu memorial, a somber place for students to mourn and reflect.

Victims of the April 16 Tragedy

Ross A. Alameddine
Christopher James Bishop
Brian R. Bluhm
Ryan Christopher Clark
Austin Michelle Cloyd
Jocelyne Couture-Nowak
Kevin P. Granata
Matthew Gregory Gwaltney
Caitlin Millar Hammaren
Jeremy Michael Herbstritt
Rachael Elizabeth Hill
Emily Jane Hilscher
Jarrett Lee Lane
Matthew Joseph La Porte
Henry J. Lee (Henh Ly)
Liviu Librescu
G.V. Loganathan
Partahi Mamora Halomoan Lumbantoruan
Lauren Ashley McCain
Daniel Patrick O'Neil
Juan Ramon Ortiz-Ortiz
Minal Hiralal Panchal
Daniel Alejandro Perez Cueva
Erin Nicole Peterson
Michael Steven Pohle Jr.
Julia Kathleen Pryde
Mary Karen Read
Reema Joseph Samaha
Waleed Mohamed Shaalan
Leslie Geraldine Sherman
Maxine Shelly Turner
Nicole Regina White

The memorial became a more permanent fixture when it was dedicated the following August. The 32 original stones were placed in mahogany boxes and offered to the families of the victims, replaced by 32 permanent stones etched with the names of those who lost their lives that day, arranged in the same order as they were in the temporary memorial.

"The stones have seen Virginia Tech continue," student Scott Cheatham said at the memorial's dedication on August 19, 2007. "The stones have seen Virginia Tech prevail. That is why these stones were the inspiration behind the design for the memorial before us today."

Each of the stones weighs 300 pounds, placed in crushed white gravel in front of neatly trimmed shrubs, and they're regularly adorned with flowers or other remembrances by people on campus. Ground lighting illuminates the stones at night, making it a poignant site.

"Hokie Stone has long symbolized the foundation of Virginia Tech," the school's website reads. "Now, it also symbolizes our relentless spirit, our courage to move forward, and our determination never to forget."

Two stone walking paths allow people to pay their respects. A memorial flower area sits at the base of the reviewing stand. At the center of the memorial is a single stone that honors all the fallen and injured victims that day. An inscription nearby reads: "We Will Prevail. We Are Virginia Tech." In 2010, two sitting benches on both sides of the memorial were dedicated to the survivors of the shooting.

Though day-to-day life continued at Virginia Tech in the years after the tragedy, as it had to, it's still something Hokies have never forgotten. That's because the community has vowed not to.

The school has annual remembrance events, including the Run in Remembrance every April and a yearly ceremony on the anniversary at the memorial site, where a ceremonial candle is lit, memorial wreaths are laid, the names of the 32 victims are read, and members of the Corps of Cadets stand guard for 32 minutes. A list of the victims' names has been placed in the football team's famed Lunch Pail since the start of the 2007 season.

The school has a "We Remember" page on its website, dedicated to honoring the memory of the victims.

"They ranged in age from 18 to 76 and represented a variety of academic areas and faith and ethnic groups," it reads. "We hope that you are able to reflect on the tremendous promise each of them embodied for our world with creativity, intelligence, humility, and humanity."

16 The Bowl Streak

Even in this age of college football, when seemingly everybody makes the postseason, Virginia Tech's run of 26 straight years qualifying for a bowl game is an impressive feat. After all, if it was so easy, why isn't everyone doing it?

It's a mark of consistency for a program that touted that for much of Frank Beamer's run and into Justin Fuente's coaching tenure. And it hasn't always been a given—four times in the last decade the Hokies have needed to win their final game of the regular season just to get to a bowl, with Tech needing to rally for two wins in both 2012 and '18 to extend its season.

But when Florida State stumbled to a 5–7 mark in 2018, falling short of the postseason for the first time since 1981, it officially ended the Seminoles' 36-year run and passed the baton to the Hokies. In fact, only FSU (36 years from 1982 to 2017), Nebraska (35 years from 1969–2003) and Michigan (33 years from 1975–2007) have had longer streaks in college football history. That's not bad company to keep.

When Virginia Tech's bowl streak started, it was still a big deal to make the postseason. The Hokies had only gone to six bowls in their history, winning just once, before Beamer's 1993 team got an invitation to the Independence Bowl to play Indiana. When bowl rep Mike McCarthy came into the Hokies' locker room after a late-season win against Syracuse to inform the team that they'd earned the invitation, the players went crazy.

"It was big at the time and it's big now," Beamer said.

In the more than quarter century since, Virginia Tech's been a fixture in the postseason, making bowls big and small. The Hokies have played in four Sugar Bowls and four Orange Bowls during the streak but also ones on the lower end of the spectrum. Regardless of the destination, Beamer looked at each one as a prize.

"Never been to a bad one," Beamer often said.

Some notable games, both good and bad, during the run include:

1993 Independence Bowl: A two-touchdown flurry just before halftime on a fumble return by Lawrence Lewis and a blocked field goal taken all the way back by Antonio Banks spurred on a very "Beamer Ball"–like effort in a 45–20 win against Indiana, just the school's second bowl win ever.

1995 Sugar Bowl: In a game that put Virginia Tech on the map, defensive end Cornell Brown terrorized Texas all night long, with three sacks and a forced fumble in a 28–10 win against the Longhorns to cap a 10–2 season. The Hokies finished the year ranked No. 10 in the country.

1998 Music City Bowl: In a foreshadowing of the magical 1999 season, the Hokies handed Alabama one of its worst post-season losses ever, a 38–7 beatdown in a freezing rain in Nashville. Tech scored 31 unanswered points, forced four turnovers, and ran for four touchdowns in the rout.

2000 Sugar Bowl: The closest the Hokies would come to a national championship, they actually led No. 1 Florida State 29–28 heading into the fourth quarter of the BCS title game. The 'Noles ended up being too talented, however, with Peter Warrick finishing with 163 receiving yards and scoring three touchdowns (one on a punt return) in a 46–29 FSU victory.

2001 Gator Bowl: The Michael Vick era came to a conclusion with a 41–20 win over Clemson, with the Hokies finishing the season ranked No. 6 in the country. Lee Suggs actually had the biggest day for a Hokie, running for three touchdowns, while Tech's defense kept Tigers quarterback Woody Dantzler in check.

2005 Sugar Bowl: The Hokies were surprise ACC champs and gave unbeaten and third-ranked Auburn all it could handle in a tight 16–13 loss. Bryan Randall threw for 299 yards and pulled the Hokies within three on a touchdown pass with two minutes left, but the Tigers held on to complete their perfect season, even though they were snubbed from a BCS title game shot.

2006 Gator Bowl: Tech handled Louisville 35–24 but this game is mostly remembered for Marcus Vick stomping on Cardinals defensive end Elvis Dumervil's leg, a last straw that got the talented but troubled quarterback dismissed from the program.

2008 Orange Bowl: Beamer's struggles in big bowl games came under more scrutiny after the favored Hokies fell behind 17–0 in an eventual 24–21 loss to Kansas, concluding an 11–3 season in 2007 when Tech had legitimate national title hopes.

2009 Orange Bowl: The Hokies snapped Beamer's four-game losing streak in major bowl games, upending Cincinnati 20–7 to finish a 10–4 season. It was Tech's first win in one of the Alliance/BCS bowls since its '95 Sugar Bowl breakthrough.

2011 Orange Bowl: Tyrod Taylor's career came to a disappointing end with a 40–12 loss to a Stanford team led by quarterback Andrew Luck, who found tight ends running free

All-Time Longest Bowl Streaks

1. Florida State, 36 years, 1982–2017
2. Nebraska, 35 years, 1969–2002
3. Michigan, 33 years, 1975–2006
4. **Virginia Tech, 26 years, 1993–active**
5. Alabama, 25 years, 1959–1983

6*t.* Florida, 22 years, 1991–2002

6*t.* Georgia, 22 years, 1997–active

8. Oklahoma, 20 years, 1999–active
9. LSU, 19 years, 2000–active
10. Georgia Tech, 18 years, 1997–2014

down the field all night. Luck threw for 287 yards and four touchdowns in the blowout.

2012 Sugar Bowl: Tech's last major bowl game was perhaps its most frustrating loss. The Hokies squandered numerous chances to put Michigan away in regulation and were robbed in overtime when Danny Coale's touchdown catch was overruled by a replay official. Tech missed its field goal in OT and the Wolverines made theirs, handing the Hokies a 23–20 loss that stings to this day.

2014 Military Bowl: Emotions were high, with Beamer sidelined for the month's leadup to the game after having throat surgery. His son, Shane Beamer, stepped in as acting head coach, with the coordinators taking on extra duties. Frank came back for the game, watching from the press box as Tech turned in quite a "Beamer Ball" performance, getting contributions in all three phases of a 33–17 win against Cincinnati.

2015 Independence Bowl: It finished where it all started, with Beamer and the Hokies going back to the Independence Bowl for the Hall of Fame coach's final game. This one was a little bit unusual. Tech won a shootout with Tulsa 55–52, sending out the retiring Beamer in style.

2016 Belk Bowl: Fuente's first bowl with the Hokies didn't look like it'd be a positive outcome when his team fell behind Arkansas 24–0 at halftime. But Tech scored 35 unanswered points in the second half, with the defense forcing four turnovers and quarterback Jerod Evans accounting for four touchdowns in the biggest comeback in school history.

17 The 1999 Season

Truth be told, the Hokies might have had the potential to do what they did in 1999 a year earlier, if not for one key missing ingredient: the quarterback.

They had a special one on the roster, all right. Michael Vick was his name and he was tearing things up on the scout team. Problem was, he was redshirting, a promise Frank Beamer had made to Vick's high school coach that he'd redshirt Vick on his first year on campus, wanting him to be prepared before being thrust into the limelight.

Beamer was a man of his word, even when injuries to Tech's top two quarterbacks in '98 forced safety and former quarterback Nick Sorensen into duty in an early-season loss to Temple. Al Clark returned later in the year but wasn't the dynamo Vick would become.

The Hokies took the restrictors off Vick in 1999, however, and the results were magical. Pairing the dual-threat Vick, who was as athletic as any player in football, with a defense that had been among the nation's best for several years transformed Virginia Tech from borderline Top 25 team to national title contender overnight.

Tech wasn't a complete afterthought—before the season, ESPN's Lee Corso actually picked the Hokies to play Florida State for the national championship, which would happen—though it certainly was not a favorite to make that kind of run, ranked 11th in the *Associated Press* poll to start the season.

Slowly but surely, the Hokies rose in the rankings. Vick debuted in memorable fashion, rushing for three touchdowns in a 47–0 win against James Madison in the opener, including a

Michael Vick (7) and Terrell Parham (86) celebrate after defeating Boston College 38–14 on November 26, 1999, to finish the regular season undefeated. (AP Photo / Steve Helber)

full-body flip that he landed on his feet in the end zone on a 7-yard run in the second quarter.

Tech was just getting started. The Hokies served notice on a Thursday night in Blacksburg against Clemson two weeks later, with defensive end Corey Moore welcoming the Tigers to "The Terror Dome" with four tackles for a loss, two sacks and a fumble return for a touchdown as a capper in a 31–11 victory. Cameras panned to Moore on the sideline, who stared into them and said, "Best in the nation."

"He just said, 'Best in the nation,'" TV analyst Kirk Herbstreit said. "I don't know if he's talking about his team or him, because he is one of the best, if not *the* best, defensive linemen in college football."

With stars on both sides of the ball in Vick and Moore, plus a strong supporting cast up and down the roster, the Hokies were close to unstoppable that year.

They beat Virginia 31–7 their next time out and Rutgers 58–20 the week after. That set up a featured matchup with No. 16 Syracuse in Lane Stadium. ESPN's *College GameDay* visited Blacksburg for the first time and Hokies fans packed a corner of the stadium for the broadcast. Tech eviscerated the Orangemen 62–0. Shyrone Stith ran for 140 yards and two touchdowns and the Hokies scored three defensive touchdowns in the beatdown.

"I've been trying to tell everyone for two years," Moore said. "Nobody plays defense like we do. We made a statement tonight, and it was important to do that on national television against them."

The country began to take notice. Virginia Tech had risen to No. 4 in the polls that week and moved up to No. 3 in the Bowl Championship Series rankings the following week, behind only Florida State and Penn State.

November 6 proved to be a mettle-testing Saturday in college football. The Nittany Lions fell out of the title picture after losing to Minnesota on a last-second field goal earlier in the day, providing an opening for the Hokies, as long as they could get past West Virginia.

That proved tougher than anyone thought. After controlling the game for much of the night, Tech gave up two late touchdowns to fall behind 20–19 with just 1:15 left. But Vick got the team into field goal range, getting a huge chunk of yards on a famous

1999: 11–1 Big East Champions, BCS Title Game Appearance

Date	Opponent	Location	W/L	Score
Sept. 4	James Madison	Blacksburg, VA	W	47–0
Sept. 11	UAB	Blacksburg, VA	W	31–10
Sept. 23	Clemson	Blacksburg, VA	W	31–11
Oct. 2	Virginia	Charlottesville, VA	W	31–7
Oct. 9	Rutgers	Piscataway, NJ	W	58–20
Oct. 16	Syracuse	Blacksburg, VA	W	62–0
Oct. 30	Pitt	Pittsburgh, PA	W	30–17
Nov. 6	West Virginia	Morgantown, WV	W	22–20
Nov. 13	Miami	Blacksburg, VA	W	43–10
Nov. 20	Temple	Philadelphia, PA	W	62–7
Nov. 26	Boston College	Blacksburg, VA	W	38–14
Jan. 4, 2000	Florida State	New Orleans, LA	L	46–29

Coach: Frank Beamer
Ranking (AP): Preseason—No. 13; Postseason—No. 2
All-American: First team—Corey Moore, defensive end; Michael Vick, quarterback; Second team—John Engelberger, defensive end; Jamel Smith, linebacker; Third team—Anthony Midget, cornerback
All-Big East: First team—Michael Vick, quarterback; Shyrone Stith, running back; Shayne Graham, kicker; Ricky Hall, punt/kick returner; Corey Moore, defensive end; John Engelberger, defensive end; Anthony Midget, cornerback; Jimmy Kibble, punter
Leaders: Rushing—Shyrone Stith (1,119 yards, 226 carries, 13 TD); Passing—Michael Vick (90 of 153, 1,840 yards, 12 TD, 5 INT); Receiving—André Davis (35 catches, 962 yards, 9 TD)

scramble up the right sideline, setting up Shayne Graham's 44-yard field goal at the gun. That lifted the Hokies to a 22–20 win and kept Tech's national title hopes alive.

The BCS wasn't Virginia Tech's friend initially, with Tennessee leapfrogging the Hokies to No. 2 after its win against Notre Dame that week. But the Vols lost at Arkansas the following week, allowing Virginia Tech to control its path to the title game.

The Hokies didn't falter, crushing No. 19 Miami 43–10 and Temple 62–7 before facing No. 22 Boston College at home in the regular season finale. Vick threw for three touchdowns, including two deep ones to André Davis early, and ran for another as Tech won 38–14 to finish the year 11–0, its first perfect regular season in 81 years, and as Big East champs.

Fans stormed the field and tore down the goal posts in celebration. In the pandemonium, Beamer stood on a makeshift platform and got on a mic to address the crowd.

"I want to know how many of you I'm going to see in New Orleans?!" he asked.

That still wasn't finalized, though. There were plenty of commenters in the sport who didn't think Tech belonged in the national title conversation, a notion *Sports Illustrated* boldly argued against in its December 6 issue with a cover shot of Davis carrying the ball high and tight, accompanied by the large headline, "They Belong!" (No. 3 Nebraska, a one-loss team, was still set to play Texas in the Big 12 title game, though the Cornhuskers didn't jump the Hokies in the end.)

"The Big East-champion Hokies, outsiders in the closed society of football powers, have crashed the party," *SI*'s Tim Layden wrote.

It became official the next week. Tech would play Florida State for the national title.

Before that game took place, Vick finished third in the Heisman voting behind Wisconsin's Ron Dayne and Georgia Tech's Joe Hamilton after throwing for 1,840 yards and 12 touchdowns and rushing for 585 and eight more scores, numbers that seem quaint by today's standards but don't completely describe how he took college football by storm that year.

Moore won the Lombardi Award and Nagurski Trophy. Fifteen Hokies graced the All-Big East teams, with eight earning first-team honors, including standouts like Stith, defensive end John Engelberger, punt and kick returner Ricky Hall, and cornerback Anthony Midget.

And while the Hokies would come up short on the biggest stage, falling to Florida State 46–29 in the Sugar Bowl that January, it doesn't change the fact that the 1999 team was the greatest in Virginia Tech history.

18 Getting into the ACC

Ever since the ACC was founded in 1953 with seven charter members, all of whom withdrew from the Southern Conference, Virginia Tech coveted membership league.

It did when it left the Southern Conference to be an independent in 1965, it did when the ACC quickly rejected the Hokies' bid for membership in 1977 and, though it eventually got into the Big East, it certainly did when the ACC decided it wanted to expand in the spring of 2003.

The time for Tech to gets its geographical, tradition, and revenue dream was within reach that year, with Hokies administrators giving a presentation for the ACC's leaders in May. There was one pesky little problem—the league's presidents targeted Miami, Boston College, and Syracuse from the Big East.

Soon, the lawyers got involved. Virginia Tech joined four other Big East schools in filing a lawsuit, accusing the ACC of conspiring to destroy the Big East. But behind the scenes, the Hokies were working to still get into their dream conference.

They had some powerful allies. Then-governor Mark Warner became an advocate for Virginia Tech joining the league. With basketball schools Duke and North Carolina against any kind of expansion, getting Virginia on board was critical. ACC bylaws required seven votes to approve expansion.

Though many in Charlottesville viewed their membership in the ACC as a trump card over their rivals in Blacksburg, Warner worked to get UVa on board.

"I had to refresh the memory of some board members that they serve at the pleasure of the governor," Warner told the *Daily Press* in 2008. "That this was not about UVa versus Tech, it was in the best interest of the state. After a few candid conversations with a couple of board members, I think they understood. And the board stood solid."

One powerful member of UVa's board was William Goodwin Jr., a Richmond native who had degrees from both Virginia and Virginia Tech. He helped convince his fellow board members to get in the Hokies' camp.

"Virginia is very much for expansion," Goodwin said at the time, "but only if it includes Virginia Tech."

After a brief stalemate, the league had a breakthrough after a June 24 teleconference. The school presidents decided to add Miami and Virginia Tech. A formal invitation came a day later. (Boston College got an invite later.)

"These two institutions represent and share the values for which the ACC has long been known," said Clemson president James F. Barker, head of the league's Council of Presidents. "We feel they will be a great addition to our family."

Virginia Tech's ACC Award Winners

Coach of the Year: Frank Beamer, 2004, 2005; Justin Fuente, 2016

Player of the Year: QB Bryan Randall, 2004; QB Tyrod Taylor, 2010; RB David Wilson, 2011

Offensive Player of the Year: QB Bryan Randall, 2004; QB Tyrod Taylor, 2010; RB David Wilson, 2011

Rookie of the Year: RB Ryan Williams, 2009

Offensive Rookie of the Year: RB Ryan Williams, 2009

Defensive Rookie of the Year: CB Kendall Fuller, 2013

Outstanding Blocker (Jacobs Trophy): OT Blake DeChristopher, 2011

It was a coup for the Hokies, conference itinerants for the longest time who'd finally found their long-desired home.

"The best thing that has ever happened to the university, both academically and athletically, is the invitation from the Atlantic Coast Conference," Virginia Tech athletic director Jim Weaver said. "There is absolutely no downside. None."

Though Miami was the headliner of league expansion, winning a national title in 2001, having four straight Top 5 finishes from 2000 to 2003, and a pipeline of talent going to the NFL, it was the Hokies who actually took the league by storm on the gridiron.

While Miami faded from the national scene for close to a decade, Frank Beamer's teams won ACC titles in four of its first seven years in the league, raising the trophy in 2004, '07, '08 and '10. The Hokies won at least 10 games in their first eight years in the ACC and won the Coastal Division in five of the first seven years after the league split into two divisions in 2005.

The revenue and exposure the Hokies got from the ACC trickled down to help all of Virginia Tech's sports.

Though former *Roanoke Times* sports editor Bill Brill once predicted Virginia Tech would not win an ACC championship in his lifetime, the Hokies have proved him wrong many times over.

They've won 27 ACC titles in 10 sports since joining the league, and while football still reigns supreme, the school's claimed multiple league championships in both men's and women's indoor track, men's and women's outdoor track, softball, and wrestling, with a single title in men's cross country, men's golf, and men's swimming and diving.

From 1994 to 2004, the Hokies best finish in the Directors' Cup all-sports standings was 63rd, with an average finish of 91st. Since the 2004–05 academic year, Tech has had an average ranking of 41st, finishing in the Top 40 nine times and reaching its highest point in 2017–18, when it came in 28th.

Academically, the school's seen graduation success rates rise rapidly among athletes, from a four-year average of 68 percent back in 1999–2000 to an impressive 92 percent in 2018, tied for first among all the public universities in the ACC.

The school's been rewarded handsomely by ACC membership with an ever-increasing revenue pot driven by its media rights deal. The Hokies reported athletic department revenue of $38.9 million in 2003–04, their final year in the Big East. Now, it's nearly $100 million, helping keep the Hokies competitive on the field and fueling a facilities boom across campus in all sports.

"The Godsend of it all, in my opinion, was Virginia Tech," ACC commissioner John Swofford told the *Daily Press* in 2012 while reflecting on the expansion of '03. "In a lot of ways, Virginia Tech should have been in the ACC a long time ago. And Virginia Tech has been a great addition to the ACC. I think it's been good for Virginia Tech and I think it's been good for the state of Virginia. It was the right thing to have happened when you take a step back and look at things."

19 Justin Fuente

Blacksburg hadn't seen a head coaching search in nearly 30 years, so Hokies fans weren't quite sure what to expect when Frank Beamer announced in the middle of the 2015 season that he planned to retire at the conclusion of the year, ending a Hall of Fame run with Virginia Tech.

What they got was a quick, relatively painless coaching search that concluded with athletic director Whit Babcock hiring Justin Fuente away from Memphis. What followed was about as seamless of a coaching transition as you'll ever see, particularly in the wake of a departing legend.

Fuente went 19–8 his first two seasons with Virginia Tech, restoring the Hokies to their historical place near the top of the ACC. And while seemingly never-ending attrition and roster upheaval caught up to the Hokies in a 6–7 campaign in 2018, Fuente still reached 25 victories in 39 games, faster than any coach at Tech since B.C. Cubbage did it in 35 games from 1921 to 1925.

"The smoothness of the process and the resulting harmony would not have been possible without two themes: the lack of ego and the presence of professionalism," Tadd Haislop wrote in the *Sporting News* about the coaching transition from Beamer to Fuente. "The fusing of relationships between all involved is rare, if not unheard of, in the world of college football."

Virginia Tech targeted Fuente for his offensive mind. A former prep standout from Tulsa, Oklahoma, Fuente went to play originally at the University of Oklahoma for Howard Schnellenberger but left after a coaching change and three seasons to play at I-AA Murray State. There, he set numerous single-season school records, earning Ohio Valley Conference Offensive Player of the Year honors.

He got into coaching, first at Illinois State for Denver Johnson, who'd coached him at Murray State, before moving to TCU under Gary Patterson, who quickly promoted him to offensive coordinator. Fuente called plays on the Andy Dalton team that went undefeated in 2010, beat Wisconsin in the Rose Bowl, and finished the season ranked No. 2.

Fuente got his first head-coaching gig at Memphis in 2012 and turned around a moribund program. After finding a recruiting gem in quarterback Paxton Lynch, the Tigers went 10–3 and 9–3 in Fuente's third and fourth seasons there, earning a share of the American Athletic Conference title in 2014, the school's first conference championship since 1971.

That caught Babcock's eye during his coaching search and, after setting up a stealth meeting between Fuente and Hokies defensive coordinator Bud Foster to make sure they could work together, he hired Fuente as Beamer's successor, officially announcing the move the day after Tech's regular-season finale against UVa.

"We all know you don't replace a legend in coaching," Fuente said at his introductory press conference. "You hope to build on what he's already done. You hope to continue to operate in the same manner with the same principals and same integrity that he's done for so many years here."

Fuente, who was 39 at the time he was hired, had some things in common with the outgoing Beamer. Both had a Murray State connection, Fuente having played there and Beamer coaching there in the late '70s and early '80s, along with Foster. Temperamentally, they both fit Blacksburg—unflashy guys in an unassuming town.

"When we met, he said, 'Whit, I may not be the flashiest guy out there.' And I thought, man, that's just perfect, actually," Babcock said. "I actually saw a lot of similarities, granted he's 39 and Coach Beamer's 69, but I like the traits.

"And I thought, one, he's the guy I want. Two, he's going to be great. And three, it can't be such a polar opposite in my eyes from Coach Beamer. Could it work? Yes. But I just like the family stuff. The Oklahoma values I thought fit Blacksburg. And I thought he and Coach Beamer have the humility. I thought that was really good."

Things started out well. Fuente brought in junior college quarterback Jerod Evans to pair with an offense waiting to break through in 2016 and helped the Hokies win the ACC's Coastal Division for the first time since 2011. Though Tech lost to Clemson 42–35 in the league title game in Orlando, the Hokies gave the eventual national champions all they could handle, driving down to the Tigers' 23-yard line in the final minutes before being stopped.

A comeback from a 24-point halftime deficit in the Belk Bowl in a 35–24 win against Arkansas gave Tech a 10–4 record and No. 16 ranking in Fuente's debut season, one in which he won ACC Coach of the Year honors, just the fourth coach in the last 20 years to do so in his first season in the league.

"Some of our fundamental messages that we were going to preach on a daily basis I believed would be in line with the same things Coach Beamer had been teaching over 29 years, maybe worded differently," Fuente said.

"But the way we were going to train, the way we were going to practice, the way we were going to eat, the way some of our schemes were organized was going to change, and for us to have a chance to have success, we needed [the players] to buy into that, and we've had great leadership from our senior class."

The Hokies lost the record-setting Evans and receivers Isaiah Ford and Bucky Hodges to the draft a year early, but a strong defense carried Tech to a 9–4 record in 2017, making Fuente one of only six FBS coaches to win nine games or more in four straight seasons, a club that included Alabama's Nick Saban, Ohio State's Urban Meyer, and Clemson's Dabo Swinney.

Another round of early NFL departures, this time on defense, and a series of player dismissals and transfers led to a nightmarish 2018 season when the Hokies' once-proud defense bottomed out and Tech had to rally just to get bowl eligible. But Fuente's team still qualified for the school's 26th straight bowl game and somehow found a way to beat rival UVa for a 15th straight time.

Still, in terms of success in the first three years, Fuente's as accomplished as any coach in Virginia Tech history, giving Hokies fans hope that he's the coach who can get the team back to the level that Beamer achieved for so long.

20 The 2004 ACC Champions

Not much was expected of the Virginia Tech football team in its inaugural season in the ACC, certainly relative to the program's level of success the previous few years, which included a trip to the national championship game.

The ACC's media contingent picked the Hokies sixth in the preseason poll, and it's hard to blame them. Tech began the year unranked after plummeting from No. 3 in the country the previous year to an 8–5 finish and out of the polls, with a 52–49 Insight Bowl loss to an Aaron Rodgers–led Cal team, leaving a bad taste in its mouth.

The off-season wasn't kind either, with cornerback DeAngelo Hall and running back Kevin Jones both leaving early for the NFL, a pair of first-round draft picks who joined center Jake Grove in going in the top 45 selections. In the spring, Virginia Tech

Eddie Royal

Of all the receivers in Virginia Tech history, the one you'd love to see in today's modern offenses the most was Eddie Royal, an electric receiver from 2004 to '07 whose biggest hindrance was how conservative the Hokies' offense was at the time.

Royal, who Frank Beamer said made more big plays than any recruit he'd ever seen on film, was a small receiver (5'10", 182 pounds), but he was a playmaker. He played all four years in his career, finishing with 1,778 receiving yards and 12 touchdowns.

The fact that he never had more than 500 yards or four touchdowns in a season was more a reflection of the Hokies' offensive struggles at the time, but Royal showed just how shifty he was as a return man.

His 1,296 punt return yards are still a school record. He averaged 14.7 yards per return and had two of his three career punt return touchdowns as a senior. His 1,386 career kickoff return yards are third on Tech's all-time list.

Royal showed his stuff a bit more in the NFL, a second-round pick by the Broncos who spent nine years in the league and had a 980-yard season as a rookie. He finished his NFL career with 4,357 receiving yards and 28 touchdowns with the Broncos, Chargers, and Bears.

suspended talented quarterback Marcus Vick for the year after several legal run-ins.

"That 2003 team was one of the most talented teams we ever had," coach Frank Beamer recalled in one of his autobiographies. "But we had no chemistry. We had some selfish guys and we had too many off-the-field things happen that year, too."

Everything that went wrong down the stretch in 2003 went right in 2004, with Bryan Randall able to play quarterback without looking over his shoulder, a selfless defense bouncing back after a rough year and a whole new conference to make an impression on.

It didn't start out auspiciously. Tech got paired up with defending co-national champion and No. 1–ranked Southern California in the opener at FedEx Field in Landover, Maryland. The Hokies stuck closer to the Matt Leinart and Reggie Bush–led Trojans than anyone thought they would, eventually fading in a 24–13 loss, but that should have been an indicator that this team had a lot more fight than the previous year.

The Hokies would drop another one in the first month, falling to N.C. State 17–16 at home on a missed field goal at the gun to fall to 2–2. It'd be the last time they'd lose for three months.

Behind Randall, who'd throw for 2,264 yards, run for 511, and account for 24 touchdowns; a decent ground game split between

2004: 10–3 ACC Champions, Sugar Bowl Appearance

Date	Opponent	Location	W/L	Score
Aug. 28	Southern California	Landover, MD	L	24–13
Sept. 11	Western Michigan	Blacksburg, VA	W	63–0
Sept. 18	Duke	Blacksburg, VA	W	41–17
Sept. 25	N.C. State	Blacksburg, VA	L	17–16
Oct. 2	West Virginia	Blacksburg, VA	W	19–13
Oct. 9	Wake Forest	Winston-Salem, NC	W	17–10
Oct. 16	Florida A&M	Blacksburg, VA	W	62–0
Oct. 28	Georgia Tech	Atlanta, GA	W	34–20
Nov. 6	North Carolina	Chapel Hill, NC	W	27–24
Nov. 18	Maryland	Blacksburg, VA	W	55–6
Nov. 27	Virginia	Blacksburg, VA	W	24–10
Dec. 4	Miami	Miami, FL	W	16–10
Jan. 3, 2005	Auburn	New Orleans, LA	L	16–13

Coach: Frank Beamer
Ranking (AP): Preseason—NR; Postseason—No. 10
All-American: None
All-ACC: First team—Bryan Randall, quarterback; Darryl Tapp, defensive end; Jimmy Williams, defensive back; Brandon Pace, kicker
Leaders: Rushing—Mike Imoh (720 yards, 158 carries, 6 TD); Passing—Bryan Randall (170 of 306, 2,264 yards, 21 TD, 9 INT); Receiving—Eddie Royal (28 catches, 470 yards, 3 TD)

Mike Imoh and Cedric Humes; a young quartet of receivers led by Eddie Royal and Josh Hyman; and a Bud Foster–coached defense that ranked No. 4 nationally, the Hokies reeled off eight straight wins to claim the ACC championship.

The run started with some unfinished Big East business, a 19–13 upset over No. 6 West Virginia that was classic "Beamer Ball"—four field goals, a defensive effort that smothered the Mountaineers and held them to 247 yards, and a blocked field goal returned for a touchdown by Vincent Fuller.

The Hokies scored 25 fourth-quarter points to win 34–20 at Georgia Tech, with Roland Minor sealing the win with a 64-yard pick six in the final minute.

The team had an emotional win against Maryland in a Thursday nighter on November 18. Beamer's mother, Herma, died in her sleep at age 86 that morning. She'd been in the hospital the previous week but made it clear to her son if anything happened to her, she wanted him to keep coaching.

With a heavy heart, Beamer did lead his Hokies on the field that night. They responded with one of the most dominating performances of the Beamer era, building a 41–3 lead at halftime on the Terps in an eventual 55–6 win.

"We take that just like she was our mother," Randall said. "It was special to us for him to be out here coaching us in a time like this."

A 24–10 win against No. 16 Virginia set up a winner-take-all matchup with fellow ACC newcomer Miami, a de facto league title game a year before the conference split into two divisions and held one annually.

The Hokies were touchdown underdogs at Miami, which was coming off one of the greatest runs in college football history and had revenge on its mind after Tech humbled the 'Canes 31–7 in Blacksburg the previous year. But the low-scoring, defensive battle was right up Tech's alley. Randall hit Royal for a 39-yard touchdown early in the fourth quarter to break a 10-all tie, and the Hokies held on for a 16–10 win.

"We've got the ACC all by ourselves," Randall said afterward. "There's no question who the champions are, who's the better team or who should have won this game."

Virginia Tech earned a Sugar Bowl bid, its third in school history, by winning the ACC and getting paired up with an unbeaten Auburn team left out of the BCS title game. The Hokies kept things close, holding an offense led by running backs Ronnie Brown and "Cadillac" Williams to half their season average in points, but Auburn completed its perfect season with a 16–13 win.

Still, the Hokies finished 10–3 in a season when not much was expected of them, winding up at No. 10 in the polls, their first Top 10 finish since 2000. It set the tone for Tech's early years in the ACC, which ran through Blacksburg. The Hokies won ACC championships in four of their first seven years in the league.

Beamer credited Randall with guiding the Hokies out of a tumultuous 2003 season and took note that simply having really good players doesn't automatically lead to success.

"When the leader of the team is also the best player, you've got something special," Beamer wrote. "And good chemistry trumps good talent every time."

21 Frank Moseley

Before Frank Beamer, there wasn't a larger influence on Virginia Tech athletics than Frank Moseley, who turned around the football program during his 10-year run as a coach and was a driving force behind a facilities push in his 27 years as the school's athletic director.

A native of Montgomery, Alabama, he lettered at the University of Alabama from 1931 to '33 in football and baseball. He had a great mentor, having served as an assistant on staffs at Kentucky and Maryland under legendary coach Paul "Bear" Bryant, who was his college teammate with the Crimson Tide.

Virginia Polytechnic Institute hired Moseley away from Kentucky in 1951 as both its football coach and athletic director, and he faced a monumental task. Virginia Tech was a football wasteland when Moseley arrived, with the Gobblers having gone 1–25–3 the previous three years under coach Robert McNeish and not having enjoyed a winning record since World War II.

Moseley was the tough taskmaster Virginia Tech needed, building the program around a strong running game, a stingy defense, and a rigorous conditioning program that players had a tough time handling. The *Techgram*, the university newsletter, described him as someone who "carries about him the air of a man who would do well in a battle with the devil himself."

The results started to show on the field, however. By 1954, he'd turned Tech into a team that went 8–0–1 and finished the year ranked 16th in the *Associated Press* poll. Moseley was named the AP Coach of the Year in Virginia that season. In 1956, when the Hokies went 7–2–1, he was named the Southern Conference Coach of the Year.

Moseley declined overtures from elsewhere to stay at Virginia Tech, though after posting a 54–42–4 record in 10 years as the football coach, the best mark by any coach in school history to that point, he stepped aside in that role to focus on being the athletic director.

He made a good replacement hire, luring Jerry Claiborne out of an assistant role with Bryant at Alabama. It was Claiborne's first stop on a Hall of Fame coaching career, one that included a

Virginia Tech Conference Affiliations

1895–1906: Virginia Intercollegiate Athletic Association
1911–1921: South Atlantic Intercollegiate Athletic Association
1921–1965: Southern Conference
1965–1978: Independent
1978–1995: Metro Conference (except football)
1991–1998: Colonial Athletic Association (wrestling only)
1991–2000: Big East Conference (football only, other sports joined in 2000)
1995–2000: Atlantic 10 Conference (except football and wrestling)
1998–2004: Eastern Wrestling League (wrestling only)
2000–2004: Big East Conference (except wrestling)
2004–present: Atlantic Coast Conference

61–39–2 mark at Virginia Tech and two Liberty Bowl appearances. Moseley would tap into that Bryant connection a couple times in his career, later hiring Alabama assistant Jimmy Sharpe to replace Charlie Coffey in 1974.

While Claiborne coached, Moseley devoted himself fully to the AD role, where he oversaw a facilities push to make Virginia Tech a better competitor around the region. He established the Virginia Tech Student Aid Foundation to that end, and during his time as AD, the Hokies' biggest building projects were completed, with Cassell Coliseum opening in 1962, Lane Stadium in 1965, and Rector Field House in 1971.

Though he yearned for ACC membership after pulling Virginia Tech out of the Southern Conference in 1965, the Hokies never got admittance during his time, spending 26 years as a football independent.

Moseley retired in 1978, the day after school president William E. Lavery fired Sharpe as the football coach, and though he died in 1979 at age 68, Moseley's legacy at Virginia Tech hasn't faded with time.

He was inducted into the Virginia Sports Hall of Fame in 1979 and was an inaugural member of the Virginia Tech Sports Hall of Fame in 1982.

Each spring the football team gives out the Frank O. Moseley Award, which, in a fitting fashion for a coach whose practices weren't for the weak-willed, goes to the players who exhibit the most hustle during the off-season and spring workouts.

Upon Moseley's death, Lavery summed up his impact on Virginia Tech athletics well.

"With the death of Frank Moseley, Virginia Tech has lost one of the pillars of its athletic program," Lavery said. "Coach Moseley brought our program from one of struggling obscurity to national prominence. His record speaks for itself."

22 The 1995 Season and an Epic UVa Game

Though the Sugar Bowl at the end of the 1995 season was Virginia Tech's introduction to the nation in a lot of ways, the Hokies' path to get there was just as important in the rise of the program and one of perseverance.

Tech had high hopes coming off a 1994 season during which it went 8–4, finished second in the Big East and went to a bowl game for the second straight year, even though it ended in a 45–23 loss to Tennessee. Seventeen starters returned from the bowl game and the Hokies opened the year ranked No. 20.

Quarterback Maurice DeShazo was gone, having exhausted his eligibility in '94, and defensive coordinator Phil Elmassian, an intense son-of-a-gun who'd brought a needed fire and toughness to the program, bolted for an assistant job at Washington.

Virginia Tech had high hopes for their replacements. Jim Druckenmiller, a 6-foot-4, 225-pound specimen who was a beast in the weight room, was the next quarterback in line. Rickey Bustle returned after a year at South Carolina to succeed Gary Tranquill as offensive coordinator.

On defense, Frank Beamer opted for a co-coordinator setup, promoting Rod Sharpless and an up-and-comer who'd followed

1995: 10–2, Big East Champions, Sugar Bowl Champions

Date	Opponent	Location	W/L	Score
Sept. 7	Boston College	Blacksburg, VA	L	20–14
Sept. 16	Cincinnati	Blacksburg, VA	L	16–0
Sept. 23	Miami	Blacksburg, VA	W	13–7
Sept. 30	Pitt	Pittsburgh, PA	W	26–16
Oct. 7	Navy	Annapolis, MD	W	14–0
Oct. 14	Akron	Blacksburg, VA	W	77–27
Oct. 21	Rutgers	Piscataway, NJ	W	45–17
Oct. 28	West Virginia	Morgantown, WV	W	27–0
Nov. 4	Syracuse	Blacksburg, VA	W	31–7
Nov. 11	Temple	Washington, DC	W	38–16
Nov. 18	Virginia	Charlottesville, VA	W	36–29
Dec. 31	Texas	New Orleans, LA	W	28–10

Coach: Frank Beamer
Ranking (AP): Preseason—No. 24; Postseason—No. 10
All-American: First team—Cornell Brown, defensive end; Third team—J.C. Price, defensive tackle
All-Big East: First team—Cornell Brown, defensive end; J.C. Price, defensive tackle; George DelRicco, linebacker; William Yarborough, defensive back; Chris Malone, offensive guard
Leaders: Rushing—Dwayne Thomas (673 yards, 167 carries, 7 TD); Passing—Jim Druckenmiller (151 of 291, 2,103 yards, 14 TD, 11 INT); Receiving—Bryan Still (32 catches, 628 yards, 3 TD)

him from Murray State named Bud Foster. Together, they created the Lunch Pail Defense tradition that's continued through today. A group featuring defensive end Cornell Brown, defensive tackles J.C. Price and Jim Baron, linebacker George DelRicco, and defensive backs Torrian Gray and Antonio Banks would be one of the best in school history.

The season got off to an inauspicious start, however. The Hokies lost their first two games, both at home, falling to Boston College 20–14 in the opener before an embarrassing 16–0 loss in a cold, steady rain to Cincinnati, the first time Tech had been shutout at home since 1981.

"This is as bad as I've ever played," said Druckenmiller, who was 12-for-32 for 135 yards with three picks. "I can't imagine it getting any worse than this."

"That was not the Virginia Tech team we are accustomed to seeing," Beamer said. "We did not play Virginia Tech football. We didn't block, our running game was stopped and our passing was not very effective either."

In his autobiography, *Let Me Be Frank*, Beamer recalled a frustrated Baron standing up in the locker room after the Cincinnati loss and yelling to his teammates: "We will not lose another [expletive] game this season!"

Who would have thought he'd be right? The season turned the following week, a Big East home game against linebacker Ray Lewis and No. 17 Miami, a team the Hokies hadn't beaten in 12 all-time matchups. But Dwayne Thomas ran for 165 yards and a touchdown and freshman cornerback Loren Johnson knocked away a fourth-down Miami pass at the 5-yard line in the final minute to preserve a 13–7 win.

It was just what the Hokies needed to jumpstart their season. They reeled off wins against Pitt, Navy, Akron, Rutgers, and West Virginia (a 27–0 final that was the defense's second shutout) to get to a showdown with No. 20 Syracuse, the conference leader featuring quarterback Donovan McNabb and receiver Marvin Harrison, in Lane Stadium to start November.

The Orangemen scored first on a Rob Konrad touchdown, but the Hokies scored 31 unanswered points in a 31–7 win. Syracuse ran for only 54 yards, with Brown wreaking havoc all day, finishing with three sacks and eight quarterback hurries. Druckenmiller threw for 224 yards and three touchdowns.

A win against Temple that included defensive touchdowns from Baron and Price clinched Tech's first Big East championship and gave the No. 20 Hokies an eight-game winning streak heading into a regular season finale at No. 13 UVa. The Cavaliers were ACC co-champions after handing Florida State its first loss in 30 games since joining the league. UVa and coach George Welsh had beaten Tech six of the last eight years.

It looked like it was about to be seven in nine after the Cavaliers took a 29–14 lead heading into the fourth quarter at Scott Stadium, but the Hokies came charging back. Druckenmiller hit Jermaine Holmes for a 10-yard touchdown that cut the lead to 29–20 early in the fourth. A Hokies field goal trimmed the UVa lead to 29–23.

After the Cavaliers missed a long field goal with 2:12 to play, the Hokies had 71 yards of field to cover. Following a clutch fourth-down completion of 14 yards to Cornelius White, Tech completed three more passes to get to the UVa 32-yard line with 58 seconds left. The Hokies went to a pump-and-go play to Holmes, who got behind the Cavaliers defense for a 32-yard touchdown with 47 seconds left and a stunning 30–29 lead.

"Jim Druckenmiller has engineered the greatest comeback I've ever seen!" bellowed Hokies broadcaster Bill Roth. "Touchdown, Tech! I've never enjoyed saying that more!"

UVa got the ball back at its 18 with less than a minute left. Cavaliers quarterback Mike Groh managed to complete three passes to get the ball to the Tech 40 with six seconds left.

Rather than try a 57-yard field goal, UVa tried to get in a quick pass to the sideline. Tech's Banks jumped the route and picked it off, racing the other direction. He eluded a couple UVa players in pursuit, as well as Cavaliers trainer Joe Gieck, who stuck out his orange pants-clad leg in a half-hearted attempt to trip Banks on the cornerback's way to a 65-yard touchdown as the clock expired. A throng of Tech fans met Banks in the end zone and the celebration was on.

The Hokies finished the regular season 9–2 and ended up getting the Big East's Alliance Bowl bid to the Sugar Bowl to face Texas, who they'd beat 28–10 in a game that helped put Virginia Tech on the map. That's a story for a different time (and chapter in this book).

Beamer sensed it coming. After the UVa victory, he was, well... beaming.

"This is a great day for Virginia Tech," he said. "Usually, you've got to get onto next week, but I think this one's going to last a while. It's another significant win for a program on the move."

23 Jerry Claiborne

Jerry Claiborne's College Football Hall of Fame inscription notes that he was famous for three things: "He was a winner. He took over washed-up programs and gave them new life. And he taught his players to be good students."

The Virginia Tech coach from 1961 to 1970 also instilled that in his protégés, one of whom was Frank Beamer, who'd carry on that legacy with the Hokies as their head coach two decades later.

A native of Hopkinsville, Kentucky, Claiborne played blocking back, end, and defensive back on the football team at the University of Kentucky under Paul "Bear" Bryant from 1946 to 1949, named outstanding senior on a 1949 team that went to the Orange Bowl. He came back to the school in 1952 to be an assistant coach on Bryant's staff.

When Bryant took the head coaching job at Texas A&M in 1954 and ran the "Junction Boys" through their famously tough training camp, Claiborne was at his side. After a one-year stint in Missouri coaching for Frank Broyles and at Alabama under Bryant again, Virginia Tech came calling with a head coaching position in 1961 after Hokies coach Frank Moseley, a former Bryant assistant who coached Claiborne at Kentucky, shifted his attention to the athletic director part of his job.

Claiborne employed the same hard-nosed approach as Moseley, both having learned a thing or two from Bryant. The Gobblers were built around running the ball and playing tough defense. Tech came around in those departments, leading the Southern Conference in total defense and pass defense in 1961 and '62.

That '63 team was a special one. After going 4–5 and 5–5 in Claiborne's first two seasons, finishing seventh and sixth in the conference, the Gobblers went 8–2 overall and 5–0 in league play to claim the school's first and only outright Southern Conference championship. He earned the league's Coach of the Year honors for his efforts.

Though Tech had gone to the postseason once before, garnering a 1947 Sun Bowl bid despite a 3–3–3 record, Claiborne got the Gobblers back into the bowl picture. Teams in 1966 and '68 earned Liberty Bowl berths.

During that time, he coached an eager young defensive back from just down the road in Fancy Gap—Beamer. Tech's future head coach arrived in 1965, had to sit out as a freshman under NCAA rules and started three years at cornerback. He found Claiborne to be a coach who drove his players hard, but he respected it.

"Coach Claiborne was a guy who was everything I thought a coach should be back then," Beamer wrote in his autobiography, *Let Me Be Frank*.

"He was tough, demanding, and you always wanted his approval. For him to say, 'Hey, you did a good job' meant the world to me. I believed in him like you're supposed to believe in a coach. I feared him at times because he was so tough, but I think it was a good fear, if that makes any sense. As I got older, I realized what a great coach he was. He could motivate us with the best of them."

Claiborne stayed in Blacksburg for 10 years, going 61–39–2 during that time to pass his boss, Moseley, and become Virginia Tech's all-time winningest coach. From 1963 to '67, Tech went 36–14–1, the 12th winningest program in the country, right behind Notre Dame.

Claiborne was out at Tech after the 1970 season before taking the head coaching job at Maryland in 1972. Before he left Virginia Tech, he gave some helpful advice to Beamer, who was thinking about trying out for a semi-pro team in Roanoke: "Frank, if I were you, I would get on with my life's work," Beamer recalled him saying.

Claiborne gave Beamer that coaching start as a graduate assistant in 1972 at Maryland. There, Claiborne turned around a terrible Terrapins team and went 77–37–3 in his 10 years before heading back to his alma mater, Kentucky. He took a Wildcats team that went 0–10–1 in his first year to a pair of Hall of Fame Bowls in his second and third seasons.

When Claiborne retired in 1989, he'd gone 179–122–8 as a coach, the 21st winningest coach of all time at that point, someone who won Coach of the Year awards in three different conferences and was honored as national coach of the year by the *Sporting News* in 1974 while with Maryland. Perhaps just as important in his eyes, he coached four Academic All-American and 87 All-Conference academics.

Claiborne was inducted into the College Football Hall of Fame in 1999, shortly before he died in 2000 at age 72, and became part of the Virginia Tech Sports Hall of Fame posthumously in 2003.

"I want to be remembered as a guy who did the best he could with what he had, and that we tried to run a program that was within the rules," Claiborne once said. "Our rules were that if that rule didn't make the kid a better person, a better student, and a better athlete, then we'd throw out the rule."

24 Hunter Carpenter

Caius Hunter Carpenter was many things all at once. He was the first star of VPI football—a fast, powerful runner whose on-field exploits would get him selected for the College Football Hall of Fame posthumously. He was also someone whose deep-seated dislike of University of Virginia football became an obsession and eventually led to the discontinuation of the budding rivalry for 18 years.

Carpenter was born in Louisa County, Virginia, in 1883 and raised in Clifton Forge, coming to Virginia Tech at age 15, weighing 128 pounds. He waited two years before he'd finally play on the football team as the team's starting halfback, initially using the alias Walter Brown because his father forbade him from playing the sport. Only once his father saw him play in 1900 against Virginia Military Institute (VMI) did he give Carpenter his blessing to play the game.

The 5-foot-11, 195-pounder thrived at it, leading VPI to a 6–1 record in 1901 and 5–1 in 1903. That year, Tech beat Navy 11–0 in a game that, according to published reports, Carpenter played much of without a jersey or stockings, which were torn from his body. (Tear-away jerseys existed before the '50s and '60s, apparently.)

Something always eluded him, however: a victory against the hated UVa. The Wahoos had started football a few years before the Gobblers and it showed on the field, with UVa winning the first eight matchups between the schools by a combined score of 175–5.

Carpenter graduated from Virginia Tech in 1904 having not beaten UVa in any of the seasons he was in Blacksburg, so he tried pursuing a graduate degree at North Carolina, which had a better team and greater chance of beating the Cavaliers. Alas, switching uniforms didn't do him any good. The Wahoos beat the Tar Heels 12–11 on a tipped extra point that went through the uprights.

Instead of sticking with UNC for another go, Carpenter returned to Virginia Tech for another year of graduate school. (Eligibility rules were looser then, not governed by a central authority like they are today.) He starred in 1905, scoring 82 points to help VPI to a 9–1 record, the school's best record to date, with wins against Army, North Carolina, and South Carolina. The Gobblers outscored their opponents 305–24 that year.

On November 4, Carpenter had his final chance to beat UVa, though the game was surrounded by controversy. Virginia complained that Carpenter was a professional at this point and was being paid by Tech to play. VPI scoffed at the notion. When UVa officials presented affidavits for several Tech players to sign saying they were eligible, the Gobblers complied.

Still, it was a major point of contention ahead of the game at UVa's Lambeth Field, which, after a bit of a standoff, was finally played. It was a fine performance with a legendary exit, chronicled

Frank Peake and the Pony Express

One of the first stars at Virginia Tech came in the mid-1920s, when running back Frank Peake headlined a group of backs that included Scotty MacArthur, Herbert "Mac" McEver, and Tommy Tomko. A sports publicist nicknamed the group the "Pony Express" as an offshoot of Notre Dame's famed "Four Horsemen."

Peake was the star, scoring five touchdowns in his first two varsity games against Roanoke College and Hampden-Sydney in 1926. In the regular season finale against VMI that year, he scored both of VPI's touchdowns in a 14–7 win.

As a junior, he rushed for nearly 200 yards and scored a touchdown in Tech's 6–0 upset of Colgate. He ran for 306, 314, and 353 yards in one three-game stretch. He injured his hip as a senior in 1928 but came back to return a punt for a touchdown against Virginia.

Peake earned All-Southern Conference honors as a senior and was inducted into both the Virginia Sports and Virginia Tech Sports Hall of Fame.

by Doug Doughty and Roland Lazenby in *'Hoos 'N' Hokies, The Rivalry*, a 1995 book on the Tech-UVa rivalry:

> It was the moment Carpenter had waited for, and he met it with fire. He broke the Wahoos' hopes with a good touchdown run, used his kicking to keep Virginia near its own goal, and impressed the newspapermen on the sidelines with his vicious tackling. As was typical of early football, the game was marked by much punching and foul language. Carpenter repeatedly warned one Virginia player to quit hitting him.
>
> Tech had built an 11–0 lead, when late in the game Carpenter broke loose on a long run. The Wahoo who had slugged Carpenter several times earlier grabbed the Tech back by the neck and took another swing. Carpenter stopped, decked his opponent, tossed the ball into the

crowd and left the field one step ahead of the official's ejection whistle.

Carpenter watched from the sideline the rest of the game, which was called with the Gobblers leading 11–0, at last giving him his long-desired victory over UVa.

The dispute over Carpenter's amateur status was the breaking point in the rivalry, however. Carpenter sued the Virginia student newspaper for libel, eventually extracting an apology. It was part of his many efforts to clear his name after his career. Relations between the schools were beyond repair, however. UVa said it wouldn't play Tech anymore, the start of an 18-year gap in the rivalry.

The original reason was forgotten over time and, when things resumed, the teams simply knew that they were supposed to dislike each other. Just like that, a rivalry was born.

Though a great player, Carpenter wasn't well-known outside of the Mid-Atlantic. He was never named to the All-American team, which was dominated by northern schools, particularly the Ivy League. Walter Camp, who did the team at the time, said he would not name a player who he had not seen play, excluding anyone from southern teams.

Carpenter's coach, Sally Miles, put him in the same category as all-time greats like Red Grange and Jim Thorpe, however, and in 1955 led a drive to get him posthumously inducted into the College Football Hall of Fame. Testimonials from players who competed against him were enough to get Carpenter inducted in 1957, four years after he died in Middletown, New York, at age 69.

"The Great Carpenter" was also an inaugural member of the Virginia Tech Sports Hall of Fame in 1982, and though his accomplishments have faded from memory with time, his spirit remains present in the heated rivalry between the state's two major football schools.

25 The 1993 Independence Bowl

Frank Beamer was on shaky ground his first six years at Virginia Tech, with a 24–40–2 record after the Hokies had a hard-luck 1992 season when they went 2–8–1.

Fortunately for him, athletic director Dave Braine was a believer in Beamer, sticking with the maligned coach and getting rewarded with a breakthrough 1993 season capped by an Independence Bowl victory that ranks among the most memorable in school history.

There were only 19 bowl games in 1993, not the 40-plus there are today, so it was a big deal for a program of Virginia Tech's stature to make the postseason. The Hokies got there after going 8–3. They beat Syracuse 45–24 in the penultimate week of the regular season, gathering in the old team meeting room to hear Independence Bowl chairman Mike McCarthy formally invite Tech to the game in Shreveport, Louisiana.

"It erupted," Hokies director of football operations John Ballein said. "It was really neat. It was one of the most gratifying moments."

Tech went into the postseason on a hot streak, topping No. 23 Virginia 20–17 in the regular season finale to move up to No. 22 in the *Associated Press* poll.

No. 21 Indiana was Virginia Tech's opponent in what was then called the Poulan Weed-Eater Independence Bowl. Little did the Hoosiers know they were about to be "Beamer Ball'd." In what would become trademark fashion, the Hokies turned the tide with a couple of non-offensive touchdowns right before halftime.

They led 14–13, but Indiana was driving at the Tech 49. Hoosiers quarterback John Paci dropped back to throw with 35 seconds left, but Hokies linebacker George DelRicco got to him, knocking loose a fumble. It got kicked backward before popping up on a bounce into the arms of defensive end Lawrence Lewis, who returned it 20 yards for a touchdown and a 21–13 lead.

That wasn't the end of it, however. A decent kick return and a quick pass set Indiana up for a 51-yard field goal with one second left on the clock. Beamer gathered his team and encouraged them to block it and take it back for a score.

"Everybody's thinking, including myself, 'Yeah right, coach,'" defensive tackle Jeff Holland said.

That's exactly what happened, though. Holland got a good push, slipping between the center and guard, leaped and got both hands up. A famous picture exists of Holland, a few inches off the ground, on the verge of blocking it.

"I like to tell people I was on my way down from my tremendous vertical leap," the 300-pound lineman joked.

He deflected Bill Manolopoulos' kick, taking a bunch of steam off it as it went only 20 yards past the line of scrimmage. There, defensive back Antonio Banks snagged it, initially running toward the Indiana sideline but reversing course to the Hokies' side of the field. With a convoy of blockers, he sprinted 80 yards for a touchdown.

The Hokies' coaches from the press box had already made their way down to the field by then, walking past the back half of the end zone as Banks crossed the goal line.

"We jumped on him," Ballein said. "[Co-defensive coordinator] Rod Sharpless tackled me. Banks hit me in the face. I ended up with a bloody nose. I tell people: That was the best bloody nose I ever had."

The Hokies built on a 28–13 halftime lead to win 45–20, the second postseason victory in school history and first since the 1986 Peach Bowl in coach Bill Dooley's final game.

Quarterback Maurice DeShazo was named outstanding offensive player after throwing for 193 yards and two touchdowns, including a 42-yarder to Antonio Freeman in the fourth quarter. Dwayne Thomas ran for 65 yards and Joe Swarm and Tommy Edwards had touchdown runs.

Tech's defense held Indiana to 296 total yards, had seven sacks and allowed an Independence Bowl record-low 11 first downs.

"It was just kind of Virginia Tech football to a T," said Shane Beamer, then the 16-year-old cord holder on the sideline for his father. "Running the football. Being efficient. Scoring on special teams. Scoring on defense."

A roster that took years to build in the face of NCAA sanctions from Beamer's predecessor finally clicked. Offensive lineman Jim Pyne wrapped up an All-American career. Receiver Antonio Freeman and cornerback Tyronne Drakeford would go on to have successful NFL careers. Tight end John Burke was an early walk-on who'd worked his way onto scholarship and also got drafted. Defensive end Cornell Brown and safety Torrian Gray were freshmen who'd become fixtures on the defense for years to come.

It was only the start for the Hokies, who have made a bowl game every season since, 26 years and counting as of 2018.

"It was: This is where we are, and we took care of the business, and this gives us an opportunity to go on to bigger things," Ballein said.

Things came full circle in 2015, with Frank Beamer's final game as the Hokies' coach being an Independence Bowl matchup against Tulsa. In a high-scoring affair, Tech outlasted the Golden Hurricane 55–52, sending Beamer out right on the same field where he had one of his biggest early wins.

"The first time I came to Shreveport I left here a happy guy," Beamer said afterward. "The last time I come to Shreveport I'll leave here a happy guy. I may come back to Shreveport just for the hell of it."

26 The Complicated Legacy of Bill Dooley

Bill Dooley the football coach was a blessing for Virginia Tech, a proven program builder at several stops in his career who did the same in Blacksburg, credited with winning a school-record 64 games at the time of his departure and taking the once-rudderless Hokies to three bowl games and their first end-of-year ranking in 32 years.

Bill Dooley the athletic director was a different story, with financial foibles, scholarship mismanagement, and academic shortcomings eventually leading to his ouster, a messy public divorce from Virginia Tech in the midst of an NCAA investigation and eventual penalties that set back the school's two most prominent sports for years.

As such, he left a complicated legacy at Virginia Tech.

The younger brother of former Georgia coach Vince Dooley, Bill Dooley was lured by Virginia Tech president Bill Lavery from North Carolina after the 1977 season with the prospect of being both the school's head football coach and athletic director. He'd turned around the Tar Heels, winning three ACC titles in 11 years, still the only coach who's ever done that at UNC.

Coming to Blacksburg was a major undertaking as well. He was Tech's fourth coach in nine years, and the Hokies had reached eight wins only once in the previous decade.

But that was Dooley's MO throughout his career. Known as "The Trench Fighter," he won with tough defenses and no-frills offenses, turning the Hokies around in short order. After going 4–7 and 5–6 in his first two years in Blacksburg, Dooley's teams ripped off seven straight winning seasons, a first for the school since the 1920s.

In 1981, he signed defensive end Bruce Smith out of Norfolk, finding an All-American anchor to his defense who would turn into one of the best players in school history and an eventual No. 1 overall draft pick.

Dooley was the one who phased out the old team nickname Gobblers in favor of Hokies, with Tech adopting the HokieBird mascot and a new VT logo during his tenure.

He got the better of in-state rival Virginia in six out of nine tries, including some of the most lopsided scores in series history. His Hokies walloped the Wahoos 48–0 in 1983 (dubbed by Tech fans as "the '83 Squeaker"), came back from a 10-point deficit to win 28–10 in Charlottesville in 1985 and crushed UVa 42–10 in Dooley's final season in 1986.

While he had the football team on an upward trajectory, however, things were falling apart in the athletic department behind the scenes. Early in 1986, Virginia Tech was being investigated for having more football players on scholarship than allowed under NCAA rules.

Bill Dooley, following his final game as coach of the Hokies, accepts the Peach Bowl Trophy after his Virginia Tech Team defeated N.C. State 25–24 on December 31, 1986. (AP Photo / JHJR)

But it was more than that. The athletic department was running in the red and had taken on more than $4 million in capital debt, a large figure back then. Academics among athletes were lagging relative to the student body. Lavery sought to split the head coaching and athletic director positions, causing friction with Dooley and protracted negotiations between the coach and the school's board.

It came to a head shortly after the season started, when Dooley sued Virginia Tech for $3.5 million, claiming the school was in violation of his contract for wanting to remove him as athletic director. They settled out of court for $1 million, with Dooley agreeing to step down at the end of the 1986 season.

"I never worry about the Virginia Tech stuff because there weren't any wrongdoings, and I was always right," Dooley told the *Roanoke Times* in 1991. "Ain't no ands, ifs or buts about it. Believe me."

After finding out their coach on the way out, the galvanized Hokies made sure he left on a high note. They won their final four games in the regular season to finish 8–2–1. (A forfeit by Temple for using an ineligible player eventually made that 9–1–1.)

Tech received an invitation to the Peach Bowl to play N.C. State, one final game for Dooley. The Hokies rallied from an 11-point halftime deficit and pulled out a 25–24 win on Chris Kinzer's 40-yard field goal as time expired to send Dooley out a winner. It was Virginia Tech's first bowl win in six tries and, retroactively, became the school's first 10-win season. The Hokies finished the year ranked 20th, their first end-of-year ranking since 1954.

The hammer came down on Tech from the NCAA after Dooley skipped town. In 1987, the Hokies were put on three years' probation and lost 20 scholarships over a two-year period, consequences that would hinder Frank Beamer early in his tenure. The basketball team was also slapped with a two-year postseason ban and saw coach Charlie Moir resign.

Robert Brown and Ashley Lee

Bruce Smith gets a lot of the attention as the Hokies' star defensive player in the early '80s, but Bill Dooley had some pretty good talent on his first few defenses at Tech.

In addition to Mike Johnson, who gets his own chapter in this book, there were standouts like defensive end Robert Brown and linebacker Ashley Lee.

After being named a junior college All-American at Chowan, Brown transferred to Virginia Tech in 1980 and quickly turned into the best player on Dooley's defense. He led the Hokies with 61 solo tackles, including 15 for a loss that year, capping his season with eight tackles in a Peach Bowl loss to Miami. As a senior captain, he earned All-South Independent First Team honors.

A fourth-round pick by the Packers, he played 11 seasons in Green Bay, making 25½ sacks in 164 games.

Lee was an undersized linebacker at just 6-foot-1, 195 pounds who played from 1980–84, but that didn't limit him. He had 129 solo tackles his first two years at Tech before tearing his ACL as a junior.

He came back to star on the defense, holding a special distinction in 1983: against Vanderbilt that year, he picked off passes and returned them 88 and 94 yards for touchdowns. His 182 interception yards broke a single-game NCAA record by one.

Brown and Lee were inducted into the Virginia Tech Sports Hall of Fame in 1998 and 2016, respectively.

That year Dooley was hired by Wake Forest, where he went 29–36–2 in six seasons, guiding the Demon Deacons to an Independence Bowl win and a No. 25 ranking in his final year. He was twice named ACC Coach of the Year during his run with Wake, bringing his career total to three. He's given a good amount of credit for raising the status of ACC football for his work at UNC and Wake Forest.

He did the same at Virginia Tech, an independent back then, even if his time in Blacksburg ended in turmoil. Billy Hite, a player and later assistant coach for Dooley at UNC who followed him to Virginia Tech, summed him up when Dooley died at age 82 in 2016.

"There's one word to describe him: He's a winner," Hite told the *Roanoke Times*. "That's all he's done everywhere he's gone. He turned this place into a winner."

27 Jim Pyne

Born into a football family, Jim Pyne seemed destined to be a success in the sport, even if he picked it up relatively late. His grandfather, George Pyne Jr., played for the Providence Steam Roller in 1931 and his father, George Pyne III, for the Boston Patriots in 1965.

So, after Jim became a standout lineman growing up in Milford, Massachusetts, it wasn't far-fetched to think it was just a matter of where he would play college ball before going on to be the first third-generation NFL player in the league's history.

After a prep year at Choate-Rosemary Hall in Connecticut, he picked Virginia Tech, coming south to play for Frank Beamer as part of the coach's fourth signing class with the Hokies in 1990.

"Usually you can tell if a guy has ability after about five plays. Jim's was a three-play tape," Beamer told Sally Jenkins in a 1993 *Sports Illustrated* profile of Pyne titled "Born to Block."

He'd be the first in a great lineage of centers in Blacksburg that includes Billy Conaty and Jake Grove.

Pyne came from a small, working-class town, where his father ran a construction and machinery company. The son took those traits to the football field.

Teammates at Virginia Tech joked that the 6-foot-2, 285-pounder looked like a 40-year-old in his college days, though that might have been in part because he was so physically developed.

Pyne was an early standout in Mike Gentry's weight room, something that showed in his famously large, size–22 neck. He had a mean streak and a physical nature that helped him thrive at an often thankless position.

"It's not a romantic position," Pyne told *SI*. "We're different people, a different breed. You're always banging your head into something. Everything falls around you. I like the word relentless."

The Hokies had their ups and downs during Pyne's four years in Blacksburg, going 11–11 his first two years before a disheartening 2–8–1 season in 1992 that almost cost Beamer his job. But Tech got to the light at the end of the tunnel in Pyne's senior year, going 9–3 and making it to the first bowl game under Beamer, an Independence Bowl win against Indiana.

Pyne was a big reason for that turnaround. He allowed one sack in over 2,700 snaps in his college career and turned in one of the best seasons for an offensive lineman in '93, selected as a unanimous All-American, the first player in Virginia Tech history to earn that honor. He also was the first Hokies player to win the Dudley Award as the state's top Division I player and was a finalist for both the Lombardi Award and Outland Trophy.

Though his playing days preceded the Rimington Trophy, which has been awarded annually to the nation's top center since 2000, Pyne was widely regarded as the best center in the country. He'd later be named to the Big East's all-time team at the end of the century.

Pyne was a seventh-round selection in the 1994 Draft by the Tampa Bay Buccaneers.

"Making the team my rookie year was a dream come true," he said.

Pyne played nine seasons in the NFL, later going to Detroit, Cleveland (as the first overall pick in the expansion draft), and Philadelphia. He played in 81 games in the NFL at guard and center and started 73 before retiring at age 30 after the 2001 season.

FOOLS

The big guys deserve some love too, or so an older gentleman who walked with the team by the tunnel and appreciated offensive line play in the 1990s thought. So, when Tech had a road-grading crew in 1993, he nicknamed them FOOLS or "Fraternity of Offensive Line Studs."

The Hokies had a bunch of them in the '90s in particular, when a power run game was the basis for the program. Though All-American center Jim Pyne was a headliner in that '93 group, it was a stout line all the way across, with tackles Chris Barry and Billy Conaty and guards Chris Malone and Damien McMahon.

Tech would have offensive linemen dot the All-Big East teams for much of the rest of the decade. Players like Malone, Conaty, Gennaro DiNapoli, and Todd Washington would earn first-team honors in subsequent years, while Jay Hagood, T.J. Washington, Dwight Vick, Derek Smith, Keith Short, Matt Lehr, and Dave Kadela got second-team recognition.

In addition to Pyne, Conaty (1996), Smith (1998), and Lehr (2000) would earn All-American honors. After Jake Grove in 2002 and '03, the Hokies haven't had a single o-linemen earn such recognition.

Perhaps trying to get back to that mentality, the team briefly resurrected the FOOLS moniker, which had faded with time, in 2015, pairing it with a meat tenderizer they called the FOOLS Hammer, a lunch pail–like token that is carried by the player who had the best week of practice. The metaphor is not subtle.

"It's to pound it out," left guard Wyatt Teller said. "It is something to symbolize how hard we're working."

He coached for three years in the NFL, first with the Bucs and then the Saints, before getting out of football and into sales, later becoming part of a start-up venture called Wheels Up, a private aviation company.

Pyne's contributions haven't been forgotten at Virginia Tech. The offensive line room in the Merryman Athletic Center is named in his honor. He was inducted into the school's athletics hall of fame in 2004 and had his No. 73 jersey retired, one of only four numbers permanently taken out of the rotation and one of nine people the school has honored with a number or jersey retirement.

"I have such fond memories of my time there. Great people," Pyne said. "I'm a proud Hokie and a big fan."

28 DeAngelo Hall

There have been plenty of athletes who have come through Virginia Tech, but few have ever been as dynamic or as versatile as DeAngelo Hall, a cornerback who dabbled in a bit of everything with the Hokies before turning in a 14-year NFL career that's among the longest for a Tech player.

Hall came to Tech in 2001 out of Deep Creek High in Chesapeake, Virginia, the same high school that also produced Hokies linebacker James Anderson and defensive end Darryl Tapp.

As a freshman, he was a specimen, capable of running a 40-yard dash in 4.37 seconds and bench pressing 300 pounds. Though he came off the bench for much of the year, he still had 42 tackles and three interceptions.

By his sophomore season, he was a starter and a cornerback you didn't want to target. Hall led the Hokies with 12 pass breakups and four interceptions that he returned for 124 yards, including a 49-yard return for a touchdown against Arkansas State.

While he was a fantastic cornerback, he was a gamechanger as a punt returner, averaging 16.0 yards per return and taking back two for touchdowns: a 49-yarder against Arkansas State and a 51-yarder against Rutgers.

The following spring, he ran the fastest hand-timed 40 ever for a Tech player (4.15 seconds). Considering how effective he was with the ball in his hands on punt returns, the Hokies had him work a little on offense too.

"I think it's a compliment to DeAngelo," coach Frank Beamer said. "I think he's a guy that can handle that. He has great skill, both as a corner and as an offensive guy. We need some more explosive power in our offense, and when you see DeAngelo Hall as a wide receiver, that's explosive."

That fall, Hall became the first Tech player in six years to play both ways in a game, getting 10 snaps on offense and 28 on defense against UCF in the opener. Hall caught two passes for 41 yards, including a 29-yard touchdown, and made three tackles in a 49–28 Hokies win.

A testament to Hall's versatility came that October in a 51–7 win against Syracuse when he scored three touchdowns, returning two punts for scores of 58 and 60 yards and adding a 24-yard touchdown run on a reverse.

He had perhaps his most famous moment three weeks later against No. 2 Miami, stripping receiver Roscoe Parrish of the ball, snatching it out of mid-air and returning it for a touchdown to jumpstart the Hokies in a 31–7 rout of the Hurricanes, ending Miami's 39-game regular season winning streak. The play led Hokies radio broadcaster Bill Roth to exclaim, "He said, 'Give it to me, Roscoe!'"

Hall, who earned second-team All-America honors that year and was a Jim Thorpe Award semifinalist, finished his Virginia Tech career with a school-record five punt returns for touchdowns.

Virginia Tech cratered to finish the 2003 season among team turmoil and Hall went pro a year early, selected No. 8 overall in the 2004 NFL Draft by the Atlanta Falcons, the third-highest Hokie ever taken in the draft behind No. 1 picks Bruce Smith and Michael Vick.

The brash, playmaking corner started off his NFL career strong, with Pro Bowl seasons in 2005 and '06, years in which he

Virginia Tech's All-Time Punt Return Leaders

	Player (Years)	Average	Yards	TD
1.	André Davis (1998–2001)	15.9	872	4
2.	DeAngelo Hall (2001–03)	15.0	839	5
3.	Frank Loria (1965–67)	13.3	813	4
4*t.*	Billy Anderson (1952–54)	13.0	557	1
4*t.*	Ricky Hall (1997–99)	13.0	534	3
6.	Jayron Hosley (2009–11)	12.0	815	2
7.	Eddie Royal (2004–07)	11.7	1,296	3
8.	Antonio Freeman (1991–94)	10.2	652	1
9.	Angelo Harrison (1995–98)	9.5	713	0
10.	Greg Stroman (2014–17)	8.7	1,108	4

had 10 total interceptions. He wore out his welcome in Atlanta, however, saddled with the derisive nickname "MeAngelo" for his selfishness and was eventually traded in 2008 to Oakland, where he was practically an exile.

After signing a huge contract, Hall played only a tumultuous half season with the Raiders before being released. The Washington Redskins scooped him up and Hall had a refreshing second act to his NFL career, changing his attitude under coach Mike Shanahan.

"Prior to Mike coming here to Washington, all I really cared about was Pro Bowls and making plays," Hall said. "I knew by making plays I would help the team win, and I thought that would be enough.

"I was always a lazy guy in practice," he added. "I always felt like I'll just get a look with my eyes and I'll play in the game. Mike told me, 'If guys see you doing that, they're going to think they can do that.'"

Hall transformed into an unexpected team leader, becoming a fixture in Washington for the next 10 years. He earned another Pro Bowl bid in 2010 at age 27 when he had six interceptions. Four of those, including one he returned 92 yards for a touchdown, came in one game against Bears quarterback Jay Cutler, tying an NFL record.

Injuries plagued the latter half of his career and he never played more than 11 games past age 30, but he still defied time by playing 14 years in the NFL as a defensive back. He finished his career with 43 interceptions, the most of any active player when he retired in 2018. He scored 10 non-offensive touchdowns in his pro career, five on interceptions and five on fumble returns, which ranks 18th all-time.

Hall's NFL accomplishments are among the most impressive for a former Hokie. Only Bruce Smith, Michael Vick, Duane Brown, and Kam Chancellor went to more Pro Bowls than Hall's three. The only position players to be a primary starter in more than Hall's 10 seasons are Smith, Brown, and Carroll Dale.

Upon his retirement, Hall reflected on his long and winding NFL career, recognizing his growth from more immature days fresh out of college and sending a message to the fans who supported him along the way.

"Thank you for putting up with a knucklehead and giving him the chance to grow and mature and learn over the years," he said.

29 Frank Loria

In terms of future coaching prowess, it's hard to do much better than the Virginia Tech secondary in the late '60s, with Frank Beamer and Frank Loria patrolling the Hokies' secondary.

The former went on to be a Hall of Fame coach at his alma mater while the latter might have had the same potential had his life not been tragically taken too soon in the Marshall team plane crash in 1970.

Loria came to Virginia Tech in 1964 from Clarksburg, West Virginia, to play for Jerry Claiborne, and though not very big at 5-foot-9, 174 pounds, he more than made up for it with his heart and physicality.

Freshmen weren't allowed to play back then but Loria started his final three seasons, quickly making a name for himself as one of Virginia Tech's most feared hitters as a safety and a standout punt returner.

"He didn't say much, but he played loud," said Beamer, who was Loria's teammate in 1966 and '67. "He stunned people when he hit 'em. I mean, he just popped 'em and it happened so quick. It was like karate, the way he hit people. He hit with such power for such a small guy. It always amazed me."

Long before Beamer Ball, Loria was a special teams standout, returning three punts for touchdowns in 1966 and four in his career, including one that went for a school-record 95 yards. His 13.3-yard career average on punt returns was a school record at the time and ranks third all-time now, behind DeAngelo Hall and André Davis.

As a senior captain in 1967, he was eighth nationally in punt returns and had three interceptions, winning the team's Williams Award for his leadership, character and influence on his teammates. He earned his second straight first-team All-America honor. Six outlets picked him, making him the first consensus All-America pick in Virginia Tech history. He also was an Academic All-American.

After his playing career, Loria joined Marshall as a defensive backs coach in 1970 at age 23. He was on Southern Airways Flight 932 when, in rainy and foggy conditions, it crashed on its approach on a hillside short of the runway at Tri-State Airport in

Huntington, West Virginia, on November 14, 1970. The chartered plane was carrying Marshall's football team back from a game at East Carolina.

All 75 people on board died, including Loria and Marshall head coach Rick Tolley, who played at Virginia Tech from 1958 to '61. It remains the worst sports-related plane crash in American history.

Beamer recalled in his book, *Let Me Be Frank*, seeing the news come across his television screen while at the house of his wife Cheryl's parents in Richmond. A sick feeling hit his stomach.

"It was a terrible time, one of the saddest days of my life," he wrote. "Frankie was just a wonderful guy and he had a heck of a career in front of him. To be (a coach) at that age tells you something about his football mind. I always thought I had a gift for figuring things out on the football field, knowing what was coming next and all that, but I know for a fact that Frankie had it."

Beamer attended Loria's funeral in Clarksburg, a particularly sad event considering Loria's widow, Phyllis, was eight months pregnant at the time. When the baby was born, she named him Frank Jr.

The emotions all came back when Virginia Tech played a game at Marshall in 2011. The Hokies wore a special sticker on the back of their helmets for that game to honor the plane crash victims. The round sticker had Loria and Tolley's initials, plus a 75 to memorialize all the lives lost in the tragedy. Beamer visited the Marshall football memorial site at Spring Hill Cemetery before the game, leaving behind a stone on behalf of Virginia Tech honoring Loria and Tolley's legacy

Though tragically taken too soon, Loria's been posthumously recognized as one of the greats in the history of college football.

In 1971, Virginia Tech retired his No. 10, one of only four numbers taken out of circulation by the Hokies. Loria was inducted into the Virginia Tech Sports Hall of Fame in the school's inaugural class in 1982 and has a prestigious award after him. Each year, the Frank Loria Award is presented by Omicron Delta Kappa to the varsity level athlete who excels athletically and academically.

In 1999, Loria got college football's highest honor: he was chosen for the College Football Hall of Fame.

"Loria was famous for his uncanny ability to diagnose opposition plays," his bio reads. "They called him a coach on the field."

It's a sad what-if of Virginia Tech history, one that Beamer's addressed several times over the years.

"I could have very easily seen him being the head coach at Virginia Tech," Beamer said. "He was a great player here, an All-American, and he was headed for a great future. His life was taken way too soon."

30 Run out of the Tunnel at Lane Stadium

"For those who have passed, for those to come, reach for excellence."

Those words on two signs flank a slab of Hokie Stone at the opening of the Lane Stadium tunnel, the last thing the Hokies see before they take the field at every home game, racing out as "Enter Sandman" blares and 65,000 Virginia Tech fans jump in unison, cheering on the home team.

It's a distinct part of the Virginia Tech football experience. ESPN glamorizes it every time it broadcasts a Hokies game, with the tunnel an integral part of one of the best entrances in college football.

Walk down the tunnel yourself and you might be surprised to see how plain it is. Painted white with retro-looking maroon and orange stripes running lengthwise, it's a conduit from Tech's practice fields to the playing surface at Lane Stadium.

Though plain in nature, Virginia Tech's spruced up the tunnel a little bit in recent years. Clear signs listing each senior class of football players now line the walls. Players who graduate (or come back to get their degree after pursuing professional opportunities) have a small graduation cap next to their name.

The Hokies' pregame routine includes what's about a 300-foot walk from the locker rooms in the Jamerson Athletic Center by the indoor practice facility to the entrance the tunnel, which is a ramp that declines slightly and turns once on its way to Worsham Field in the northwest corner of Lane Stadium.

Tech's players get lined up in the tunnel before games, waiting as the "Enter Sandman" entrance gets cranked up before spilling onto the field as the song completely kicks in. It's not for the claustrophobic, only about seven feet wide or so, and, with the echoes, gets quite loud. On the way in, each player slaps the Hokie Stone slab above the exit, keeping in mind the phrases on the signs above. The stone suspended above the opening has been a part of the tunnel since 1965.

It's become an iconic part of the university's athletic grounds, and, despite its purpose, it's not just reserved for football games. The school holds graduation ceremonies in Lane Stadium. First lady Michelle Obama had her photo taken touching the Hokie Stone when she was the commencement speaker in 2012.

It's a popular photo spot when fans are allowed on the field, which has been the case on occasion when the team has its annual Fan Appreciation Day in August. You can't go to a game without seeing some fans with field access stopping to take their picture reaching up at the end of the tunnel.

The tunnel's become a notable part of other university events, like the annual Run in Remembrance each April. Things get backed up—that many people can only get through a skinny tunnel so quickly—but getting to run out like the Hokies do at every home game is something every Virginia Tech fan should experience.

31 Carroll Dale

Virginia Tech has had numerous players appear in a Super Bowl, with 12 different players earning rings for winning it. But only one was there for the very first one: receiver Carroll Dale.

Dale was part of the Green Bay Packers teams that won both Super Bowls I and II, and, had it not been for a flag for illegal motion, would have hauled in a 64-yard touchdown in Super Bowl I.

"Honestly, after it was over, we looked at it over and over and there was no motion or movement," Dale recalled 50 years later to the (Fredericksburg) *Free Lance-Star*. "It was solid. That was one of my memories. I had the record for the longest touchdown called back (in a Super Bowl)."

As it was, Dale finished those two Super Bowls with eight catches for 102 yards, the Packers' second-leading receiver in those games behind Max McGee, the surprise star of the first AFL-NFL World Championship Game. Green Bay rolled in both games, beating the Chiefs 35–10 in what's now called Super Bowl I in Los Angeles and the Raiders 33–14 in Super Bowl II in Miami.

"It was a business atmosphere. I guess that's the best way to put it," Dale said. "Maybe it wasn't so much all the joy and all the hype that you see teams have now. Our reaction was, 'Wow, we got it done.' We passed the test, so to speak. It was a burden off our minds."

Dale got his start at Virginia Tech, however. A native of Wise in the far southwest part of Virginia, the 6-foot-2, 200-pound

Dale played for the Hokies from 1956 to '59, an ironman in his day, playing both offensive and defensive end and missing only two practices in his four years in Blacksburg. He started 39 straight games and all but one in his career—his very first game as a freshman.

Though his totals are modest by today's standards, Dale led Virginia Tech in receiving all four years he played, catching 25 passes for 459 yards and six touchdowns as a junior and 17 for 408 and six more scores as a senior captain.

He had 67 catches for 1,195 yards and 15 touchdowns in his career, averaging 17.8 yards per catch and leaving school as Tech's all-time leading receiver, a mark that stood until Ricky Scales broke it over a decade later.

Dale was Virginia Tech's first All-American, making teams as a junior and senior. He earned first-team honors in 1959 from the Football Writers Association of America and the Newspaper Enterprise Association and was named the Southern Conference Player of the Year in both 1958 and '59.

The Los Angeles Rams took him in the eighth round with the 86th overall pick in the 1960 NFL Draft and it began one the most successful pro careers for a former Tech player. He spent five losing seasons with the Rams, but his career really took off when he was traded to the Packers in 1965, putting the speedster on a team that featured quarterback Bart Starr and coach Vince Lombardi, who'd constructed a championship force in the NFL.

"He was intimidating to the point that you didn't want to get on his chew-out list, so that was motivation to do your job," Dale said of Lombardi. "He was consistent. You knew where you stood with him."

Dale was on the 1965 Packers team that won its third NFL championship in five years, then had the good timing to be on the Green Bay teams that dominated the first two Super Bowls in

Hokies in the Super Bowl

Super Bowl XLIX	Kam Chancellor, SS, Seahawks
Super Bowl XLVIII	Kam Chancellor, SS, Seahawks*; Vinston Painter, OT, Broncos (IA)
Super Bowl XLVII	Tyrod Taylor, QB, Ravens*
Super Bowl XLV	Chris Ellis, DE, Steelers (IA); Jason Worilds, LB, Steelers (IA)
Super Bowl XLIV	Pierson Prioleau, S, Saints*
Super Bowl XLIII	Eric Green, CB, Cardinals (IA)
Super Bowl XXXVII	Todd Washington, C-G, Buccaneers*
Super Bowl XXXVI	Nick Sorensen, CB-S, Rams
Super Bowl XXXV	Cornell Brown, LB, Ravens*
Super Bowl XXXIII	Vaughn Hebron, RB, Broncos*; Ken Oxendine, RB, Falcons
Super Bowl XXXII	Antonio Freeman, WR, Packers; Vaughn Hebron, RB, Broncos*
Super Bowl XXXI	John Burke, TE, Patriots; Antonio Freeman, WR, Packers*
Super Bowl XXIX	Tyronne Drakeford, CB, 49ers*
Super Bowl XXVIII	Bruce Smith, DE, Bills
Super Bowl XXVII	Bruce Smith, DE, Bills
Super Bowl XXVI	Bruce Smith, DE, Bills
Super Bowl XXV	Bruce Smith, DE, Bills; Roger Brown, CB, Giants*
Super Bowl XIX	Don Strock, QB, Dolphins
Super Bowl XVII	Don Strock, QB, Dolphins
Super Bowl XVI	Rick Razzano, LB, Bengals
Super Bowl XIV	Tom Beasley, DT, Steelers*
Super Bowl XIII	Tom Beasley, DT, Steelers*
Super Bowl VIII	Carroll Dale, WR, Vikings
Super Bowl III	Jim Richards, S, Jets*
Super Bowl II	Carroll Dale, FL, Packers*
Super Bowl I	Carroll Dale, FL, Packers*

(IA) - inactive for the game, * - Super Bowl champion

the 1966 and '67 seasons against the Chiefs and Raiders when the leagues merged.

The game was an experiment of sorts back then, with owners unsure how well it would work. The Los Angeles Memorial Coliseum was only two-thirds full for the first Super Bowl, a far cry from the worldwide event it has become today.

"It really is amazing how many great football players play in a 10- or 15-year career and never win the division, let alone the Super Bowl," Dale said. "The odds of a player winning it are really slim.

"It's really mind-boggling what it's become. I'm overwhelmed just by how the game has changed over the past 50 years—and the Super Bowl is a prime example of that."

Dale played 14 seasons in his NFL career, long enough to appear in Super Bowl VIII with the Vikings in his final year in 1973, though Minnesota lost that game to the Dolphins 24–7.

He made three Pro Bowls, catching the winning touchdown in the 1970 game from Roman Gabriel. In his career—which included five years with the Rams, eight with the Packers, and one with the Vikings—Dale had 438 catches, 8,277 yards, and 52 touchdowns.

After retiring, Dale's made numerous halls of fame, inducted into the Virginia Sports in 1976, the Packers in 1979, and the College Football Hall of Fame in 1987. He was also an inaugural member of the Virginia Tech Sports Hall of Fame in 1982, going in with Hokie greats like Hunter Carpenter, Frank Loria, and coach/administrator Frank Moseley.

Dale's one of only nine people in Virginia Tech history to have his jersey retired, with his No. 84 one of only four numbers taken out of circulation by the Hokies, joining Loria (10), Jim Pyne (73), and Bruce Smith (78).

He holds an exclusive spot in Hokies history with regards to Super Bowls. Seven Tech players have been a part of multiple Super Bowls, but only Dale, Pittsburgh Steelers defensive tackle Tom

Beasley, and Denver Broncos running back Vaughn Hebron have two rings to their credit.

32 The Lunch Pail

Blacksburg's a blue-collar town in a blue-collar part of the state in foothills of the Blue Ridge Mountains in Southwest Virginia. Hall of Fame head coach Frank Beamer embodied much of that spirit in the way he constructed his football team, which wasn't always the biggest or fastest but was one that out-worked its opponents.

As such, the Hokies needed a blue-collar symbol.

With that, the Virginia Tech Lunch Pail was born, something that's become synonymous with the defenses that longtime defensive coordinator Bud Foster has put on the field.

"What the Lunch Pail is about is going out and earning success and deserving victory, whatever it is, whether it's on the field or off the field," Foster said.

Foster's popularized Virginia Tech's Lunch Pail, an idea born from his childhood when his family moved 40 minutes outside of St. Louis when he was 12 to a farming and coal community that was as blue-collar as Blacksburg.

The original pail was actually procured by his co-defensive coordinator Rod Sharpless' mother-in-law, who in 1995 acquired it from an actual coal miner in New Jersey.

Those '95 Hokies had a lockdown defense led by defensive end Cornell Brown, tackle J.C. Price, linebacker George DelRicco, defensive back William Yarbrough, and others, helping Virginia Tech break through on the national scene by qualifying for the

Reggie Floyd poses with the Lunch Pail after the Hokies defeated the Duke Blue Devils 31–14 on September 29, 2018. (Jay Anderson / Icon Sportswire via Getty Images)

Sugar Bowl and beating a Top 10 Texas team. As a result, the pail stuck.

The symbol's grown in popularity over the years. There have been many iterations of the pail, though they usually have a similar look. "Team"—which stands for "Together Everyone Achieves More"—is typically painted in orange on one end of the box, with the word "WIN" on the side, an acronym for "What's Important Now."

The pail holds the defense's mission statement, keys to success, and goals. After victories on the road, Hokies players collect turf from the field to put in the weathered box as a keepsake.

Players take great pride in carrying the pail, with Foster originally bestowing the team's MVP from the previous week's game with the honor of toting it to and from the practice field. In 2005, defensive end Darryl Tapp staked claim of the pail and never gave it up, the only player to receive it on a permanent basis. That role, which is unofficially called "The Keeper of the Pail," seems to go more often to the defensive captains these days.

"It's just coming to work every day, practicing hard, not taking any plays off, doing things right in the weight room, and even going to the training room to get rehab or going to class," said defensive tackle Ricky Walker, a frequent carrier of the pail in his final two seasons in 2017 and '18. "It pretty much comes down to one thing: what you do off the field translates on the field."

How much does it mean to players? Defensive tackle Tim Settle went as far as to get the Lunch Pail tattooed on his right bicep in 2017.

"For them to give me a second chance, and for me to able to play on a defense like this, I think I should have it a part of something that I will never forget," he said. "So, this is going to be a part of me forever.... I can remember what I stand for and who I represent every time I look at my tattoo right here."

Given its special meaning, it's fitting that the pail was used to help guide Virginia Tech through one of its darkest hours. When the Hokies first played in Lane Stadium the September after the tragic campus shooting of April 16, 2007, the Lunch Pail contained the names of the 32 victims on a laminated card with a maroon ribbon in the middle. Underneath the ribbon is the phrase the school used as it began its healing process: "We will remember. We will prevail. We are Virginia Tech." The names on the card remain in the pail to this day.

"I think it taught us tomorrow is never guaranteed," Foster said at the time. "You can't take anything for granted. These people, something was taken away from them and their families.... Obviously, the victims were part of the Hokie Nation. They were a part of the program when they were in the stands. Now, they're going to be a part of it in spirit."

The Lunch Pail has become so synonymous with Foster that it's on the name of a non-profit organization he started called the Lunch Pail Defense Foundation. Its dual purpose is to fund academic scholarships for eligible high school students from the New River or Roanoke Valley areas, in addition to assistant families awaiting organ transplants in conjunction with Duke University Medical Center. The scholarship recipients embody all the characteristics associated with the pail: spirit, character, work ethic, and determination to succeed in all areas of life.

An incarnation of the pail is now in the lobby of the Merryman Athletic Center for viewing, while a duplicate resides in the College Football Hall of Fame in Atlanta.

33 Vince Hall and Xavier Adibi

Virginia Tech's had its share of standout linebackers over the years. Mike Widger, Rick Razzano, Mike Johnson, Ken Brown, George DelRicco, Myron Newsome, Jamel Smith, Ben Taylor, James Anderson.

You'd be hard-pressed to find a better linebacking duo than Vince Hall and Xavier Adibi, a pair that terrorized ACC offenses in the mid-2000s on some of the best Bud Foster defenses in Virginia Tech history.

The duo started side-by-side for three years in the middle of the Hokies' defense from 2005 to '07, finishing their careers with 606 tackles, 51 tackles for a loss, and 17½ sacks.

They came to Virginia Tech from different parts of the 757. Hall was from Western Branch High in Chesapeake, where he played for coach Lew Johnston and was a SuperPrep All-American. Adibi, the younger brother of Tech defensive end Nathaniel, was across the water on the peninsula at Phoebus High in Hampton, a U.S. Army All-American Bowl selection who helped the Phantoms win state titles in 2001 and '02.

Both signed with Virginia Tech in a deep 2003 recruiting class that included defensive linemen Barry Booker, Chris Ellis, and Carlton Powell; eventual offensive tackle Duane Brown; defensive back D.J. Parker; and receivers David Clowney and Josh Hyman.

They'd soon become the backbone for Foster's defense, but not before a redshirt year, with Hall settling in at Tech's "mike" position and Adibi working at "backer."

Hall, a stout 6-foot, 244-pounder, got into the starting lineup first alongside Mikal Baaqee, making 12 starts on the 2004 ACC championship team and making 64 tackles. Adibi, the more athletic of the two at 6-foot-2, 221 pounds, got a taste that year, making an appearance in seven games.

With Baaqee graduating in 2004, it opened up for the dynamic duo to be the heart of Tech's defense. The two quickly fell into a comfortable partnership. Hall always had the higher tackle count, as the mike typically does in Foster's defense, plugging running lanes. As the rangier defender, Adibi was more of the playmaker, tasked with covering tight ends and backfield receivers.

If a run came up the middle, Hall was usually there. Go to the outside and it was Adibi.

"Playing with Vince Hall kind of makes my job a little bit easier," Adibi said. "Just having another linebacker on the field who is just as good as I am and being able to fly around and having a knack for just getting the ball makes my job easier."

They got off to a good start in 2005, when they combined for 181 tackles and 15½ tackles for loss on a Hokies defense that ranked No. 1 nationally. Tech went 11–2 that year and, after a disappointing loss in the inaugural ACC title game, beat Louisville in the Gator Bowl to finish No. 7 in the final *AP* poll.

"We are pretty confident that we can come back and be the number one defense in the nation," Hall said. "That's our goal. That's been the goal since we first got here. We've just got to uphold that tradition."

Sure enough, they repeated as the country's top-ranked defense in 2006, holding opponents to 219.6 yards per game and just 3.84 yards per play. Saddled with a 99th-ranked offense, however, the Hokies fell short of the ACC title game, finishing 10–3 and ranked 19th.

They had statistically their best season as seniors in 2007, combining for 215 tackles, 18½ tackles for a loss, and 6½ sacks, even though Hall missed four games with a broken wrist suffered against Clemson.

About Those Other Linebackers

Hall and Adibi built on a linebacker legacy that had been long established at Virginia Tech, and while there's probably not a duo as good as those two, the Hokies have had some tackling machines who came before them, including:

- **Mike Widger:** An undersized linebacker who was actually Frank Beamer's roommate for two years, Widger's instincts and effort earned first-team All-America honors in 1968. He flew under the radar as a pro, one of the best linebackers in the Canadian Football League who spent seven of his nine years with the Montreal Alouettes.
- **Rick Razzano:** There's no real way to know exactly how accurate a lot of the college stats back in the '70s were, but Razzano was a tackling machine, leading Tech for four straight years and finishing his career with (get this) 634 tackles. He spent five years with the Bengals.
- **Ken Brown:** A 1990 recruit who went to Fork Union, he was on the early Beamer teams that first got to a bowl game. He was a two-time All-Big East pick who was a first-teamer in 1994 and went on to be a fourth-round pick by the Broncos.
- **George DelRicco:** Hardly a heralded recruit, DelRicco turned himself into a mainstay on the Hokies' first Big East championship team in 1995. He had 267 tackles in 1994 and '95 and was a first-team All-Conference pick that second year.
- **Brandon Semones:** He wasn't a physical marvel by any means, at 6-foot, 200 pounds, but he produced, leading the team in tackles as a senior in 1996 with 88 and earning second-team All-Big East honors in 1995 and '96.
- **Myron Newsome:** Another undersized linebacker (sensing a theme here?), Newsome came to Tech from Butler Community College. Bud Foster called him "probably the best football player, pound-for-pound, that I've ever coached." He was a second-team All-Big East pick as a senior in 1996, finishing second on the team in tackles.
- **Jamel Smith:** A starter on the 1999 national title game team, Smith was a three-year starter who finished his career with 301 tackles, 27 tackles for a loss, and six sacks. He was a

second-team All-American in '99, a first-team All-Big East pick, and a semifinalist for the Butkus Award.

- **Ben Taylor:** There a lot of first-team All-Conference picks on here, but Taylor's the only linebacker who made the first team twice, getting those honors in the Big East in 2000 and '01. He had 318 tackles in his career and was twice named an All-American, getting third- and second-team honors his junior and senior years. He played five years in the NFL, four with the Browns.
- **James Anderson:** He never quite got his due in college, never making an All-Conference team despite making 82 tackles and 8½ for a loss as a senior in 2005. A 10-year NFL career, mostly with the Panthers, shows how good this prototype whip linebacker was.

"I think I've got a little more edge on my Senior Day because I've been missing," Hall said ahead of his final home game against Miami. "I feel like I'm off the map right now. I've got to let people know I'm still here."

The pair certainly showed up down the stretch that year. They combined for 12 tackles and 2½ tackles for a loss in a 33–21 win in the regular season finale against UVa, the fourth time they beat the Cavaliers in their careers. They made 20 combined tackles and each had an interception in a 30–16 ACC title game win in Jacksonville against a Matt Ryan-led Boston College, with Adibi sealing the deal with a 40-yard return for a touchdown in the final minute.

In their last college game, they made 15 total tackles and forced a fumble, though it wasn't enough for the Hokies, who lost to Kansas 24–21 in the Orange Bowl.

Neither went on to have much of an NFL career, though Adibi was a fourth-round pick by Houston in 2008 who'd play five pro seasons with the Texans, Vikings, and Titans. Hall made the practice squad with the Bills briefly before a stint with an indoor league in Richmond.

Nevertheless, their college credentials make them the greatest linebacking duo to ever come through Blacksburg. The pair made five All-ACC teams in their career, Hall a first-teamer in 2006 and Adibi in '07. Adibi also got a first-team All-America nod by the America Football Coaches Association as a senior.

"I've seen a lot of football," Foster said. "I think this is the best linebacking core we've had at Virginia Tech, and I'd like someone to show me two better linebackers in the country than them."

34 Billy Hite and Virginia Tech's Lineage of Great Running Backs

When Frank Beamer suffered chest pains in 1989 and had to undergo a pulmonary angioplasty, it kept him off the sidelines for the Hokies' next game against Tulane. There was one logical option to step in and serve as acting head coach—Billy Hite.

Beamer's longevity at Virginia Tech is often mentioned when his career is brought up, and 29 years at the same school is a long time, no doubt. But Hite, who'd come to Tech as an assistant coach under Bill Dooley in 1978, worked for the Hokies for 36 years until his retirement in 2014.

Hite took the big whistle for the Tulane game, expecting to give a rah-rah pregame speech. Instead, Beamer showed up and gave a little speech in the locker room before going home to watch the game on TV, under doctor's orders. Hite went out and coached the Hokies to a 30–13 victory.

"I'm just glad we won this game for Frank Beamer," Hite said afterward. "Now I can retire."

Beamer's glad the quick-witted Hite was only joking. In his 36 years at Tech, 33 as an assistant coach, 31 in charge of the running backs and 10 as associate head coach, Hite was many things—a loyal aid and tell-it-like-it-is sounding board for Beamer, not to mention someone with a discerning eye for ballcarriers who had talent.

He coached 30 running backs that would go on to sign with NFL teams. Of the 18 top rushers in Virginia Tech history, Hite mentored 14 of them, including nine of the Top 10.

That's one way to stay in the same place for more than three decades. Hite started his coaching career at North Carolina in 1974 and came to Virginia Tech in '78 when Dooley did. He'd been married seven months to his wife, Anne, and bought his first house in Blacksburg.

"I told her not to get to know anybody in this town because we were going to be here a year or two and we were going to be out of here," he said.

Umm...about that. Instead, Hite became the longest-tenured assistant coach in the country, coaching 397 games, going to 21 bowl games, and producing some really good running backs.

When Beamer was hired in 1987, Hite figured he wouldn't be retained, but Beamer kept hearing about all the work Hite did around the program, so he kept him on staff. When Beamer knocked on his door that March, Hite figured it was so Beamer could fire him face-to-face. Instead, Beamer asked if Hite wanted to watch the NCAA basketball tournament together.

"I was with Bill Dooley nine years, and he never once knocked on my door and wanted to come in," Hite told *Sports Illustrated* in 2015. "Old school coaches, they separated themselves from the assistants. They never socialized with them. Not Frank Beamer. I'd been with him three months, and there he was. Frank's the most down-to-earth football coach I've ever seen. He did not have an ego whatsoever."

It was the start of a strong partnership and allowed Hite to continue the great work he was doing with running backs. His successes included:

- **Cyrus Lawrence:** Still the school's all-time leading rusher with 3,767 yards from 1979 to '82, he was a workhorse back for Tech. Perhaps too much. Hite began to split carries to a number of backs after Lawrence broke down physically at the end of his college career.
- **Maurice Williams and Eddie Hunter:** Tech's famed "Stallions" backfield from 1983 to '86, Williams ran for 2,981 yards and Hunter 2,523, numbers that rank fourth and 10th on the Hokies' all-time list today.
- **Vaughn Hebron and Tony Kennedy:** Another tailback duo from 1989 to '92, Hebron ran for 2,327 yards before going on to win two Super Bowl rings with the Broncos, standing out as a kick returner. Kennedy ran for 2,259 yards in his college career and scored 26 touchdowns.
- **Dwayne Thomas:** The featured back of the early bowl teams under Beamer, Thomas finished his career with 2,696 yards, which ranked fourth all-time at Tech at the time. He ran for 1,130 yards in 1993 when the Hokies won the Independence Bowl
- **Ken Oxendine:** A load of a back at 230 pounds, "Ox" ran for 2,653 yards from 1994 to '97, with 27 career touchdowns.
- **Brian Edmonds:** Yes, fullbacks get their credit too, and Edmonds was as fine of one as Tech's ever had. On the power-rushing teams of the mid-1990s, he helped clear the way for Oxendine, Shyrone Stith, and Marcus Parker. He also ran for 1,154 yards and 11 touchdowns and was a pretty good pass-catcher.
- **Shyrone Stith:** Oh, what could have been had he stayed for his senior year in 2000, but Stith was the Hokies' featured back

during their 1999 run to the national title game, rushing for 1,187 yards and 14 touchdowns.

- **Lee Suggs and Kevin Jones:** "The Untouchables" were just that, both on the field and in Hokies history. Suggs was a touchdown machine who found the end zone 56 times in his career, an amazing 21 more times than any other Hokie. He also ran for 2,767 yards, despite missing a year with an ACL tear.

  Jones was perhaps the finest back in Tech history, a former No. 1 overall recruit nationally who lived up to the hype. The 6-foot, 227-pound specimen ran for 3,475 yards in three years, setting the school's single-season record with 1,647 yards in 2003. He's No. 2 on Tech's all-time rushing list, only because he went pro a year early.

Notable Virginia Tech Rushing Records

Rush attempts in a game: Cyrus Lawrence, 42 (against Memphis State in 1981)

Rush attempts in a season: Cyrus Lawrence, 325 (1981)

Rush attempts in a career: Cyrus Lawrence, 843 (1979–82)

Most net rushing yards in a game: Darren Evans, 253 (against Maryland in 2008)

Most net rushing yards in a season: David Wilson, 1,709 (2011)

Most net rushing yards in a career: Cyrus Lawrence, 3,767 (1979–82)

Most touchdowns scored in a game: Tommy Francisco, 6 (against VMI in 1966)

Most touchdowns scored in a season: Lee Suggs, 27 (2000)

Most touchdowns scored in a career: Lee Suggs, 53 (1999–2002)

Highest yards-per-carry average in a season (min. 100 carries): Andre Kendrick, 6.26 (1999)

Highest yards-per-carry average in a career (min. 300 carries): David Wilson, 5.76 (2009–11)

- **Branden Ore:** He quietly ran for 2,776 yards in three seasons and had a great chance of breaking Lawrence's all-time mark if he hadn't gotten the boot from the program for ongoing issues ahead of the 2008 season.
- **Darren Evans, Ryan Williams, and David Wilson:** It's hard to believe these three were all in the same backfield at one point. Evans ran for 1,265 yards in 2008 before suffering a knee injury. Williams, one of the best all-around backs in Tech history, set the single-season school rushing mark with 1,655 yards in 2009.

Though Hite had moved into an off-field role when Wilson eclipsed Williams' single-season mark with 1,709 yards in 2011, he was still the running backs coach when Wilson arrived in Blacksburg.

Hite did all that coaching with a great sense of humor and an endless supply of stories, never afraid to say what everybody was thinking—and precisely what needed to be said in some situations.

As for why he never went anywhere else, even when a couple of I-AA head coaching offers came up, there was never a reason to with Beamer in charge.

"The way he treated us, the way he treats our families, that's why no one wants to leave there," Hite said. "As for the coaching, we always respected that he trusted us to coach our players. He'd offer suggestions, talk to you about things, share his thoughts. But he always let us coach."

35 John Ballein

Every great coach needs a right-hand man, someone to do the little things that can slip through the cracks. For Frank Beamer, that man was John Ballein.

A Virginia Tech athletics staffer for more than 30 years, Ballein is now an executive associate athletics director, one who oversees football and baseball and has a secondary role for men's basketball. But for most of his time in Blacksburg, he was Beamer's director of operations in football.

While Beamer was in the limelight, the face of the program, Ballein worked out of the spotlight's glare, taking care of, well, anything that needed to be done. Whether it was directing recruiting visits, making travel arrangements for the team's road games, making sure players made curfew or anything else, Ballein generally had a hand in it.

"The guy that I think [is] the best in the country in what he does is John Ballein," Beamer said at his retirement press conference in 2015. "He gives me advice whether I want it or not. I talked with him and I think he is sensible about things."

Ballein did it with an unwavering belief in everything Beamer did, his loyal aid up through his retirement and beyond.

Ballein joined Virginia Tech as a graduate assistant coach in 1987 shortly after Beamer was hired, rising up the ranks over the years. He served as the departmental recruiting coordinator from 1989 to '96 and moved to football operations in 1996, a role he'd hold until Beamer's retirement in 2015.

He played an important counterbalance to Beamer's affable, outgoing ways. In short, he was the one who said "no" for Beamer.

Ballein handled some of the disciplinary measures required of a football program. When freshman center Keith Short broke curfew at the 1995 Sugar Bowl, it was Ballein who sent him back to Blacksburg on a Greyhound bus, a 23-hour ride that became the standard punishment for breaking curfew on Hokies bowl trips under Beamer.

Ballein didn't only operate with a stick, however. Short ended up leaving the Hokies prior to graduation, hoping to catch on with an NFL team. When he didn't and wanted to come back to get his degree, Ballein was the man he contacted. Ballein got him financial assistance to finish his degree in return for 20 volunteer hours a week in the athletic department. Short got his bachelor's degree not long after and his master's two years after that.

"He was Frank's secret weapon," said Chris Colston, the editor for years of Tech's in-house publication, the *Hokie Huddler*, who also wrote Beamer's first autobiography. "People have no idea how important he was to that program. He handled so many things.

"Without (defensive coordinator) Bud Foster and John Ballein, I don't think Coach Beamer would have had the same level of success. Ballein is the most underrated administrator that's been there in a long time. It's immeasurable his contributions. It's all behind the scenes. And he'll never take any credit."

As the years went on, Ballein became one of Beamer's closest confidants, his office adjacent to the head coach's. When Beamer made his daily lunchtime walks around campus, Ballein was always at his side.

Sometimes those conversations weren't serious. Sometimes they were, like when they were walking shortly after the shooting tragedy on campus in 2007. Beamer's wife, Cheryl, was with them when they came upon a young female student who was sobbing with her head down. Beamer sat down and talked with her.

"She needed to be able to talk to someone that hopefully made her feel better and made her feel like things are going to be okay," Beamer said. "And we are. We are going to get through this."

As Beamer's career wound down, Ballein was there every step of the way, including after the coach's retirement. Ballein was the first to know about Beamer's election into the College Football Hall of Fame in January 2018, stopping by the Beamers' house to check their mail while they were out of town. He called them while they were on the road to inform them of the good news. They all burst into tears.

The same happened when Ballein sprung the surprise on them that Virginia Tech was going to put up a statue of Beamer outside of Lane Stadium. He'd worked hard behind the scenes to make it happen and had the idea to eschew a pedestal and make it approachable, just like the coach himself.

After Beamer retired, Ballein moved up in Virginia Tech's athletic administration, promoted to associate athletic director under Whit Babcock. He wears several hats and continues to play a major role in the Hokies' football scheduling.

"He obviously can cover a lot of complex issues," Babcock said. "He's loyal, he works hard, he's very smart and, shoot, I'd be crazy not to lean on him. It's public knowledge that he was interested in the athletic director job, but he handled that with such class and grace. I think the world of John."

36 Jim Weaver

No athletic director in Virginia Tech history presided over a more successful period of sports than Jim Weaver. Not only was he with the Hokies during their rise to national prominence in football, but he helped shepherd Tech from the Big East to the ACC, oversaw a facilities boom, and made sure the athletic department was on sound fiscal footing.

Weaver was the second-longest serving AD in Hokies history to Frank Moseley, on the job from 1997 to 2013 before complications from Parkinson's disease forced his retirement. He died at age 70 in 2015 after a nearly decade-long battle with the disease.

"He's going to go down as a legend," Hokies wrestling coach Kevin Dresser said upon Weaver's passing. "As time goes on and people look at where Virginia Tech was when Jim took over and where Virginia Tech was when Jim resigned last year, it's pretty daggone legendary."

Weaver was a 1967 graduate of Penn State, where he played for Joe Paterno, later serving on Paterno's staff as an assistant coach. But he found his calling in sports administration, starting as an associate AD at Florida in 1983 before getting athletic director gigs at UNLV and Western Michigan.

He was hired at Virginia Tech in 1997 at a unique time in the school's athletics history. The Hokies were already on their way to becoming a national football force under Frank Beamer, having won two Big East titles by that point, but the Tech's sports programs were still scattered among three leagues: the Big East for football, Colonial Athletic Association for wrestling, and the Atlantic 10 for all other sports.

Every sport but wrestling got into the Big East in the 2000–01 season, a boon to the school's non-marquee programs.

"You look at baseball, softball—everyone's benefited by Jim being here," Beamer said. "All sports."

Of course, football was and remains the big dog on campus, with Tech playing in the national title game in 2000. And though Beamer had the Hokies on an upward trajectory when Weaver arrived, the AD helped by giving the coach all the support he needed, be it facilities or, in the one contentious moment of their relationship, during Beamer's contract negotiations, when the coach sought increased salaries for his assistants.

"I can't ever think of a day, except when we were trying to do my contract, that he didn't give me everything I wanted," Beamer said.

On the facilities front, Weaver was instrumental in the athletic department committing to over $200 million in upgrades during his time, including the Lane Stadium south end zone expansion in 2002 and west side renovation of the press box and luxury seating completed prior to the 2006 season.

He also oversaw the building of the Hahn Hurst Basketball Practice Center, a new football locker room and the baseball hitting facility, which was posthumously named in his honor. He pursued building an indoor football practice facility for years, with construction beginning at the end of his run. (Through it all, he was always blunt, particularly during the spat with the Stadium Woods proponents when the indoor facility was being planned.)

"His legacy is always going to be facilities and student-athlete welfare," former Hokies broadcaster Bill Roth said.

Weaver also was instrumental in getting Virginia Tech into the ACC in 2004, having the Hokies in a position athletically, academically and financially to be a viable candidate when the league was seeking to expand. The Hokies were a surprise addition along

Virginia Tech Athletic Directors

R. M. Brown (1908)
Branch Bocock (1909)
L. W. Riess (1910)
Post abolished (1911–19)
C.P. "Sally" Miles (1920–34)
William "Monk" Younger (1935–50)
Frank Moseley (1951–77)
Bill Dooley (1978–86)
Dale T. "Dutch" Baughman (1986–87)
Raymond Smoot (interim, June–December 1987)
David Braine (1988–97)
Sharon McCloskey (interim, 1997)
Jim Weaver (1997–2013)
Sharon McCloskey (interim, 2013–14)
Whit Babcock (2014–present)

with Miami and Boston College, getting the initial invite instead of Syracuse.

After many itinerant years, Virginia Tech finally found its home smack dab in the middle of the ACC's footprint, a move that looks even better with the benefit of hindsight, as the Big East imploded upon further raids by the ACC. Virginia Tech won 16 ACC championships during Weaver's run.

"I hope people recognize that he and his staff had Virginia Tech's finances and teams and compliance and operation in shape so it was attractive to the Big East and later attractive to the ACC," Roth said.

Weaver did much of his work while battling the crippling effects of Parkinson's disease, a degenerative disorder of the central nervous system that impairs speech and coordination. Diagnosed in 2004, he revealed his battle with it in 2006. He had multiple back surgeries and chronic pain from the disease, limiting his office hours by the end of his tenure.

Still, he left the athletic department in great shape when he left. The Hokies had annual revenues of $17 million when Weaver took over in 1997. That figure was north of $70 million by the time of his retirement, with Weaver running Virginia Tech in the black every year since 2000.

He also upgraded Tech's football schedule, agreeing to marquee non-conference games with USC, Alabama, Nebraska, Ohio State, LSU, Texas A&M, Boise State, and others during his time. After years of talks, he finally helped make a reality the Battle at Bristol, a game against Tennessee at the Bristol Motor Speedway that was agreed to in 2013 and played three years later. Future series with Penn State, Wisconsin, and West Virginia were also Weaver's handiwork.

"He's just a very sound, very good decision-maker," Frank Beamer said upon Weaver's retirement. "Treated all the sports with interest. I mean, I think he was perfect for Virginia Tech."

37 Thursday Night Games

Though the idea has since been co-opted by the NFL, college football used to be the only game on Thursday nights. Virginia Tech's Frank Beamer was one of the first coaches to recognize the power of the platform that the game afforded on ESPN, and the Hokies' success in mid-week games helped raise the profile of the program.

"I like that it's the only game on," was an often-said phrase of Beamer.

Since ESPN's Thursday night package began in 1991, the Hokies have appeared 33 times, going 23–10 in those contests, a .687 winning percentage.

Beamer was a remarkable 21–9 in those games, including a 6–0 record against frequent Thursday night foe Georgia Tech.

The Hokies first appeared in the Thursday night slot the year after their first bowl appearance under Beamer in the 1993 Independence Bowl. In 1994, No. 14 Tech hosted West Virginia in a mid-week showdown in September and ran the Mountaineers out of Lane Stadium with a 34–6 win in which the Hokies held WVU to 238 yards and forced four turnovers.

"I think when we started, there was as much talk about the fans and the atmosphere, and we happened to play pretty good in a couple of them," Beamer said. "It kind of gave us our identity here."

Virginia Tech opened the 1995 season at home on Thursday night, losing a tight one 20–14 to Boston College, but by then the tradition was gaining traction. They soon became a staple in Blacksburg, with Tech having at least one home Thursday nighter on the schedule every season from 2002 through 2012.

Athletic director Jim Weaver requested not to have a Thursday night home game in 2013, leading to a backlash from a portion of the fan base that had grown accustomed to them.

Weaver said he did it as a "thank you" to many season ticket holders who find it difficult to make it down for a yearly game in the middle of a work week, though that explanation was met with a quick and negative reaction from many of the team's younger supporters, including students who saw attending Thursday night games as an annual Hokie tradition.

Though Friday nights have gained popularity and frequency on the ACC schedule in recent years, Thursday nights are still special to a Virginia Tech fan base that's experienced some big moments (and one soul-crushing loss) in the mid-week showcase game, including:

- 1999 vs. Clemson: Defensive end Corey Moore welcomed the Tigers to "The Terror Dome," finishing with four tackles for a loss, two sacks, and a 32-yard touchdown return on a fumble he forced in a 31–11 Tech win, which was its first big one on the way to the national title game.
- 2003 vs. Texas A&M: Hurricane Isabel made landfall just ahead of this much-anticipated Thursday nighter against the Aggies, knocking out power for 1.5 million people along the coast, but it didn't deter a rain-soaked crowd of 65,115 from showing up in Blacksburg to watch the Hokies win 35–19. Running back Kevin Jones ran for 188 yards and three touchdowns and quarterback Bryan Randall made big plays down the stretch, including a 12-yard touchdown run in the fourth quarter.
- 2004 vs. Maryland: Beamer's mother, Herma, died in her sleep overnight before this game, but the coach, at her request, pushed on, leading his Hokies on what was an emotional night. Virginia Tech responded with an absolute thrashing of the Terrapins, building a 41–3 lead at halftime of a 55–6 win. It was Tech's largest margin of victory in an ACC game until 59–7 rout of North Carolina in 2017.
- 2005 vs. Boston College; Marcus Vick threw for 280 yards and a touchdown and the No. 3 Hokies held the No. 13 Eagles to 183 yards in what was Tech's 11th straight Thursday night victory.
- 2006 vs. Clemson: The Hokies snapped a two-game ACC losing streak by smothering a No. 10 Tigers offense that featured running backs C.J. Spiller and James Davis, holding it to 166 total yards. Running back Brandon Ore did the heavy lifting for Tech, running for 203 yards and two touchdowns.

- 2007 vs. Boston College: The game whose mere mention raises Tech fans' collective blood pressure, this 14–10 loss was like a punch to the stomach for a team with national title hopes. The Hokies led 10–0 well into the fourth quarter, having held quarterback Matt Ryan in check. A touchdown and onside kick recovery set the stage for Ryan to scramble, pull up and find running back Andre Callender for a 24-yard touchdown with 11 seconds left, an improbable win that stunned Lane Stadium into silence.
- 2007 vs. Georgia Tech: Someone stole the uniforms of Sean Glennon, Tyrod Taylor, Kam Chancellor, and Brandon Flowers before the game, so the quartet had to wear white Yellow Jackets jerseys provided by the home team trimmed in blue and gold. Hokies equipment managers blacked out the team name and Russell Athletic logo on the front and used a marker to write the players' surnames on tape as nameplates. That was more interesting than the game, a 27–3 Hokies blowout.
- 2010 vs. Georgia Tech: Things were tied at 21 late in the fourth quarter when David Wilson sprinted into every Hokies fan's heart, taking a kickoff back 90 yards for a touchdown and leaping into the air once he reached the end zone in a 28–21 victory.
- 2011 at Georgia Tech: The game when Logan Thomas wouldn't go down. Momentum turned when the Hokies quarterback refused to be taken to the ground on a sack on third-and-long, frustrating Georgia Tech defensive end Jeremiah Attaochu into slugging the quarterback in the facemask after the whistle. The personal foul call kept a critical third-quarter drive alive and Thomas shined the rest of the way, accounting for 279 yards and five touchdowns in a 37–26 win in Atlanta.
- 2015 vs. Georgia Tech: The game after Beamer announced he would retire at the end of the 2015 season just so happened

to be on a Thursday night at Georgia Tech. He did what he always did on that night against that team, beating the Yellow Jackets 23–21 in a game that the Hokies held Georgia Tech's option offense to only 161 rushing yards. It spurred on a run to the coach's 23rd straight bowl appearance.

38 Catch a Glimpse of Frank Beamer on a Walk (or Just Take a Picture at His Statue)

Frank Beamer has always been known as a down-to-earth football coach, the kind of person who treats a CEO the same way he would a janitor—with kindness. It was the Beamer Way, and he maintained it even through his fame as one of college football's most recognizable faces.

That's extended to his post-coaching career, in which he's an ambassador for the athletic department, always eager to have a chat with anyone and never turning away a photo request.

He's always been approachable, a man of the people who cemented that status with his daily, lunchtime walks around campus. He's done it for years with his most-trusted advisor, John Ballein, the football program's longtime director of operations who moved into an assistant athletic director role following Beamer's retirement. Beamer is never shy about stopping for photos with students.

As affable and available as Beamer is to the public, he's not always strolling about, so your best bet to get a souvenir photo is probably at the statue Virginia Tech put up in the fall of 2018 just outside of Lane Stadium.

The idea was pushed by Ballein. Not wanting a statue up on a pedestal, like most are, he wanted to honor Beamer with something that was just like the man—approachable. "Just like the man who was taught the values of hard work and loyalty on his family's farm in rural Fancy Gap," Virginia Tech declared in a press release ahead of the statue's unveiling.

The bronze sculpture, done by South Carolina artist Tom Gallo, is of a life-sized Beamer standing on the ground looking stern, his leg up along a long bench and a headset hanging around his neck. He's wearing his trademark sideline gear, a Nike jacket, and of course has a giant ACC champion ring on one of his fingers.

He's got a piece of paper in his left hand that includes the words commitment, trust, responsibility, caring, and respect. It also includes his accomplishments—280 career wins, 238 at Virginia Tech, 23 straight bowl games, four ACC titles, three Big East titles, and 19 All-Americans.

The idea is that anyone can sidle up to the statue and be on the same level as the venerable coach, easily able to take a picture. It's interactive, playing into the "we are all in this together" mantra that Beamer espoused his entire career.

"I love the way they did it," Beamer said. "That's the way I would've wanted it."

The Hokies unveiled it before the Notre Dame game in 2018. Beamer's son, Oklahoma assistant coach Shane Beamer, had to go to great lengths to get him to stay in Blacksburg and not spoil the surprise. Oklahoma was playing Texas in the Red River Shootout that same day, and Frank was intent on coming to Dallas to watch the rivalry game for the first time in person.

"I said, 'Well, you know they're honoring you for the Hall of Fame. They're recognizing you during the game. You've got to be there for that,'" Shane said. "I wanted to tell him, 'There's going to be a lot more than that, too!'"

Eventually Frank got the news. Ballein called to tell him about the statue. Tears started streaming down Frank's face as he handed the phone to his wife, Cheryl. When Ballein told her, she started crying, too.

That statue stands in Moody Plaza, in the southwest corner outside of Lane Stadium next to, what else, Beamer Way, the road renamed in his honor in 2015. It's quickly become a hot spot for photo seekers, a must-stop destination on game days in Blacksburg. Do it when the Hokies are at home and you'll probably have to stand in line, though the keepsake will be worth it.

39 George Preas, Buzz Nutter, and the 1958 NFL Champion Colts

Though the offensive linemen took different paths to get to the famous 1958 National Football League championship game, George Preas and Buzz Nutter both started in the same place in college—on Virginia Tech's offensive line.

Madison "Buzz" Nutter got to Blacksburg first, an offensive lineman during a rough period in Gobblers history. The teams he was on went a combined 7–24 from 1950 to '52, but it didn't stop Nutter from being selected by the Washington Redskins in the 12th round in the 1953 Draft.

He was only the fifth player ever drafted in any league from Virginia Tech, following Herman "Foots" Dickerson (Chicago Cardinals, 1937), John Maskas (Boston Yanks, 1944), Frank Ballard (Buffalo Bills in the AAFC, 1948), and Sterling Wingo (L.A. Rams in 1951).

He'd be joined at VPI by Preas, a big tackle who grew up in Roanoke, played locally there at Jefferson High and turned down offers from Georgia Tech and Army to come to Blacksburg. He went on to star with the Gobblers from 1951 to 1954, a key part to the turnaround under coach Frank Moseley.

Tech went 0–10 in 1950, the year before Moseley and Preas arrived. By Preas' senior year in 1954, after he started 40 straight games, the Gobblers went 8–0–1 and finished No. 16 in the final national poll. Preas, who played on both sides of the ball in the trenches, was honored as an All-American, All-Southern, and All-State selection.

"Preas can block and tackle with the best of them—and his drive and experience make him one of the top players in football," the 1954 Tech *Gridiron Guide* said.

He too went to the NFL, drafted in the fifth round by the Baltimore Colts in 1955. It was the start of an 11-year pro career in which he played alongside Colts greats like quarterback Johnny Unitas, receiver Raymond Berry, running back Lenny Moore, left tackle Jim Parker, defensive tackle Art Donovan, and defensive end Gino Marchetti.

Nutter joined him in Baltimore. After failing to make the Redskins right after the draft, he returned to his hometown of Summersville, West Virginia, to work in the steel mill but got back into football when the Colts signed him in 1954.

Together, they were both starting offensive linemen on Baltimore's 1958 and '59 NFL Championship teams, Nutter at center and Preas at right tackle, helping clear the way for the Colts' strong running game.

They blocked for fullback Alan Ameche's game-winning touchdown plunge against the Giants in a 23–17 overtime victory in Yankee Stadium, which has become known as "The Greatest Game Ever Played." Preas, who was voted by his teammates as the team's Unsung Hero Award winner, cleared the path for Ameche, wiping his defender out of the picture with a block.

"That picture [of the touchdown] sums up George," teammate Alex Sandusky told the *Baltimore Sun* upon Preas' passing in 2007.

"He did a hell of a job for years and nobody knew it, except for the guys who played with him."

Nutter stood out in that game, too, helping secure a little piece of history in the game's aftermath. After Ameche threw the football following his game-winner, Nutter chased after a security guard to retrieve the keepsake. In the locker room, Nutter presented the ball to Marchetti, who'd broken his leg during the game.

Preas played all 11 years of his career with the Colts before retiring in 1965. Nutter was traded to Pittsburgh in 1961, making the Pro Bowl in 1962. He was traded back to Baltimore for one year before he too retired in 1965.

"Let's face it, Buzz didn't get enough credit," teammate Dick Szymanski told the *Baltimore Sun* when Nutter died in 2008. "Buzz was a vastly underrated center and a good pass blocker who never got hurt—and when he did get hurt, he stayed in the game."

Both were honored with induction into the Virginia Tech Sports Hall of Fame, Preas in 1983 and Nutter in '85. Preas is also an inductee in the Virginia Sports Hall of Fame.

Virginia Tech's football team honors Preas' legacy every year when it hands out the George Preas Award to the team's MVP of spring practice.

40 The Fuller Brothers

When Vincent Fuller, a safety from outside of Baltimore, signed to play for the Hokies all the way back in 2000, little did anyone know it'd be the start of one of the greatest family pipelines that Virginia Tech football would ever see.

The Hokies had great success with 25 sets of brothers playing for the school during Frank Beamer's time, but, with apologies to the Edmunds brothers, none of those groups had quite the influence as the Fuller foursome—Vincent, Corey, Kyle, and Kendall.

"Virginia Tech is better because the Fuller brothers were Hokies," head coach Frank Beamer said. "Vinny, Corey, Kyle, and Kendall were all different, but they were all the same in that they were smart, competitive, very athletic, and great teammates who possessed great character.

"Those qualities are all a tribute to their parents. The Fullers are what college football players should be. It is an honor to me that each of them followed their brother to Virginia Tech. It was my privilege to coach all four of them."

All four went on to the NFL, joining the Browners (Ross, Jim, Joey, and Keith, who played in the 1970s and '80s) as the second foursome of NFL brothers in the Super Bowl era, since joined by the Gronkowskis (Dan, Chris, Rob, and Glenn).

Neither of those other NFL quartets all played at the same college. The Fullers did, their time at Virginia Tech spanning from 2000 to 2015.

"They've been good to us. I think we've been good to them," said their father, Vincent Sr.

"They're in the best hands," their mother, Nina Dorsey-Fuller, said. "They really are. The staff is like family."

Vincent came first, a defensive back who played in 50 games with the Hokies from 2000 to '04, finishing with 142 tackles, eight interceptions and touchdowns on a 50-yard fumble return and a 74-yard blocked field goal return. He was a fourth-round pick by the Titans who'd play seven years in the NFL.

He'd be a trendsetter. Kyle, the third-oldest, actually came next, signing with the Hokies in 2010 and, despite not being the most-touted recruit, finding a path to the field early in his career as a nickelback and starting six games. He was a full-time starter as a cornerback by his sophomore year in 2011 and went on to have a memorable career, a first-team All-ACC pick by his senior year who was also a second-team All-America pick by the Walter Camp

In this August 10, 2013, photo, Virginia Tech senior Kyle Fuller (left) mock interviews his younger brother, freshman Kendall Fuller, during the annual media day in Blacksburg. (AP Photo / *The Roanoke Times*, Matt Gentry)

Football Foundation. Kyle had 173 tackles and six interceptions in his college career, which overlapped with two of his brothers.

The second-oldest, Corey, took an unusual path to Tech, originally going to Kansas as a track athlete. He transferred to Tech in the fall of 2010 to be with Kyle and walked on to the football team, again bucking the Fuller family trend by playing on offense at receiver. He eventually earned a scholarship and became a key contributor who had 45 catches, 834 yards, and six touchdowns over two seasons.

Kendall, the youngest of the four, came next, molded by the paths forged by his older brothers and the endless advice they gave him.

"Whatever Corey and Kyle did, Kendall was trying to do it," Vincent Sr. said. "And I can stop saying tried to do it. Kendall was doing it. Whenever they'd be playing, he was able to play with them, and he was able to fit right in."

A five-star recruit, Kendall picked Virginia Tech over Clemson, playing as a freshman in 2013 while Kyle was a senior, often in the same defensive backfield. He too thrived in college, with 119 tackles and eight interceptions, a first-team All-ACC corner and second-team All-American in 2014 before a knee injury cut short his final year in 2015.

All three of the youngest brothers made it to the NFL, too. Corey was a sixth-round pick by the Lions in 2013 who had a cup of coffee in the league.

Kyle went the highest in the draft of the four, a first-round pick by the Bears with the 14th pick in 2014 who, after some injuries early in his career, flourished in 2018, tied for the league lead with seven interceptions and was selected as a first-team All-Pro.

Because of his injury, Kendall slid to the Redskins in third round of the 2016 draft, though he's done well as a nickelback, first with Washington and then after being traded to the Chiefs as part of the Alex Smith deal.

Brothers Who Played at Virginia Tech

Nathaniel Adibi (lettered 2000–03), Xavier Adibi (lettered 2004–07)

Ken Barefoot (lettered 1987–88), Jason Barefoot (on 1988–90 teams)

Mike Borden (lettered 1979–80), Karl Borden (lettered 1987–88, 90)

Nekos Brown (lettered 2006–09), Wiley Brown (lettered 2010–11)

Trey Edmunds (lettered 2013–15), Terrell Edmunds (lettered 2015–17), Tremaine Edmunds (lettered 2015–17)

Vincent Fuller (lettered 2001–04), Kyle Fuller (lettered 2010–13), Corey Fuller (lettered 2012), Kendall Fuller (lettered 2013–15)

Eric Gallo (lettered 2015–17), Nick Gallo (signed in 2019)

Kirk Gray (on 1990–92 teams), Keith Gray (lettered 1994)

Chad Grimm (lettered 2006), Cody Grimm (lettered 2006–09)

Danny Hill (lettered 1976–79), Scott Hill (lettered 1986–89)

Antoine Hopkins (lettered 2009–12), Derrick Hopkins (lettered 2010–13)

Bill Houseright Jr. (lettered 1995), Jake Houseright (lettered 1998–2001), Jonas Houseright (lettered 2006–08)

Connor Kish (on 2015–18 teams), Kevin Kish (on 2015–18 teams)

Kevin Lewis (lettered 2000–04), Jonathan Lewis (lettered 2002–05)

Orion Martin (lettered 2005–08), Cam Martin (lettered 2006–09)

Vinny Mihota (lettered 2015–18), Louis Mihota (on 2018–19 teams)

Andrew Moss (lettered 1990), Billy Moss (lettered 1992)

D.J. Parker (lettered 2004–07), Matt Wright (on 2006 team)

Willie Pile (lettered 2000–02), Ben Barber (on 2009 team)

Ryan Shuman (lettered 2006–08), Mark Shuman (lettered 2013)

Terry Smith (lettered 1990), Eric Smith (lettered 1992)

Sidney Snell (lettered 1977–80), Donald Wayne Snell (lettered 1984–86)

Billy Swarm (lettered 1991–92), Joe Swarm (lettered 1992–93)

Anthony Thibodeau (lettered 2000), John Thibodeau (on 2003–04 teams)

Ronny Vandyke (lettered 2012, 2014–15), Devin Vandyke (on 2012–14 teams)

Michael Vick (lettered 1999–2000), Marcus Vick (lettered 2003, 2005)

Ed Wang (lettered 2006–09), David Wang (lettered 2011–14)

Blake Warren (lettered 2002–05), Brett Warren (lettered 2004–05, 2007–08), Beau Warren (lettered 2007–10)

T.J. Washington (lettered 1994–96), Todd Washington (1995–97)

Rich Williams (lettered 1987–88), Ryan Williams (1991–94)

As Kendall's time at Virginia Tech wound down, Vincent Sr. and Nina got wistful about their run at Virginia Tech coming to an end.

Asked if there were any more Fullers in the pipeline, Nina simply laughed and said, "I wish. I'm going through that Empty Nest Syndrome right now. Sometimes I look at my husband and go, 'We'll try one more time?' He's like, 'No.'"

"We get that all the time," Vincent Sr. said. "'Are you going to have any more?' It's funny. My wife and I just laugh. But we're finished and right now we're enjoying them and trying to enjoy our life at the same time."

41 DBU

Pinning down one school as Defensive Back University is a tough task, though no shortage of outlets have offered up their own rankings over the years.

Virginia Tech, which has had 27 defensive backs drafted in the last 23 years, has as good of a claim to the "DBU" moniker as anyone.

"I know there's talk about who's had the best group of DBs over the years," Foster said in 2013. "But in the last 20 years, I don't think we're second to anyone in terms of the type of kid we put out there and how our productivity has been."

The consistency the Hokies have had producing quality defensive backs in the last quarter century has been remarkable. Since Pierson Prioleau earned third-team All-America honors in 1997, Tech has had 11 different All-Americans in the defensive backfield.

Jimmy Williams, Victor "Macho" Harris, Brandon Flowers, and Jayron Hosley all earned first-team All-American recognition honors during that stretch. Since Frank Beamer took over the program in 1987, eight Tech defensive backs have been taken in the first two rounds of the NFL Draft, with DeAngelo Hall, Kyle Fuller, and Terrell Edmunds going in the first round.

Since 2000, the Hokies have finished in the Top 40 in passing defense 15 times. They've been a Top 10 unit in yardage allowed five times.

No one quite knows when the "DBU" nickname first started, though the Hokies really embraced it after then-secondary coach Torrian Gray heard Jon Gruden say it during the Hokies' 2011 Orange Bowl appearance against Stanford when Hosley intercepted Andrew Luck.

"As soon as I heard him say it, I was like, 'Well, let's just take it and run with it then,'" Gray said. "If he feels that way, if we think that way, then we're DBU."

Since then, it's been a calling card for the program and a way of life for the defensive backs.

"Once you get here, you just feel the vibes," said Detrick Bonner, a safety with the Hokies from 2011 to '14. "You know how focused everyone is. You know everyone has got one goal on them. And that's to be great, to be exact as possible. And you just feel like you've got to uphold it."

The foundation was laid long ago. Tyronne Drakeford was one of the first big names in the secondary during the Hokies' bowl run, a three-time All-Big East pick from 1991to '93 whose 16 interceptions were two shy of the school record set and still held today by Gene Bunn. Drakeford would be a second-round NFL Draft pick by the 49ers in 1994 and played eight pro seasons.

Gray, long before he was a coach of DBU, was a member, an All-Big East safety who had two interceptions in the Hokies' program-defining Sugar Bowl win against Texas in 1995. He and fellow defensive back Antonio Banks both were selected by the Vikings in the 1997 draft.

In 1999, Prioleau went in the fourth round to the 49ers, starting a streak of 14 straight years that Tech had at least one defensive back selected in the NFL Draft.

Anthony Midget and Ike Charlton were starting corners on the 1999 team that went to the national title game, both earning All-Big East honors.

Hall, who was an all-around talent who starred on special teams and dabbled on offense, has the distinction of being the highest draft pick of a cornerback in Virginia Tech history, going to the Falcons with the eighth pick in the 2004 draft.

Williams became Tech's first unanimous All-American at defensive back in 2005, the same year he was a finalist for the Jim Thorpe Award.

Flowers—a third-team choice in 2006 before making several teams in 2007, including the first team by the American Football Coaches Association—became the Hokies' first two-time All-American in the secondary since Frank Loria. He'd go pro his junior year and be a second-round pick by the Chargers.

Interceptions came in bunches over the years. Harris had 15 in four years from 2005 to '08, taking four of them back for touchdowns, which is a school record. Hosley burst on the scene in 2010, leading the nation with nine interceptions, which broke Tech's single-season record.

Kam Chancellor might not have been the most heralded player in college, but he redefined the safety position at the pro level after being drafted by the Seahawks and headlining Seattle's famed "Legion of Boom" secondary that keyed back-to-back Super Bowl appearances.

The Fuller brothers played an enormous part of DBU's history, with three alums in the family—Vincent (2000–04), Kyle

Victor "Macho" Harris

When the Hokies landed Victor Harris in the 2005 signing class, it was a big get. The kid called "Macho" was the state's No. 1 recruit out of Highland Springs, Virginia, someone Tech prized for a while.

His time in Blacksburg showed why. Harris turned himself into a first-team All-American cornerback and two-time first-team All-ACC pick over his four-year career.

He had a knack for finding the end zone. He had 15 career interceptions, third most in Hokies history, and took four of them back for touchdowns, a school record. Showing off his versatility, he took a kickoff back 100 yards for a touchdown in Tech's "Beamer Ball' masterpiece of a 41–23 win against Clemson in 2007.

Though Harris didn't latch on for long in the NFL, he carved a five-year career in the Canadian Football League, with four interceptions in parts of five seasons from 2012 to '16.

(2010–13), and Kendall (2013–15) all playing for the Hokies. Kyle and Kendall both were All-Americans.

Two players joined Hall as first-round picks in the last five years. Kyle Fuller went 14th overall by the Bears in 2014, with safety Terrell Edmunds the 28th overall pick by the Steelers in 2018.

It's been part of a great run recently for Tech in the draft. After no DBs were taken in 2013, eight have been picked in the last six years, accounting for nearly half the players the Hokies have had selected in the NFL Draft in that span.

What's been remarkable in the defensive backfield in the last quarter century has been that the performance has stayed consistent across several coaches, From Lou West to Lorenzo Ward and Gray to now Brian Mitchell, with only Foster, as the coordinator, being the constant all those years.

"I think it goes back to our scheme a little bit and obviously who we're recruiting," Foster said.

Mitchell, who was hired from West Virginia prior to the 2016 season to coach cornerbacks, said Tech's DBU reputation precedes itself, and he wasn't put off by the challenge of living up to lofty standards.

"That tradition is embedded here, and hopefully it's not going away anytime soon, at least not while I'm here," he said. "Anytime you can attach yourself to a legacy, or to an ongoing tradition that everyone in America has known about and read about and respect, that's special in my book. That doesn't come along that often."

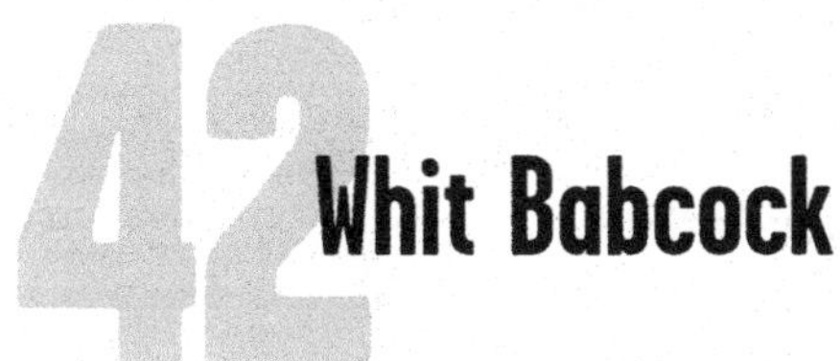

42 Whit Babcock

It had been 16 years since Virginia Tech last hired an athletic director, with Jim Weaver filling the role until health reasons forced him to retire late in 2013. That time frame saw the Hokies' rise to a national power in football, transition from the Big East to the ACC, and get on the right side of the ledger financially.

In that sense, Whit Babcock stepped into a pretty good situation when he was hired as Virginia Tech's new athletic director in January 2014. But Babcock's still gone about modernizing the Hokies' athletic department, making coaching hires in almost all of Tech's biggest sports and spearheading a restructuring of Tech's donation process to help the school sit on better financial ground from a competitive standpoint.

Coming to Virginia Tech was a homecoming of sorts for Babcock, a Harrisonburg native who attended James Madison and played baseball, earning his degree in 1992.

"It was appealing to me primarily because of two reasons—fit and opportunity," Babcock said at his introductory press conference. "My Virginia heritage—I'm a fifth-generation Virginian—certainly helps with fit and understanding the culture, and coming home is a big component.

"But it's more than that. It's also the opportunity to compete against the best and to join a championship-caliber program that is and will continue to be a leader in the ACC athletically and academically."

His career took him to several stops as a sports administrator, including West Virginia (where he got his master's), Auburn, Missouri, and finally Cincinnati, where he got his first athletic director gig.

His background fit precisely what Virginia Tech needed when he was hired at age 43. Babcock was a seasoned fundraiser at Auburn and Missouri and oversaw an $86 million renovation to the Bearcats' football stadium, so finances were his strong suit.

Upon his hire he set out an ambitious plan to deepen Tech's financial resources and broaden the Hokies' lagging donor base. Two years into his tenure, Virginia Tech launched its "Drive for 25" campaign, a fundraising initiative aimed at expanding the Hokies donor base from 11,000 to 25,000 members, which would put it among the ACC's leaders. As of late 2018, that number was north of 16,000, with the Hokies raising $7 million more for scholarships than they did in 2016.

He's shepherded several large donations to completion, including one for $15.2 million, the school's largest ever, from an anonymous donor in late 2017 to fund an all-sports, state-of-the-art student-athlete performance center that includes an enhanced dining area.

"This is a big step in our journey to being the best in the ACC," Babcock said when the gift was announced. "That's what we aspire to, is to be a leader across the board, and we will get there in our conference."

In 2013, the year before his hire, Virginia Tech had an athletic department revenue of $70 million. That figure was up to $87

Sharon McCloskey

In more than three decades at Virginia Tech, Sharon McCloskey was a pioneer in athletic administration, working up from her start while an undergraduate on the grounds crew (she literally cut grass at Lane Stadium) to being the No. 2 person in the athletic department.

The 1979 Virginia Tech graduate from Falls Church, Virginia, got her first full-time job at the school as the football office receptionist. She rose up the ranks, becoming recruiting secretary, then senior woman administrator. In 1988, she became the first woman in college athletics to be named football recruiting coordinator at a Division I school.

Athletic director Dave Braine promoted her to senior associate AD in 1995. She twice served as interim AD, after Braine left for Georgia Tech in 1997 and after Jim Weaver retired for health reasons in 2013. McCloskey herself had a health scare, first diagnosed with stage IV, non-Hodgkin's lymphoma in 2014. She underwent a stem-cell transplant that proved successful.

By the end of her career in 2015, she oversaw football, women's basketball, women's soccer, sports medicine, and strength and conditioning, and she was inducted into the Virginia Tech Sports Hall of Fame in 2012.

million in 2017, which is still 44th nationally of public schools, showing the inherent challenges in Blacksburg.

"We're fine to overachieve, and we'll beat them with what we have, but it would be a little bit easier if we could jump that up there," Babcock said.

It helps to have the right coaches in place. Babcock's put his stamp on the athletic department there, too. Most impressively, he gracefully handled Frank Beamer's exit and the transition to new coach Justin Fuente, securing one of the more in-demand coaches in that cycle, easing out a coaching legend with no acrimony and managing to keep beloved defensive coordinator Bud Foster in the fold.

The Beamer-to-Fuente transition has been hailed as one of the most seamless exits for a coaching great, an often tricky dance. Fuente went 19–8 in his first two seasons at Tech, winning one Coastal Division title.

Babcock helped make Hokies basketball relevant again by convincing Buzz Williams to leave Marquette for a program that had finished in last place of the ACC three straight seasons. After a transition season, Tech won 20 or more games for four straight seasons, making the NCAA Tournament in back-to-back years for the first time in more than 30 years in 2017 and '18. The 2018–19 squad, which had a Top 10 ranking early in the season, made it three straight for the first time in school history.

Babcock's also made hires in women's basketball (Kenny Brooks), baseball (John Szefc), and several other sports. Additionally, he, along with assistant AD Tom Gabbard, has overseen a facilities push that's included a renovation to Rector Field House, a vast upgrade to the baseball stadium paid for in part by a naming rights deal and necessary infrastructure expansion for the ACC Network that launched in August of 2018.

He's got big plans for Virginia Tech's future, too.

"As far as something big that we're working on, I say it a lot, but continued momentum to the top of the ACC across the board," he said in the spring of 2018. "And I think we've moved it forward as a group each of the last four years and I believe we're just hitting our stride. So, I wouldn't say that there's any one project, but it's more morale, momentum, culture, everyone knowing their role. But it's fragile. We take a lot of pride in that."

43 The Day the Yankees Came to Blacksburg

When Virginia Tech suffered the deadliest shooting tragedy in U.S. history in 2007, the country came together to mourn. Pro sports played a part in the healing process.

Joe Saunders, a former pitcher for the Hokies who played for the Angels at the time, got permission from Major League Baseball to wear a Virginia Tech hat four days after the shooting when he took the mound, inscribing "VT" on his cleats and drawing the school logo on the back of the pitching mound.

It's hard to be more generous than the New York Yankees were, however, donating $1 million to the Hokie Spirit Memorial Fund a month after the tragedy and agreeing to come to Blacksburg to play an exhibition game against Virginia Tech the following spring.

On March 18, 2008, the Yankees made that trip, helping a Blacksburg community still healing from the previous spring. They flew into Roanoke and took buses through the mountains to Blacksburg, stopping at the Drillfield at Virginia Tech to visit the memorial site for the 32 victims from the shooting.

The Yankees, who were nearing the end of spring training in Tampa, brought nearly their entire team, including their best players. Derek Jeter, Alex Rodriguez, Johnny Damon, Jason Giambi, Jorge Posada, and others made the trip, many feeling the same emotions they did after the September 11 attacks in New York.

"People always ask, well, what can you do? How does this help?" Jeter said. "I really don't know. If it just makes people smile or enjoy themselves for the three hours that we're here, it's all worthwhile."

"There are certain things that happen that are so devastating that time stops," Rodriguez said. "For me, this is one of them. This is probably the proudest day I've ever had to wear a Yankee uniform."

The Yankees had no real connection to Virginia Tech. The only Hokie to ever suit up for the Yankees was catcher Johnny Oates late in his career in 1980 and '81. But the franchise felt it necessary to visit an area in mourning.

"The tragedy was of such great proportion that it didn't matter if there was a connection between the Yankees and Virginia Tech prior to the event," said Randy Levine, the Yankees president. "We all had to rally around these brave people."

Dave Smith, Virginia Tech's longtime sports information director, remembered the Yankees running off the bus and into Lane Stadium, where their locker room was set up, eager to see where the Hokies played football and came out to "Enter Sandman."

He knew how difficult the logistics of a large-scale event like that could be, especially when dealing with a professional franchise, but tears came to his eyes years later recalling how amenable the team was to everything.

"The Yankees players were great. Whew," Smith said, fighting back tears before managing a whisper. "Great."

The visit called for an exhibition game at Virginia Tech's English Field, with families of the survivors and first responders from that fateful day among the 5,000 packed in attendance, an overflow crowd after the school added temporary seating to the stadium.

The teams lined the baselines before the game as 32 oversized orange balloons were released into the air as a tribute to the victims.

"We're trying to do something as a club, as in win a championship, and to me, this should move you to do everything you can to reach your goals, because you never know what tomorrow's going to hold—for any of us," Yankees manager Joe Girardi said. "I think it's something our players will talk about for a long time."

New York, which wore maroon and orange "NY" hats during batting practice, won the game 11–0, though nobody cared much about the outcome. Virginia Tech coach Pete Hughes got everyone into the game, starting sixth-year senior Andrew Wells, who'd missed two seasons because of injuries. Wells pitched one inning, giving up a run after facing, in order, Damon, Jeter, Bobby Abreu, Rodriguez, and Giambi. He called it a "once-in-a-lifetime opportunity."

The Yankees' starters stayed in for two at-bats, but when they were done, they hung around the field. Rodriguez went over to the Hokies' dugout for a few innings, signing bats and balls for the team. The players stayed after the game and headed to the outfield fence to sign autographs for every fan that wanted them, with Damon sticking around the longest.

"You didn't see anybody leave and not sign," Smith said. "From a professional standpoint, I cherish it. And I'm proud probably of that even more so than the [football] championship game. But it was the Yankees that made it."

It might have been one afternoon exhibition game, but it was much more than that for those in Blacksburg who had been through so much in the previous year.

"It's on the forefront of everyone's daily lives around here," Hughes said. "Just to have some fun and laughs for three hours, it's pretty special."

44 Attend a Basketball Game at Cassell Coliseum

There are bigger and glitzier basketball arenas around, especially in a hoops-crazy league like the ACC, but when Virginia Tech's playing well at home and there's a good crowd on hand, the cozy confines of Cassell Coliseum can be one heck of a homecourt advantage.

Cassell, which sits at the intersection of Washington Street and Beamer Way on the edge of campus that includes all of Virginia Tech's athletic facilities, has been the Hokies' men's basketball home since 1962, in addition to hosting the women's basketball, volleyball, and wrestling programs.

Construction began on the building in 1961, with the school seeking a replacement for the outdated War Memorial Gymnasium, which was built in 1926.

The project for the arena, originally called Virginia Tech Coliseum, was spearheaded by Stuart K. Cassell, a 1932 alum and the school's chief business officer at the time who'd eventually rise to vice president for administration. He got the state legislature to approve building an 8,000-seat arena, though he found a seat manufacturer that made smaller seats and squeezed in an extra 2,000 to bring the capacity to 10,000. The final cost? $2.7 million.

The school renamed the building in Cassell's honor in 1976 after his death.

"He was *the* driving force behind the project," said T. Marshall Hahn, the former president at Tech from 1962 to '74.

The men's basketball team played its first game in the building before construction was even completed. Cassell and Tech athletic director Frank Moseley wanted to open the arena in December 1961 against national-power Kentucky, but the project fell behind and the team changed the schedule. Instead, its inaugural game came on January 3, 1962, when Virginia Tech hosted an Alabama team coached by Wimp Sanderson.

How ragged of an unveiling was it? The seats hadn't arrived yet, forcing the nearly 8,000 fans in attendance to sit on concrete to watch their team.

They got a good show, however. Virginia Tech rolled 91–67, getting 22 points from Bucky Keller and 20 from Howard Pardue. Fans continued to pack the still-unfinished stadium the rest of the year, and Tech posted a 19–6 record, winning every single home game. In fact, Tech won the first 16 games in the arena.

With its steep seating setup and single-bowl design, Cassell's been a good homecourt advantage over the years. The Hokies have won more than 75 percent of their games in the building, which has had its share of big moments.

In 1983, Tech beat No. 1 Memphis State 69–56 in front of 10,000 fans. The Tigers were the first No. 1 team ever to play in Cassell and it was Tech's first win over a top-ranked squad.

Seth Greenberg's teams in the 2000s had several noteworthy wins on the home hardwood, knocking off No. 7 Duke 67–65 in 2005, the Hokies' first win against Duke since 1966. Tech knocked off No. 1 North Carolina in 2007 by a 94–88 final, once leading by as many as 22. In 2011, Virginia Tech did it again, dropping No. 1 Duke 64–60 at home.

The building hasn't just been home to sports events, though. The university uses it for commencement exercises, presidential inaugurations, concerts, and speeches. On April 17, 2007, after the tragic shooting on campus, a memorial convocation was held at Cassell, one attended by President George W. Bush and his wife, Laura. It was there that Tech professor Nikki Giovanni read her poem "We Are Virginia Tech" to the over-capacity crowd, helping heal a campus. After a standing ovation, chants of "Let's Go Hokies!" broke out in the arena.

Cassell Coliseum Facts

Capacity: 9.275

Seasons: 58th in 2018–19

Construction Began: 1961

Opened: 1962

All-Time Tech Men's Basketball Games: 798 as of the end of the 2018–19 season

Tech's Men's Basketball Record: 602–196 (.754)

The old arena has had some renovations over the years to bring in some of the creature comforts of the modern sports world. A recent update came in 2013, when two video boards with high-definition LED displays were put on opposite ends of the arena. Tech's since replaced some of the old, light-brown wooden seats, which weren't the most comfortable to sit in, with cushioned, maroon seats that even have cup holders. The capacity of the building, which was once 10,500, is now 9,275.

A trip to Cassell is a must for every Virginia Tech fan, certainly with the Hokies' recent run of success. The building has a very '60s vibe to its exterior—especially next to its more modern looking neighbor, the Hahn Hurst Basketball Practice Center, which was built in 2009—though the concrete arches that extend from the main building are a unique look. (Legend has it that former Hokies running back David Wilson traversed the arches by foot and got up on the roof, though the Virginia Tech police department doesn't recommend such an action, certainly for anyone of lesser athletic ability than the acrobatic Wilson, which is everyone.)

Once inside, take a look at the laminated wood arches that support the roof and the giant fans that help keep the sometimes steamy building a little bit cooler. Ingratiate yourself enough and maybe you'll be welcomed into the "Cassell Guard," Virginia Tech's raucous student section. Don't dally or you'll miss out on one of the milkshakes sold by The Dairy Club of Virginia Tech, a particular favorite of frequent courtside observer Frank Beamer.

But most of all, wear maroon and orange and be loud. Hokies fans have been doing it in Cassell Coliseum for nearly 60 years.

45 The First Game in 1892 and Early Years of Virginia Tech Football

Football came to Virginia Tech over 125 years ago, though the humble beginnings were a far cry from today's game.

Back in 1891 when the school was called Virginia Agricultural and Mechanical College, school president John McBryde approved and supported an athletic association to be formed on campus. The efforts during the early years were centered on football.

Students split into a pair of teams in 1891 to play rugby football, doing so on a field behind Number One Barracks, which is now Lane Hall. The teams liked the game so much they decided to field a football team the following year.

In September 1892, through the efforts of physics professor W.E. Anderson, biology professor E.A. Smyth, and cadets H.B. Pratt and J.W. Stull, a call for football players was issued. Enough players showed up that they were split into two teams.

Anderson, who also played right tackle, was elected captain, while Smyth was selected as the first "trainer" (coach) and business manager. Smyth, who earned the role after reading a book of rules, is now referred to as the father of modern football at Virginia Tech.

He had a tough time keeping the team together, having to go into the barracks every day to beg cadets to come play. Those who were not placed on the first team one day would refuse to return the next. (And people say *today's* players are entitled.) As a result, each of the two teams got a chance to play in one of the two games scheduled that first year, both against St. Albans Lutheran Boys School of Radford.

The team practiced and later played in a wheat field located close to where Shanks Hall is today. It was cleared by a plow and was described as "about as level as a side of Brush Mountain," which is to say not very flat. Team members got up at 6:00 AM and took a cross-country run before breakfast to stay in shape. This was a military school, after all.

"It was not football and yet we had some fun. Suits were ordered, footballs of various descriptions bought and general enthusiasm prevailed," read the *Bugle*, Virginia Tech's yearbook, describing the first football practices in 1892.

The first game took place October 21 that year against St. Albans. Fans lined the sidelines to watch the game, a 14–10 VAMC victory. Anderson scored the first touchdown in Tech history.

A week later, on October 29, St. Albans evened the ledger with a 10–0 win in a game in Radford that was never completed. Both teams' captains agreed to call the game off at halftime after a number of disputes and disagreements. (The score was listed as 12–0 in one newspaper account, though officially it's listed as a 10–0 final.)

Smyth coached again in 1893 when VAMC played two games and lost both, 6–0 at Emory & Henry and 34–6 against Randolph-Macon in Bedford.

In 1894, McBryde offered part of the horticulture farm, then located where today's Memorial Chapel is, to be used by both the athletic and military departments. They called it Sheib Field.

Both of Virginia Tech's longest-running rivalries began in the 1890s, too. VAMC played Virginia Military Institute for the first time in 1894, with VMI winning 10–6 in Staunton.

By 1896, the school was rebranded Virginia Agricultural and Mechanical College and Polytechnic Institute, or more commonly

Virginia Polytechnic Institute or VPI. That was a year of firsts for the football team.

The first game with the University of Virginia was played in Charlottesville in 1896. UVa won 44–0. Later that year, the first game in Roanoke between VPI and VMI was played on Thanksgiving Day. VPI won 24–0, with the *Roanoke Daily Times* devoting multiple writeups before and after the game.

VPI finished 5–2–1 that season and posted a winning record 24 times from 1894–1919, claiming South Atlantic championships in 1909, '16, and '18.

In that time frame, the school enhanced its facilities, too, adding a grandstand to its field in 1902 and renaming it Gibboney Field. The grandstand was enlarged and the field graded and leveled in 1909 when the stadium was renamed Miles Field, which stood as the Hokies' home through 1925.

46 The Black Diamond Trophy and West Virginia Rivalry

Virginia might be Virginia Tech's most disliked annual rival, but when it comes to pure, distilled hate, it's tough for Hokies fans to get more worked up than in the more sporadic rivalry games against West Virginia, the winner of which takes home the Black Diamond Trophy.

The trophy didn't debut until 1997, decades after the series began, sponsored by Rish Equipment Company, a construction equipment company from Bluefield, West Virginia, that donates scholarship money to both schools. The trophy symbolizes the Appalachian region's coal heritage, with a black, coal-shaped top sticking out of a glass bowl.

The Hokies celebrate as coach Justin Fuente hoists the Black Diamond Trophy after the team's 2017 defeat of the Mountaineers. (Scott Taetsch / Cal Sport Media via AP Images)

The rivalry predates the trophy by quite some time, however. Virginia Tech and West Virginia first met on the football field in 1912, a 41–0 VPI victory. The teams didn't start playing annually until 1973, with the rivalry ratcheting up a notch when Don Nehlen and Frank Beamer were the coaches, even more so once they became Big East rivals in 1991.

The Hokies spoiled Nehlen's introduction to the rivalry in 1980 with a 34–11 win thanks to Cyrus Lawrence's 173 rushing yards, the most ever by a Virginia Tech back in the series. West Virginia would own much of the next decade, however, winning seven of the next eight matchups.

After the No. 7 Mountaineers won the 1988 game in Blacksburg 22–10, Nehlen remarked, "Playing here is like airplane landings—any one you can walk away from is a good one."

The Hokies won the next three games in the series, their first three-game winning streak in the matchup at the time. Virginia Tech won 12–10 in 1989, upending the unbeaten No. 9 Mountaineers led by quarterback Major Harris. It was Tech's first win in Morgantown since 1967.

"West Virginia was at a point in their program where they were at a level above and where we aspired to be," said Bud Foster, who was a Hokies linebackers coach that year. "I'm just talking everything, from their stadium to their facilities to where they were in the rankings and those kinds of things. And if we wanted to get to that point, we had to beat somebody like that. So yeah, that was a big game in us taking that next step...of where we wanted to go as a program."

The teams met as Big East foes for the first time in 1991, with Tech pulling out a 20–14 win in Morgantown on a goal-line stand when Hokies defensive end James Hargrove forced a fumble from quarterback Chris Gray on an option play.

They met for the first time when both teams were ranked in 1996, when Jim Druckenmiller threw for a pair of touchdowns and Ken Oxendine ran for two more in a 31–14 Virginia Tech win that clinched a share of the Big East title.

West Virginia got revenge in 1997, scoring 24 straight points in the second quarter in an eventual 30–17 win when Amos Zereoué ran for 153 yards. That was the first year the Black Diamond Trophy was awarded.

The most memorable game, certainly from Virginia Tech's perspective, came in 1999. The Hokies, who had national title aspirations, led comfortably for much of the night in Morgantown, but West Virginia scored two touchdowns in a flurry in the fourth quarter, one after a Tech fumble, to take a late 20–19 lead.

The Military Classic of the South

Though it has faded with time, Virginia Tech's rivalry with Virginia Military Institute used to be a big deal. Because both schools had a corps of cadets and a military heritage, it was dubbed the "Military Classic of the South."

It started all the way back in 1894 and finally became an annual game in Roanoke beginning in 1913 and lasting all the way through 1971. In 1921, it became a Thanksgiving Day fixture, with the corps of cadets from both schools marching to Victory Stadium in Roanoke from the team hotels. The schools played for the 22-inch high Chamber of Commerce Trophy.

The series began to move around in 1973, played in Blacksburg, Richmond and Norfolk over the next 10 years. With the Hokies taking off as a football power and VMI still in I-AA, the series ceased after 1984, when the teams met in the Oyster Bowl in Norfolk and the Hokies won 54–7. Tech leads the all-time series 49–25–5, and at 79 games, it's the second longest series in Hokies history.

Though the schools are in vastly different football worlds today, they agreed to a one-off meeting in Blacksburg in 2026.

That set up the most dramatic drive in Hokies history, with quarterback Michael Vick scrambling for a 26-yard gain to get close to field goal range and Shayne Graham booting a 44-yarder as time expired in a 22–20 win later dubbed the "Miracle in Morgantown." It kept Tech's perfect season alive and allowed it to make it to the national title game.

"Everyone wearing blue and yellow that day was screaming and yelling, and I had the control and power at that moment to basically make them drop their heads and get quiet," Graham said. "All the West Virginia fans went silent, but you just heard this faint uproar [from Virginia Tech fans] come from that corner. And it wasn't the loudest in the world, but yet it was the loudest in the world, if that makes any sense."

The annual series petered out after Virginia Tech left the Big East for the ACC, with a 2005 game in Morgantown as the last game for a while. The Hokies won that one 34–17, though it was becoming clear the rivalry was getting a bit too heated for anyone's good.

Tech quarterback Marcus Vick extended his middle finger to the West Virginia fans after being run out of bounds on a play in the game, later apologizing for his actions. The fans weren't always innocents in everything that went on. Virginia Tech players were told to keep their helmets on whenever they visited Morgantown.

"Their fans may deny it, but it's true: we got hit with stuff," former offensive lineman Dwight Vick said. "Liquor bottles, but they weren't filled with liquor. Little ones. Some of them were filled with urine. I remember driving from the hotel into Morgantown for pregame warmups, we got mooned by elderly women. Flicked off by women.

"They just trash talk and it's nasty, it's old-school. It's kind of like a scene from *Glory Road* or *Hoosiers*, and those small gyms, when they're on top of you. I know venues where it's tough to play, but Morgantown in my day was a very hostile environment. We saw fights in the stands. The fans would lean over the stands and they'd hassle you or just really get on you if you dropped a ball or made a bad play. I mean, it was tough."

The schools cooled things off by not scheduling the series for a while, though the faded feud was rekindled in a 2017 matchup at FedEx Field in Landover, Maryland, a 31–24 thriller that Tech barely held on to win after Will Grier marched the Mountaineers into the red zone in the final seconds.

The rivalry will come back on a limited basis in 2021 and 2022, first with a game in Morgantown and then one in Blacksburg. West Virginia leads the overall series 28–23–1, though the Hokies have won seven of 10 games since the Black Diamond Trophy debuted.

"It's not the same level as Alabama-Auburn or Ohio State–Michigan, but it's one of those things where you have to experience it," Dwight Vick said. "It meant so much to beat West Virginia, because the hatred is real."

47 The Edmunds Brothers

The Edmunds family was all decked out for the 2018 NFL Draft in AT&T Stadium in Arlington, Texas. Tremaine Edmunds, a 6-foot-5, 250-pound linebacker out of Virginia Tech, had been invited to sit in the green room ahead of his presumed first-round selection.

The entire Edmunds clan joined him. His parents, Ferrell and Felecia, sat close by along with both of Tremaine's older brothers. Both played with him at Virginia Tech. Trey, the oldest, had just finished his first season with the New Orleans Saints after signing as an undrafted free agent, and middle brother, Terrell, was a safety who was in the same draft class, expecting to hear his name called a few picks later.

Sure enough, it didn't take long for Tremaine to be taken, selected by the Buffalo Bills with the 16th overall pick. As he went through the pomp and circumstance of being a first-round pick, getting his picture taken again and again, including a photo session from high up in the concourse, the Edmundses were hit with a welcome surprise.

With the 28th overall pick, the Pittsburgh Steelers selected Terrell, making the Edmundses the first set of brothers ever to be selected in the first round of the same draft.

How caught off guard was Terrell? He was in the bathroom when Steelers coach Mike Tomlin called him.

"I promise on everything, I ran out of the bathroom, my pants unzipped, my belt undone, and I just ran to my parents," Terrell said. "I couldn't even tell them was going on. I was just pointing to the phone, so excited and so ready. I'm just blessed for the opportunity."

With that, the Edmunds brothers had made history, though they had been doing that for a while. The relentlessly upbeat trio from Danville followed in the footsteps of their father, Ferrell, who was an All-Pro tight end in 1989 and two-time Pro Bowler with the Dolphins before later finishing his seven-year NFL career with the Seahawks. Felecia was no slouch of an athlete herself, having won three Missouri Valley Conference hurdles and sprint championships at Southern Illinois, so it's no wonder their sons all turned out to be tremendous athletes.

Ferrell III, also known as Trey, came first, matriculating at Virginia Tech in 2012 after being a Parade All-American who played both sides of the ball at Dan River High in Ringgold, Virginia, where he was coached by his father. The Hokies turned him into a running back and, after a redshirt year, he started, running for 132 yards, including a 77-yard touchdown in his debut against No. 1 Alabama.

Trey ran for a team-high 675 yards with 10 touchdowns that season but broke his tibia in the regular season finale against Virginia, a major injury that was the first in a long line of them during his college career.

It was just the start of the Edmundses' run at Virginia Tech. Terrell signed as a defensive back in 2014 and Tremaine as a linebacker the following year, both recruited by Frank Beamer and Bryan Stinespring. In 2015, all of them played for the Hokies, lining up next to one another on the team's kickoff coverage team in the season opener against Ohio State.

"They are equipped athletically to do what each position calls for, so I said, 'What the heck? Let's line 'em up side-by-side and let 'em roll,'" Beamer said.

In doing so, they became just the third set of brothers to take the field together in the same game since 1970, joining the Selmon brothers (Lee Roy, Lucious, and Dewey) who played on Oklahoma's defense in 1972 and '73 and the McCray brothers (Cliff, Jordan, and Justin) who played on UCF's offensive line in 2010 and '11.

Trey would leave after graduating that season, spending his final year of eligibility at Maryland, where he got off to a fast start but suffered a fractured foot that cut short his season. Terrell and Tremaine stayed at Virginia Tech during the coaching transition from Beamer to Justin Fuente and served as leaders on the first defenses of the Fuente era.

Terrell was an indefatigable free safety who earned third-team All-ACC honors as a junior in 2017, a versatile hard-hitter who set the tone in the Hokies' secondary and had 196 tackles and six interceptions in his three years.

"He's an incredibly hard worker, but I just have never seen a guy that can't get tired," Fuente said. "He just doesn't.... There's just something different about him in terms of his stamina, his strength, his work ethic, his intelligence. He's a pretty special kid."

Tremaine was a unicorn, with a size and speed at the linebacker position rarely, if ever, seen in Blacksburg. In his two years as a starter he had 202 tackles, 30½ tackles for a loss, and 10 sacks, earning first-team All-ACC honors and being a third-team All-America selection as a junior in 2017.

"The guy is an eraser out there on the field," defensive coordinator Bud Foster said. "Because of his length, because of his quick burst and then having the size and things, you're just seeing a special guy that we just haven't had here, in my time particularly as a linebacker."

The Edmunds era at Virginia Tech ended in 2017 when both Tremaine and Terrell went pro a year early, setting the stage for their historic draft night, but the family's football careers are really just getting started.

Tremaine, who turned 20 after the draft, made a team-high 121 tackles for the Bills, just shy of a franchise rookie record. Terrell was named the Steelers' Rookie of the Year after finishing with 78 tackles, an interception and a fumble recovery. Trey, meanwhile, was on the Steelers' practice squad most of the year, getting a brief late-season promotion to the 53-man roster.

However their pro careers play out, their time at Virginia Tech was a memorable one, both for the brothers and for the Hokies.

"That's a great family," Beamer said. "It starts at home with mom and dad. They're very respectful kids, very mannerly kids. They're very athletic kids. They're a delight to have in the program. I'm really glad we've got all three of them in the program."

48 Hokie Stone

Walk around Virginia Tech's campus and you'll notice a familiar aesthetic, with a stone facade on the majority of buildings. The Hokies' athletic facilities are no exception, with accents and trim on Lane Stadium, the indoor facility, the baseball stadium, and others all in the rock.

It's Hokie Stone, a native dolomite formed from calcium and magnesium carbonate that's found in the Appalachian Mountains, mostly in Virginia, Tennessee, and Alabama.

It used to be called Tech's "native stone" but has since been nicknamed Hokie Stone for its close ties to the school. It's mined in a quarry not far from the Blacksburg campus to the east. Though gray from a distance, it's produced in muted shades of pink, red, gray, brown, and black.

In 1975, Virginia Tech purchased a 40-acre quarry near campus that had been in operation since 1958. It provides 80 percent of the stone used in campus construction, with another 20 percent from a farm in Montgomery County to ensure some variation in color.

Each week, the quarry produces 25 to 50 tons of stone, with miners using black powder to dislodge the stone before cutting it into blocks for construction projects on campus. The quarry makes around 2,600 tons a year, with a ton covering about 35 square feet on a building. Normal campus buildings use about 1,500 tons of it, with more than 82,000 individual stones.

The first building on campus that used the native limestone was the YMCA, constructed in 1899. Though the campus moved to a more modern look with its architecture in the 1960s and '70s, in 1990 the school's board of visitors moved toward having Hokie Stone be in all buildings constructed on the central campus. A resolution passed in 2010 made that official policy.

It's an aesthetic that Virginia Tech athletics has embraced, both in its architecture designs and uniforms.

Since 1965, when the Hokies run out of the tunnel in Lane Stadium onto Worsham Field, players slap a two-foot slab of Hokie Stone above the exit, flanked by the signs that say, "For those who have passed, for those to come...reach for excellence." The exit of the tunnel's been lined with an archway of Hokie Stone too.

Look on the outside of Lane Stadium and it's everywhere, mixed into the design of the west-side renovation. When the Beamer-Lawson indoor practice facility was finished on the existing practice fields between Lane Stadium and the Jamerson Athletic Center next to Stadium Woods, it was done with Hokie Stone in the design along the base of the support columns along the outside.

Though Cassell Coliseum was constructed during a more modern period of architecture on campus and doesn't have Hokie

Stone in its exterior design, the school has subtly made it a part of the interior. When a new basketball floor was finalized prior to the 2017–18 season, the border to the court was designed with a Hokie Stone pattern in shades of maroon.

The look has worked its way into Virginia Tech's athletic uniforms as well. In 2013, at Georgia Tech, the football team debuted Hokie Stone-inspired helmets featuring a gray rock pattern and the school's famed pylons and founding date as a logo. Later versions included the standard VT logo instead.

"The outside world may have to do a double-take, but the Hokie Nation will know exactly what it is: Hokie Stone! And it's something we're proud of," Beamer said in a Virginia Tech release when the uniforms debuted. "The reason I like it is because it represents what this program and this university are built on. Each piece, in its place, serving its purpose, doing its job, and when it's all working together, it's rock solid and it's something special. That Hokie Stone represents what we're all about, a foundation that we're proud of, built on brotherhood, loyalty, leadership, *Ut Prosim*, sacrifice, service, honor, and duty."

Though unique, those uniforms were met with mixed reviews—it was an interesting look but was somewhat mismatched with the team's standard maroon jerseys and pants—but a more integrated set of Hokie Stone uniforms went over much better a few years later. For the game against Tennessee in the Battle at Bristol in 2016, Virginia Tech debuted black-and-gray uniforms with a Hokie Stone pattern on the jerseys, in the VT logo on the helmet and as an accent on black pants. Tech released a version with a white helmet and pants for a home game in 2017.

While the basketball team has incorporated Hokie Stone into a couple of its uniform designs, the football team made more subtle use of the pattern in its redesign ahead of the 2018 season, with a hint of it faintly in the numbers that you can see better when close up.

In short, Virginia Tech is Hokie Stone and Hokie Stone is Virginia Tech, and the rock is woven deeply into not only the campus but the school's athletics teams too.

49 Duane Brown

When Duane Brown arrived at Virginia Tech as a 250-pound tight end, there was little to indicate that he'd go on to be one of the most successful NFL players in Hokies history, and certainly not on the offensive line.

But more than a decade and a half after the Richmond product got to Blacksburg, that's exactly what he's become, a four-time Pro Bowl selection and 2012 first-team All-Pro pick who's been one of the most reliable left tackles in the NFL in the last decade.

Brown's success story hits many of the same notes as a lot of Hokies over the years. He wasn't the most touted recruit after breaking his ankle as a senior in high school, a three-star prospect out of Hermitage High who Rivals.com ranked as the No. 22 recruit in the state in 2003. (He was also a decorated shot putter and discus thrower.) He picked the Hokies over an offer from UVa.

Though he caught a touchdown pass against Western Michigan in 2004, the coaching staff finally convinced the reluctant big man to switch to offensive line. They liked his agility and footwork at that size, thinking that would translate well at the left tackle position. History and over $80 million in career earnings proved them right.

"He needs to thank us just about every other day, because he's made a lot of money at offensive tackle," joked former Tech coach Frank Beamer, who used Brown as an example to future big men of how lucrative of a career they could have protecting a quarterback's blind side.

Brown took to the position quickly. His first start there was the 2005 season opener against N.C. State and All-American defensive end Mario Williams, a future No. 1 overall pick and someone who'd be Brown's NFL teammate in a few years. Brown held his own, holding Williams without a sack, though he had some growing pains that day.

He'd iron those out, starting 40 games the next three seasons. Virginia Tech went 42–11 and won a pair of ACC titles during his career. Brown was a second-team All-ACC pick his junior and senior years.

"My freshman year, I was about 265 pounds," Brown told the *Houston Chronicle* ahead of a return to his hometown of Richmond for a preseason camp in 2015. "Everybody kept telling me to move to tackle and that I would make a lot of money. I wasn't trying to hear it. I was catching touchdowns, and I wanted the glory of having my name in the stat line. I'm very fortunate that they gave me that insight early on."

Perhaps it finally sunk in when the Houston Texans took him in the first round of the 2008 NFL Draft. To date, he's still one of only two Hokies offensive linemen to be selected in the first round, joining Eugene Chung in 1992.

The 6-foot-4, 315-pounder became a fixture on the Texans' line, starting all 16 games as a rookie and protecting the blind side for Matt Schaub, who threw for an NFL-best 4,770 yards in 2009. His tireless work ethic, technical mastery, and mean streak made him one of the best tackles in the game.

In 2011, he didn't allow a single sack or get flagged for a holding penalty. Houston rewarded him with a six-year, $53.4 million extension with $22 million guaranteed ahead of the 2012 season. Brown was a first-team All-Pro that year and made the Pro Bowl each year from 2012 to '14.

After a knee injury limited him in 2016, he held out during training camp and the first six games of the year in 2017, wanting a new contract. In the middle of that season, the Texans traded him to the Seattle Seahawks.

Brown earned his fourth Pro Bowl nod that year and the Seahawks locked him up on a three-year deal worth $36.5 million in the off-season.

"Duane made an immediate impression on us when he got here," Seattle coach Pete Carroll said. "This is a real leader. He's a real man in that huddle and in the locker room, and we're very, very fortunate to have him. He's a great worker. He's really, really an astute ballplayer. He's got a great voice and perspective that's gonna help other guys."

Brown was a second-team All-Pro pick in 2018, his first year into the new deal, helping lead a revamped Seattle offensive attack that led the league in rushing.

After Bruce Smith and perhaps Michael Vick, you can make an argument that Brown has had the best career of any Hokie in NFL history—a career that, as of 2019, was still going strong.

50 Brandon Flowers

There have been plenty of defensive back standouts at Virginia Tech, as you'd imagine at a school that fashions itself DBU, so many that it's hard to pick the best in the Hokies' quarter-century run of producing stars in the secondary.

When his arm was twisted, defensive coordinator Bud Foster landed on one name.

"Brandon Flowers is one of my favorites because he was a complete football player," Foster said. "Just a great football IQ, being durable, being physical, and doing a great job in the passing game."

With apologies to DeAngelo Hall, it's hard to argue. Flowers, a 5-foot-9, 187-pound player, wasn't the biggest corner, but he checked all the boxes of what Virginia Tech looks for in a defensive back. And his story hits many of the beats common to the Hokies in the mid-2000s.

Flowers came to Virginia Tech from Atlantic Community High in Delray Beach, Florida, a school that's served as a pipeline to Tech over the years. He wasn't the first to take that route, though he and classmate David Clowney started a run in the 2000s. Clowney beat Flowers to Blacksburg by a year, since Flowers had a one-year stop at Hargrave Military Academy, a prep school that served the Hokies well during that era.

Once Flowers got to Tech, it was clear he'd be a player. He returned a pick for a touchdown in his very first defensive series in 2004, taking back an interception against Western Michigan for a 38-yard touchdown. He fractured his right fibula later in that game, however. Still, he gave everyone a glimpse.

"I just felt like that momentum just jumpstarted my career," Flowers said. "That gave me so much confidence, so much respect amongst the coaches coming into the next season when I was coming off my injury."

He played 13 games as a redshirt freshman in 2005, intercepting one pass, then took over the starting boundary corner spot as a sophomore in 2006. He never looked back, starting the final 27 games of his career and twice earning All-American honors, the first Virginia Tech defensive back to do so since Frank Loria in the '60s.

He had 51 tackles, 7.5 tackles for a loss, and three interceptions in 2006, earning third-team All-America honors from the *Associated Press* and first-team All-ACC honors.

Brandon Flowers cradles a fourth quarter interception against the Miami Hurricanes in a game where Virginia Tech defeated Miami 17–10.
(Doug Benc / Getty Images)

In 2007, he was even more active, getting in on 86 tackles, with eight tackles behind the line, and intercepting five passes. Lest you think he could only cover, he could lay the lumber, too. In Tech's notable first win against Florida State in 2007, he knocked out 'Noles starting quarterback Drew Weatherford with a big hit in the second quarter.

People took notice nationally. Despite being a second-team All-ACC pick, Flowers was a first-team All-America selection by the American Football Coaches Association and a second-team pick by two other selectors.

Though he had a year of eligibility remaining, Flowers decided to go pro, and the Chiefs made him a second-round pick with the 35th choice overall in the 2008 NFL Draft. He turned in a strong pro career, playing nine years for the Chiefs and Chargers, intercepting 21 passes, four of which he returned for touchdowns, and earning a Pro Bowl trip in his final year in Kansas City in 2013.

Virginia Tech All-Time Interception Leaders

	Player (Years)	INT	TD
1.	Gene Bunn (1976–78)	18	0
2.	Tyronne Drakeford (1990–93)	16	1
3.	Victor "Macho" Harris (2005–08)	15	4
4.	Willie Pile (1999–2002)	14	2
5*t.*	Lenny Smith (1968–70)	13	0
5*t.*	Ron Davidson (1966–68)	13	0
7*t.*	Jayron Hosley (2009–11)	12	0
7*t.*	John Granby (1987–91)	12	0
7*t.*	Mike Widger (1967–69)	12	3
10*t.*	William Yarborough (1992–95)	11	0
10*t.*	Ashley Lee (1980–84)	11	2
10*t.*	Mike Johnson (1980–83)	11	1

Flowers had close to $50 million in career earnings but, upon his retirement in 2017, came back to Virginia Tech to complete the degree he'd left unfinished when he went pro nearly a decade earlier

"I always preach to kids: go to college, get your education," said Flowers, who mentors kids in his hometown of Delray Beach. "And even with myself, I always felt something in me, like I need to make sure I go finish. I can't just tell these kids to go get a college education. I need to practice what I preach."

Flowers finished up his last semester at Tech, earning a sociology degree before pursuing his MBA at Miami.

During his time back in Blacksburg going to school, he had several sit-downs with Foster, with the athletic department producing a pair of videos of their chats reminiscing about the good old days. Though Flowers had a long, prosperous NFL career, Virginia Tech holds a special place in his heart.

"Man, it gave me goosebumps," Flowers said. "Because the NFL is fun. That's my dream. But you can ask any NFL football player—unless they had just a terrible college football experience, not anything competes with college. College football was some of the best times of my life playing on the field. So just going back down memory lane with Bud Foster, man, I just wish I could play one more down for Virginia Tech.

"In the NFL? I'm done. I don't care about playing one more snap. I retired on my own terms. I don't miss it at all. But running out of this stadium at Virginia Tech, that's one thing I do miss."

51 Do the Hokie Pokie (Or at Least Be Loud in the Cheer That Replaced It)

It was a fun little quirk, though a bit outdated, that Virginia Tech's band, the Marching Virginians, always used to perform the "Hokie Pokie" in the break between the third and fourth quarter at Hokies football games. The sousaphones always took a leading role in the playing of the song, which was arranged by former director James Sochinski and first played in 1980, and a good portion of Lane Stadium always participated.

Now, if you're going to do it, it's just a little bit earlier in the game.

Virginia Tech made the decision ahead of the 2017 season to move the Hokies' take on the children's song and dance to halftime of games, clearing the room for an alternate cheer at the end of the third quarter.

No harm, no foul, right? After all, the song's the same. It's just at a different time of the game.

Well, things are never quite that simple. The school got a good deal of blowback from the move, certainly from the traditional set of Hokies fans. In fact, an online petition titled "Save the Hokie Pokie" garnered over 2,000 signatures.

Virginia Tech stuck with its decision, however, trying to start a new tradition after the third quarter that so far has been hit or miss. Now, when the clock expires on the third quarter, the Marching Virginians play the "VPI Victory March," followed by a blast from "Skipper," the Corps of Cadets' cannon.

After that, an honorary guest takes the field to lead the crowd in a "Let's Go, Hokies!" cheer alternating between the east and west stands, with "Tech Triumph" following to set the stage for the fourth quarter.

Early reviews were, well, not great.

Some blowouts early in 2017 mostly in the Hokies' favor sapped the stadium of most of its energy (and many fans) during the first few test runs of the new cheer.

"I'll say this: You can't, quote, 'make a new tradition,'" athletic director Whit Babcock told the *Roanoke Times* after the new cheer's debut. "I don't believe anybody in 2000-whenever-it-was when we played 'Enter Sandman' said, 'Today we're starting a new tradition.' It just took off."

Things have gone a little bit better with the cheer since. Frank Beamer was a natural choice early in the first year to give it a shot. With Tech leading Old Dominion at the time 31–0, it was hardly a rowdy, capacity crowd he was egging on, but the retired coach gave the moment a lasting image with an exaggerated mic drop once he completed his task.

Although a number of former players have brought plenty of energy to the chant since, particularly Darryl Tapp, who screamed words of encouragement to try to get the crowd pumped in a game that had gotten away from the Hokies, the best version of the cheer probably came during the Virginia game in 2018, when beloved former fullback and consummate team leader Sam Rogers returned to Blacksburg and fired up the crowd.

"This is our game! This is our field! And most important, this is our state!" he yelled before starting the chant, just about getting the 60,000-plus in attendance jacked up enough to run through a wall. Perhaps related, Virginia Tech pulled out a 34–31 come-from-behind overtime victory against UVa, the Hokies' 15th straight win in the series.

Maybe that will be a launching pad for the new tradition at Tech. If it is, the Hokies have one more signature moment to get Lane Stadium rocking.

Regardless, the "Hokie Pokie" hasn't gone away. And when the band belts out the familiar Virginia Tech rendition of the song at halftime, you certainly won't be alone if you stand up and show them what it's all about.

52 Bryan Randall

Virginia Tech's debut season in the ACC wouldn't have been as special had the Hokies not been ushered into the new league by a quarterback universally respected around Blacksburg.

Bryan Randall fit the bill.

Randall went down as not only one of the most beloved but also accomplished players in Virginia Tech history, guiding the Hokies to the ACC championship in their first year in the league and finishing his career as the school record holder in total offense (8,034 yards), touchdown passes (48), and passing yards (6,508).

Randall came to the Hokies as a two-sport star out of Bruton High in Williamsburg, Virginia, where he broke school records in total offense and touchdown passes and was a member of the state championship basketball team.

His path to Virginia Tech legend wasn't always a smooth one. He got a taste of action as a freshman before starting 12 games as a sophomore, with some success (2,134 yards, 12 touchdowns, 11 interceptions), including a 504-yard, five-touchdown pass effort in a triple-overtime loss at Syracuse. The former's the second-most in Tech history. The latter's still a school record.

Randall started all 13 games in 2003, throwing for 1,996 yards and 15 touchdowns to 10 interceptions, but his status as Tech's starter wasn't set in cement. That's because former five-star recruit Marcus Vick, Michael's younger brother, was on the scene, stealing snaps here and there and looking good in the process.

It prompted Randall to declare at one point, "Why am I still having to prove myself?"

The Hokies cratered at the end of the year, losing four of their last five after upsetting Miami, and though Randall threw for 398 yards and four touchdowns and added a rushing touchdown in a

Darryl Tapp and Jimmy Williams

When Virginia Tech first got into the ACC, two defensive stars from the 2002 signing class played a big part in helping the Hokies achieve instant success.

Defensive end Darryl Tapp and defensive back Jimmy Williams were both All-Americans from the 757 who made the All-ACC first team in both 2004 and '05.

Tapp, from Deep Creek High in Chesapeake, became a full-time starter as a junior in 2004, when he had 60 tackles and team highs with 16½ tackles for a loss and 8½ sacks, helping the Hokies win the ACC in their first year in the league. He had 14½ tackles for a loss and 10 sacks as a senior, the last Tech player to reach double digits, and was a first-team All-America pick by the American Football Coaches Association.

Williams, who was from Hampton, was as decorated of a defensive back as the Hokies have had. He played both safety and cornerback in his career, intercepting nine passes and returning two for touchdowns.

As a senior in 2005, he was a finalist for the Jim Thorpe Award and was named a unanimous first-team All-American by all five of the major selectors.

The two had vastly different NFL careers, with Tapp, a second-round pick by the Seahawks in 2006, carving out a 12-year run with six teams and finishing with 29 career sacks. Williams was a second-round pick by the Falcons but watched his career fizzle out after just a few seasons.

52–49 Insight Bowl loss to an Aaron Rodgers-led California, he still didn't have the starting job locked down. (He also dabbled on the basketball team that winter, averaging 3.1 points in 18 games.)

Everything changed in the spring when he held off a challenge from Vick, who was taken out of the competition altogether when he was suspended for a season by the university for several off-field incidents.

Given full reins of the offense, Randall turned in a dream senior season, guiding the Hokies to a 10–2 regular season record and a surprise ACC championship in their first year after switching from the Big East.

Randall earned ACC Player of the Year honors, the first of three Hokies to earn that distinction, after throwing for 2,264 yards and 21 touchdowns. He also ran for 511 yards and three scores, having a knack for coming up big when the Hokies needed it the most. He led fourth-quarter comebacks against both Wake Forest and Georgia Tech.

"He plays his best when the game is on the line," Virginia Tech coach Frank Beamer said.

He beat Virginia for a third time as starter by throwing for two second-half touchdown passes in a 24–10 win, then did just enough, going 11-for-18 for 148 yards and two touchdowns, in the Hokies' 16–10 upset at No. 9 Miami in a de facto ACC title game, clinching a spot in Tech's third Sugar Bowl in a decade.

Randall accounted for 344 yards in a 16–13 Sugar Bowl loss to No. 3 Auburn, which finished the season unbeaten, though it didn't mar his stellar career.

Though he never latched on with an NFL club beyond practice squad or off-season stints with the Falcons, Steelers, and Buccaneers, he kept his football dream alive, spending a year in the Canadian Football League before playing eight years in various indoor football leagues, with stops all over the country—like Richmond,

Virginia; Allen and Laredo, Texas; Allentown, Pennsylvania; and Albuquerque, New Mexico—and out of it when he had a one-year stint in a newly-formed league in China in 2016.

In 2015, he was inducted into the Virginia Tech Sports Hall of Fame, a no-brainer of a selection.

Kevin Rogers, Tech's quarterbacks coach during his career, summed up Randall's impact well, saying he would be "forever remembered here as a walking advertisement for Virginia Tech. [He's] a guy of strong moral fiber and an incredible leader. What more could you ask for?"

53 1986 Peach Bowl

By 1986, Virginia Tech had been to five bowl games in its history, including a Peach Bowl trip in 1981 and an Independence Bowl appearance in 1984 under coach Bill Dooley.

But the Hokies had yet to break through and win a bowl game—until 1986, that is, when Chris Kinzer's 40-yard field goal as time expired lifted Virginia Tech to a rousing 25–24 win against No. 18 N.C. State in the Peach Bowl at Atlanta-Fulton County Stadium.

The Hokies got there after going 8–2–1 during the regular season, winning four straight down the stretch and getting the invite after a 29–21 victory against Vanderbilt. They'd face an N.C. State team coming off three losing seasons and under first-year coach Dick Sheridan.

The coaching drama was all on the Hokies sideline, however. Dooley, who was both the athletic director and head coach, was coaching in his final game. University president Dr. William E. Lavery had sought to separate the head coaching and athletic director positions after the department's financial woes came under scrutiny. (The NCAA was also investigating the school for having more football players on scholarship than allowed.)

Just before the season, school officials informed Dooley he wouldn't continue as athletic director but they'd like him to continue as head football coach. Dooley responded by suing the university for $3.5 million, alleging breach of contract. In an out-of-court settlement, Dooley agreed to quit his position as coach after the season, giving the Hokies a rallying cry to send him out on a high note.

They did just that in the Peach Bowl, rallying from a 21–10 halftime deficit in a down-to-the-wire game against the Wolfpack.

Tech running back Maurice Williams, who had a 77-yard run earlier in the game, scored on a 1-yard run just before the end of the third quarter to cut N.C. State's advantage to 21–16.

Kicker Chris Kinzer (4) is knocked off his feet by a number of N.C. State players after his field goal to give the Hokies a 25–24 win in the Peach Bowl. (AP Photo / JHJR)

The Hokies took a 22–21 lead with 9:36 remaining on a touchdown pass from Erik Chapman to tight end Steve Johnson. Johnson tossed the ball into the stands in celebration, earning a 15-yard penalty. Years later, as a successful commercial developer, he donated $1 million to the Virginia Tech athletic department, plus another $25 to cover the cost of the football he threw into the crowd.

N.C. State answered with a 33-yard field goal from Mike Cofer to take a 24–22 lead midway through the fourth.

Eventually, Tech had one last-gasp drive to win it, starting at its own 20 with 1:53 left on the clock. Chapman hit Johnson for a pair of first-down passes but, after several more plays, the Hokies faced a fourth-and-3 at the N.C. State 37 with just 20 seconds left. Chapman again hit Johnson, this time for nine yards, to the Wolfpack's 28 with 15 seconds remaining.

A holding penalty backed Tech up to the 38 on the next play, but a pass interference put the ball at the N.C. State 23-yard line with four seconds left. That set the stage for Kinzer, a Pulaski County native who'd grown up rooting for the Hokies.

He'd already kicked field goals that proved to be the difference in five wins and a tie during the regular season, making 17 straight at one point. And he'd already made a 46-yarder earlier in the game, the second longest in Peach Bowl history. This one, from 40 yards, wasn't any tougher, even with N.C. State trying to ice him by calling a timeout.

After Dooley gave him a thumbs up on the sideline, Kinzer drilled it perfectly between the uprights as time expired, giving the Hokies a 25–24 victory, their first in a bowl game and the last for Dooley at Virginia Tech, where he went 64–37–1, the winningest coach in school history at the time.

Kinzer's teammates smothered him on the field. He managed to get out of the scrum near the N.C. State sideline, where several

Wolfpack players started giving him the finger. Kinzer shot a one-finger salute right back—on national TV, no less.

Atlanta Journal-Constitution columnist Furman Bisher, in a throwback to an earlier era, had this old-school account of the finish:

> In the end the play that did decide it all was left to the man in the clean uniform with the number "4" brightly shining, as if he had just stepped out of the laundry room, his person bearing no traces of the stains and gore of combat.…As the clock came up on triple zero, Kinzer's 40-yard placekick sailed high and majestically between the iron pipes, and Virginia Tech won with no time left for rebuttal, 25–24. Never has there been such a finish in any Peach Bowl, and the climax had this old house, and its 53,668 occupants, in a frenzy. It was no place for cardiograms.

54 Jake Grove

If there's a prototype for the nasty kind of offensive lineman Virginia Tech had in its heyday, it's Jake Grove, an unheralded high schooler out of Jefferson Forest High who turned himself into the nation's best center in Blacksburg.

A late bloomer, Grove's only other offer coming out of high school other than Virginia Tech was a partial scholarship to VMI, but he more than made the most of his opportunity with the Hokies.

"The first thing I thought about was, 'Did I belong?'" Grove said. "That Coach Beamer took a chance on me because, to be honest, I didn't think I could play. I mean, I didn't know if I could. I just wanted to show him that it was worth his time offering me a scholarship. Even if I couldn't play, I was going to at least work hard."

Grove signed with the Hokies in 1998, a year before their run to the national title game but didn't find his way into the starting lineup until 2001. By then, he'd worked tirelessly with strength coach Mike Gentry to become the 6-foot-3, 300-pounder that would anchor the Hokies' offensive line for his final three years.

What Grove lacked in overwhelming physical traits he made up for with his attitude. Quiet and reserved off the field, he was anything but when stepped on the field, where he earned the nickname "Nasty."

"If you watch him, he's got a big, strong, flexible body and he's a smart guy," Beamer said. "He's just got a nastiness and relentlessness to him. To me, that's the way the game is played."

With linemen, there's always a fine line between aggressive and dirty, and Grove tightroped it most of his career. After the Hokies crushed then–No. 2 Miami 31–7 in 2003, Hurricanes coach Larry Coker accused Grove of delivering a cheap shot on defensive tackle Santonio Thomas.

Grove thought it was a preposterous accusation.

"When the whistle blows I stop playing, but the whistle hadn't blown," Grove said. "If you want to call me dirty for playing aggressive and playing hard, then I really don't care, but I would never try to hurt anybody."

If anything, Grove leaned into his nasty reputation.

"I want to be a guy who people don't like," he said. "I'm just the kind of player who loves contact, that's all, and I'm going to keep riding you until somebody separates us.... I want (defensive linemen), after we're done, to know they were in a dogfight. I don't care if people call me dirty. As long as they don't call me soft, that's all."

That attitude served Grove well. He was the headliner on a line that cleared holes for some of the most productive rushing seasons in Virginia Tech history, with Lee Suggs and Kevin Jones putting up monster stats running behind him.

Grove got some kudos for his play, too. He was a two-time All-American, a unanimous pick in 2003, only the third in Virginia Tech history at the time. He also won the Rimington Trophy as college football's best center during his senior season, a year in which he graded out at 91.8 percent on over 700 offensive plays and led the Hokies with 48 knockdowns.

That success led him to be a second-round draft pick by the Oakland Raiders in 2004, the 45th pick overall and first center off the board. Grove played six seasons in the NFL—five with the Raiders and one with the Dolphins—playing 66 career games before retiring due to nagging knee and shoulder problems.

His accomplishments weren't forgotten at Virginia Tech, which had a jersey retirement ceremony for him in 2006, honoring the No. 64 he wore during his time with the Hokies.

Grove never strayed far from his roots. In retirement, he retreated to a 260-acre farm with his wife and kids in his native Forest, Virginia, but he didn't get far from the game. In 2014, he accepted an assistant coach job at his old high school, Jefferson Forest, working for his old coach, Bob Christmas. He coaches with the same mindset he did as a player.

"Every single week is going to come down to whether the offensive line can get it done," Grove told the *Roanoke Times*. "If we get it done, we've got a really good shot to win. If we don't get it done, we are going to lose. That's the way it goes every week at any level of football."

55 How Worsham Field Got Its Name

Wes Worsham is easy to spot on Hokies gamedays, a fixture on the Virginia Tech sideline for years whose custom-made khakis with sewn-on HokieBirds stood out. It's hard to believe that for most of his life, the man who the Lane Stadium field is dedicated to knew next to nothing about Virginia Tech.

A friendship made during his deployment in the Korean War led to an unlikely connection to the school, where he'd be one of the biggest supporters of Frank Beamer during the coach's early days.

Worsham, who was born in 1932 and grew up in Powhatan, Virginia, was shipped off to the Korean War in 1950 when he was only 17 years old. It was there that he met a fellow soldier, 11 years his senior, named Arthur Fleet, a veteran of World War II from Blacksburg. Fleet saw Worsham's jacket with "Virginia Kid" scrawled on the back and the two quickly became friends.

Worsham saved Fleet's life in a skirmish on the Pusan Perimeter, shooting dead a North Korean who had Fleet in his sights as he climbed a hill. As thanks, Fleet offered Worsham a beer ration—one can of Pabst Blue Ribbon—when they got back to headquarters that night. Worsham declined but said the two would share a beer when they reached the Yalu River, which was on the northern border of North Korea, 500 miles away.

The two got close but never made it. As they approached the goal following General Douglas MacArthur's amphibious landing at Inchon, Chinese forces pushed the U.S. back from the China–North Korea border.

In a Chinese spring offensive in 1951, Worsham and Fleet ran from tank to tank as the last ones off the battlefield during a retreat, covering each other as they made a dash back to safer ground. During one sprint, Worsham saw Fleet get shot in the chest. He circled back to put his wounded friend on a U.S. tank that was pulling out before running ahead.

Later, while searching for Fleet, another soldier told Worsham that Fleet was in a nearby body bag. Worsham didn't look inside but said a prayer for his friend.

"I thought he was dead," Worsham said. "We went on with our fighting, And I never heard from him or saw him again."

Worsham's war continued and he was taken prisoner by the North Koreans in April 1951, held for three months and 23 days before being liberated by a Turkish army and a U.S. tank column. His parents were told he was dead, but he survived, weighing only 92 pounds when he returned to the States.

He healed up and re-entered life as a citizen, getting into the fire protection business and founding Worsham Sprinklers in 1964. He visited some of the men he'd served with over time but, feeling some guilt, never worked up the courage to visit Fleet's family until 1970. Finally, he looked up Fleet in the phone book and called Arnold, Arthur's brother.

"Did you have a relative killed in Korea?" Worsham asked.

"No, but I had one in Korea," Arnold answered. "He died here."

Arthur Fleet wasn't in that body bag. He'd survived the Korean War, making it back to the U.S. in 1953. He settled down in Blacksburg, got married and started a family. Two wars had taken their toll on him, though. He was in constant pain, his back littered with shrapnel that couldn't be removed. In 1964, he died from a heart attack at age 43.

Worsham visited Fleet's family in Blacksburg for the first time around 1970, becoming close friends with them and trading stories with Fleet's son Bob.

He also fell in love with Virginia Tech, becoming a super fan of the Hokies. The successful businessman donated in the Jimmy Sharpe and Bill Dooley days, but he had a special fondness for Beamer, who he thought was the real deal. In 1991, when Beamer was struggling to turn a corner and Tech's athletic department was desperate for money, Worsham and his wife Janet gave their biggest donation of $1.3 million.

"I figured they needed it," Worsham said.

The sum was substantial, especially in 1991, so much so that Virginia Tech named the Lane Stadium field after Worsham in 1992.

"Every time I see that Worsham name on that field, it makes me proud to know that," Bob Fleet said. "It also makes me proud of my dad. Because in some way, I see my dad having something to do with that."

Beamer was so grateful for Worsham's support that he let the booster roam the sidelines before games and be in the locker room afterward. In fact, Virginia Tech gives out the Wes Worsham Award annually each spring to a player who exceeds expectations or surprises everyone with his performance. In retirement, Beamer's a frequent guest in Worsham's luxury box at games.

Worsham never forgot his friend Fleet. He shares that beer they were supposed to have at the Yalu River at his friend's gravesite in Blacksburg every August 10, Fleet's birthday. He cracks a PBR and sets an unopened one on Fleet's headstone, whispering a few words to his late friend.

An unfortunate miscommunication cost them more than a decade that they could have been together.

"I would give anything if those two could just get together," Bob said. "And I could sit there and shut up and listen to them laugh."

56 David Wilson

He did backflips with ease, ripping off 10 in a row as though he was walking down the street. He'd chase rabbits at football practice just for the heck of it. Legend has it he scaled the arches outside of Cassell Coliseum up onto the roof during his freshman year, about as close as you can get to Superman leaping a building in a single bound.

"Nothing surprises me with him," former Hokies running backs coach Shane Beamer said of David Wilson, a one-of-a-kind ballcarrier. "He plays like a superhero sometimes, so that's probably a good comparison in my opinion."

There have been many outstanding running backs throughout Virginia Tech's history, though none probably had as much sheer athleticism and personality as Wilson, a 5-foot-9, 205-pound dynamo who earned All-America honors in both football and track during his three years with the Hokies.

Wilson was one of the last offensive jewels recruited by Frank Beamer, the top recruit in the state in 2009 out of Danville who was champing at the bit to get on the field from the moment he arrived in Blacksburg. The problem was, Tech had a logjam at running back. Darren Evans ran for 1,265 yards in 2008 and Ryan Williams made a school-record 1,655 in 2009.

Wilson ran for 619 yards as a sophomore in 2010 in a backfield-by-committee by default with Williams battling a hamstring injury. But he really began to make his mark on kickoff return, averaging 26.5 yards per return and taking two back to the house, including a 90-yarder in the final minutes to break a 21-all tie against Georgia Tech, when he leaped into the air after crossing the goal line.

Williams and Evans both went pro after the 2010 season, leaving the starting tailback job at long last open for Wilson. He didn't disappoint, rushing for a school-record 1,709 yards and scoring nine touchdowns as the Hokies went 11–3 and made it back to the Sugar Bowl.

Wilson was named ACC Offensive Player of the Year after setting the Hokies single-season record for most 100-yard games (10) and the career mark for yards per carry (5.76).

He did it with a flair that you'd expect from someone who wore a shirt and tie every day to class and drove a 1978 orange Thunderbird with Ostrich leather-covered seats.

Against Clemson early in the year, he did a very good impersonation of one of his idols, Barry Sanders, reversing field twice on one run while spinning out of a tackle and retreating 20 yards in the process before breaking free and turning the corner up the left sideline. By the time he finished the amazing run, he'd covered over 100 yards on what ended up being a 19-yard gain.

Wilson would earn All-America honors on the gridiron that year, a second-team pick by the *Associated Press*. It was his second sport earning All-America honors. In the spring of 2011, he earned it after finishing sixth in the triple jump at the NCAA championships with a personal-best leap of 16.20 meters.

"I love competition," Wilson said. "That whole thing is like, 'Let me get a better number than my whole group.' You see everybody and you want to separate yourself. That drive, that will get my adrenaline going."

He took the leap into the NFL after his junior season, snatched up by the New York Giants with the 32nd pick in the 2012 Draft. His NFL career was sporadic and brief, marred by fumble problems in his rookie year and cut short by spinal stenosis early in his second season, which required neck surgery. He risked serious injury if he played again, prompting his early retirement.

But in that short time as a pro, he showed off his out-of-this-world athleticism. It was all on display on December 9, 2012, when Wilson set the Giants team record for all-purpose yards with 327 in a 52–27 home win against the Saints. He returned four kickoffs for 227 yards, including a 97-yarder for a touchdown. He also ran for 100 yards and two touchdowns on 13 carries.

He punctuated one of his touchdowns with his signature backflip, prompting the *New York Post* to publish his photo, mid-backflip as he was upside down, with the headline, "Over Easy: 'Flip' Wilson leads Giants in 52–27 romp."

Wilson retired at age 23, dressed dapperly in a suit as he almost always was, wiping tears away from his eyes.

"These are tears of joy," Wilson said. "Don't think I'm sad. There's no need to dwell on the negative, because if you do, then you feel sorry for yourself and you're not living. I'm still healthy. I'll still be able to do the things that I could always do, except play football."

Wilson hasn't slowed down in retirement. He made a track and field comeback as a triple jumper, though he came up short of his Olympic goal. Now he's pursuing a music career.

"I really try not to put limits on me," he said recently, something that seems to apply to all aspects of his life.

57 Kam Chancellor

Virginia Tech's had its share of big hitters over the years, at all levels of the defense. Nobody quite laid the lumber in the secondary like Kam Chancellor, who became the big, physical archetype of the NFL safety that teams still seek today.

It's a career that, given the hurdles it took to get there, almost never happened. Chancellor grew up in a rough part of Norfolk, pitching in by sweeping floors at a barbershop to help his mother,

Karen Lambert, a single parent who worked two or three jobs in order to provide for him and his five siblings.

Chancellor wasn't the most recruited athlete coming out of high school, a three-star quarterback whose only other offers were from James Madison and Kent State. But Virginia Tech plucked him out of the 757, and a position switch started him on a career that, including his pro exploits, turned out to be one of the best ever by a Hokie.

Tech didn't tab Chancellor as the hulking safety he'd eventually be, initially having him work as a cornerback before moving him to rover as a sophomore, when he first excelled, registering 79 tackles and an interception. Finally, the 6-foot-4, 230-pounder ended up at free safety in Bud Foster's defense for the final two years of his career.

All the moving around slowed his development and probably cost him some All-Conference accolades, but he eventually earned second-team All-ACC honors as a senior in 2009, perhaps coming up short of secondary coach Torrian Gray's declaration that Chancellor would become the greatest safety in Virginia Tech history.

"I think it could have been better [in 2008]," Chancellor said as his career winded down. "Maybe I took a step backward, but I finished strong. I had to start trusting my instincts and speed and technique a little more."

His college career was just a taste of what was to come, however. A perfect NFL fit finally unleashed all his talents. Chancellor went lower than expected in the 2010 NFL Draft, selected in the fifth round by the Seattle Seahawks. It was a fortuitous fall. He ended up being a key cog in the "Legion of Boom" secondary that was so instrumental in Seattle's back-to-back Super Bowl appearances.

He modeled his game after the late Sean Taylor, a Miami product who was a star for the Washington Redskins before his murder in 2007. Chancellor watched his highlights on YouTube before games as motivation and might have been as close as the NFL had to Taylor since his untimely death.

By Chancellor's second year in 2011, he was a Pro Bowl safety anchoring the Seahawks' secondary, which included fellow safety Earl Thomas and cornerbacks Richard Sherman, Brandon Browner, and Byron Maxwell. During the era of the "Legion of Boom" (a name coined during a radio show visit Chancellor did), the Seahawks won three division titles, two NFC championships and one Super Bowl.

Chancellor, the tallest and heaviest safety in the NFL, set the tone. In eight seasons, the big hitter made 641 tackles and had 12 interceptions. He and the "Legion of Boom" hit their peak in 2013, when the Seahawks beat the Broncos and Peyton Manning for the franchise's first Super Bowl victory.

Chancellor starred during the playoff run, finishing with 14 tackles and two pass deflections in a divisional round win against the Saints. He had 10 tackles and an interception in the Seahawks' 43–8 rout of the Broncos for the title.

He'd end up being a four-time Pro Bowl selection, tied for the second most by a Virginia Tech player behind Bruce Smith's 11 appearances, and was a two-time second-team NFL All-Pro (2013, '14).

Only months after signing a three-year, $36 million contract in 2017, Chancellor suffered a neck injury that would eventually end his career. The former Hokies standout announced he was walking away from the game because of the risk of paralysis in the summer of 2018, though he was careful never to use the word retire.

The Norfolk native never forgot his roots along the way. He gives back annually, hosting football camps and his annual Memorial Day Barbecue in the area to raise money for his non-profit, the Kam Cares Foundation. He donates money to the Boys

& Girls Clubs of Southeast Virginia, which were so instrumental in his upbringing.

He also rewarded his mom for all her hard work raising him and his siblings. In 2013, after he signed his first big contract extension worth $28 million over four years, he bought her a car, telling her they were going to pick it up from a guy in a nice neighborhood.

When they arrived, Chancellor told her she had to go knock on the door to get the keys. Once she stepped inside, a huge gathering of her family members surprised her, with Chancellor informing her that the house was hers, too.

"She was so happy and it just felt good," Chancellor said. "She deserves it."

58 What's a Hokie?

You might see Virginia Tech's famed HokieBird and assume that's always been the school's mascot, but that's not the case. In fact, the name "Hokies" didn't even derive from a bird. It was the other way around.

To get to the root of the university's nickname, you have to go back to 1896, when the school, then called Virginia Agricultural and Mechanical College, changed its name to Virginia Agricultural and Mechanical College and Polytechnic Institute, commonly known as Virginia Polytechnic Institute or VPI.

With a new name, the school felt it necessary to come up with a new cheer to go with it and a contest was opened up to the student body. A senior by the name of O.M. Stull, class of 1896, won a first prize worth $5 for coming up with a new spirit cheer, now known as "Old Hokie," which is still used today. Originally, it went:

Hoki, Hoki, Hoki, Hy.
Techs, Techs, V.P.I.
Sola-Rex, Sola-Rah.
Polytechs - Vir-gin-ia.
Rae, Ri, V.P.I.

Later, an "e" was added to "Hokie" to make it "Hokies" and "Team! Team! Team!" was tacked on to the end of the cheer.

Stull noted that the term "Hokie" didn't have any special meaning, saying it was solely a made-up word used as an attention-getter for his yell. But it stuck, eventually becoming the nickname for all the school's athletic teams and their fans. The official definition of "Hokie" is "a loyal Virginia Tech Fan."

Hokie wasn't always the most popular team nickname, however. For the longest time, starting in the early 1900s, athletes were called the Gobblers, a nickname whose origin is disputed. One story claims it was because athletes would gobble up their food so quickly. By 1909, football coach Branch Bocock initiated players into the "Gobbler Club."

However it started, it stuck for a long time, gaining popularity when a local resident named Floyd "Hardtimes" Meade trained a large turkey to pull a cart during a football game in 1913. In subsequent years, trained turkeys would gobble on command and perform stunts at games, up through the 1950s. By 1924, the nickname "Gobblers" was commonly used by reporters covering the team.

In 1962, the first permanent costumed Gobbler appeared at football games, created after a civil engineering student named Mercer MacPherson raised $200 for a costume. It looked like an unusual turkey, with a head that looked like a cardinal and real turkey feathers dyed in the school colors. It debuted at the Thanksgiving Day game between VPI and VMI. A different version

HokieBird Facts

5'10"—Average HokieBird height

10 pounds—The most weight a HokieBird has lost during a single day of performing

$5,000—The total cost of the suit

$2,500—The cost of the head alone

54—Weddings the HokieBird was invited to in 2017

85—Number of hugs the HokieBird received to break the Guinness World Record for mascot hugs given in a minute in 2015

5—HokieBird suits

35 pounds—The weight of the suit

5 pounds—The weight of the feet alone

15—HokieBird shoe size

3—Average number of HokieBirds to graduate each year

was modified in 1971 to include a long neck, making it more than seven feet tall. By then it was called the Fighting Gobbler. (ESPN's Lee Corso has famously worn this headgear three times while picking the Hokies to win on *College GameDay*.)

The nickname Gobblers stayed in fashion until football coach and athletic director Bill Dooley arrived in 1978. Dooley disdained the Gobblers nickname, stung by insults other teams' fans would hurl at Virginia Tech's athletes calling them a "bunch of turkeys." He spearheaded a campaign to reinstate the nickname "Hokies," removing the gobbling sound made by the scoreboard during games after Virginia Tech scored a touchdown and having the sports information department have reporters refer to the team as the Hokies.

The mascot was renamed the HokieBird, getting a redesign when student George Willis sketched a new one as part of a class project. That model, which looked like a maroon cardinal, appeared at a football game for the first time in September 1981.

The current HokieBird costume, an anthropomorphic, turkey-like bird, debuted in 1987, the same year Frank Beamer returned as the football team's head coach, and has become a famed symbol of Virginia Tech's sports programs.

The wearers of the costume follow some strict rules. They're never supposed to speak and aren't ever to lose their head in public. A famous story goes that one person was changing into the suit in a bathroom stall and placed the head on top of the toilet lid, walking out to get the rest of the costume. A child walked in, saw the head and began screaming that the mascot had been flushed down the toilet.

Anonymity is held in high regard, so much so that students who dress as the HokieBird remain anonymous until commencement, when they reveal their secret by wearing the costume's feet during the procession into Lane Stadium.

Back to the unusual nickname, though. It's strange enough that outsiders often have the same question when they encounter Virginia Tech fans: what exactly is a Hokie? The school's faithful fans have adopted a popular, catch-all response: "I am."

59 Miracle in Morgantown

Virginia Tech's special 1999 season was taking shape, but landmines remained on the schedule, with games against ranked Miami and Boston College still in the way. But so too was a pesky trip to Morgantown, where the Hokies and Mountaineers had waged some memorable Big East battles.

November 6, 1999, ended up being a night when Michael Vick showed just how special he could be under pressure, kicker Shayne

Graham etched his name forever in Virginia Tech annals, and Virginia Tech vaulted itself into serious national title contention. So monumental was this game that the Tech athletic department made a documentary short about it years later titled *Miracle in Morgantown*.

The game didn't seem like it should give the Hokies much trouble. West Virginia was 3–5 while the Hokies came in 7–0 and ranked third in the BCS rankings, though still behind a pair of unbeaten blue bloods in Florida State and Penn State. Earlier that day, however, unranked Minnesota upset the No. 2 Nittany Lions 24–23 in State College on a last-second field goal, creating an opening.

Though a tight game at halftime, tied 7–7, the Hokies broke things open in the second half, getting a field goal, a safety and a 6-yard Bryan Stith touchdown run with just under five minutes left to take a commanding 19–7 lead.

West Virginia rallied, however. The Mountaineers scored a quick touchdown to pull within 19–14, then caught new life when a hard hit on Stith popped the ball up the air for a fumble as Tech was trying to run out the clock. Four plays later, Brad Lewis hit Khori Ivy for an 18-yard touchdown on third-and-13, giving WVU a shocking 20–19 lead with 1:15 to play.

As it turned out, that was just enough time for Vick to save the day. He got things going with completions totaling 23 yards to Terrell Parham and André Davis, getting the Hokies out to their own 38. Then came the play that truly began his legend.

"I was ready to get on the field," Vick said. "I was ready to go because that's the way I play. I live for moments like that. It's just in me. It's in my blood. Once I stepped on that field, I knew everybody was watching. I just wanted to make good plays for the team and for the coaching staff."

With 36 seconds left on the clock, and moments after the TV announcer said, "Michael Vick is wasting too much time right now," the redshirt freshman dropped back, couldn't find anyone open and scrambled to his right away from pressure, still looking downfield for an open receiver.

Nobody got free, so Vick took off down the sideline, turning on the jets as he darted for extra yards, finally getting pushed out as he did a giant leap at the West Virginia 36 to finish a 26-yard gain with 23 seconds left on the clock.

"I don't know how fast he was going, but if we'd had a watch, it would have been the fastest 40 he's ever run, I promise you," Hokies coach Frank Beamer said. "He was moving."

Tech still had some time to play with and make a field goal for Graham a bit easier. A 9-yard completion to Ricky Hall got the Hokies more yards but kept the clock moving. Vick hustled everyone to the line and spiked the ball with five seconds remaining.

That set the stage for Graham, a senior kicker from Tech's own backyard from Pulaski County High in Dublin. Graham hadn't made a game-winning kick since the state semifinals when he was a freshman in high school, but nothing compared to the magnitude of the one he was about to attempt—a 44-yarder from the right hash with his team's national title hopes on the line.

"If I had to bet my life, I'd bet my life on Shayne Graham," defensive end Corey Moore said. "Those are kicks he makes every day in practice."

Sure enough, he drilled it, dead center, for a 22–20 win as time expired, sending the Tech sideline spilling onto the field. Players hoisted Graham on their shoulders.

"The instant it hit my foot, it's like when a golfer knows he hit a good shot," Graham said years later. "A kicker knows when he hit a good hit. I picked my head up, I saw the ball going in and I instantaneously threw my arms up and started jumping."

Beamer watched the kick with his hands on his knees and didn't jump for joy when it went through, instead simply exhaling. He took an exasperated step and shook hands with his security detail, police captain Jody Falls, who put his arm around the coach as they walked toward midfield in a bit of a daze.

Sideline reporter Michele Tafoya tracked Beamer down afterward and asked him what was going through his mind during the kick.

"I was praying," Beamer said. "Quite honestly, I just said a little prayer."

The kick didn't clinch anything for the Hokies, who were actually jumped in the BCS standings a few days later by Tennessee, which had beaten Notre Dame. But it only lasted a week, with Virginia Tech seizing the No. 2 spot the following week after the Vols lost and holding onto it the rest of the way to qualify for the national championship game.

"This was the one that kept us going and got us to the national championship game," Beamer said. "Without this win, we never would have gotten there."

60 Bill Roth

"From the blue waters of the Chesapeake Bay to the hills of Tennessee, the Virginia Tech Hokies are on the air."

With those 21 words, broadcaster Bill Roth let you know he was going to be a part of your life for the next couple hours, calling either a Hokies football or basketball game. For 27 years, Roth was a fixture over the airwaves in Blacksburg, the "Voice of the Hokies," who for many fans is as indelible a part of Virginia Tech football as Frank Beamer, Lane Stadium, or "Enter Sandman."

The suburban Pittsburgh native arrived in Blacksburg as a fresh-faced 22-year-old in 1988, less than a year removed from college at Syracuse. Then-athletic director Dave Braine noticed him after Roth got a full-time gig as Marshall's play-by-play man.

Roth quickly became synonymous with Virginia Tech football, and a pairing with color man Mike Burnop not only hit a perfect note in the broadcast booth but was the start of a lifelong friendship. They were roommates on the road for decades, a bond strengthened with the twin tragedies that befell their families in 2012, when Lynda, Roth's sister, and Ellen, Burnop's wife, died within a month of each other from asymptomatic lung cancer.

The close friends would call 337 consecutive football games together, with Burnop, a former Hokies tight end, joining the basketball radio crew in 1996.

"They make such a good team," Beamer said. "They've done it for so long. That's not an easy job. I've always been amazed. You've got to remember names and make things interesting and you've got to fill in time sometimes, and I've always been amazed how professional Bill Roth has been and how well he's served Virginia Tech."

Roth called more than a thousand football and basketball games, coinciding with the rise of the football program under Beamer. What stood out most was his professionalism. He eschewed over-the-top stylings and blatant homerism of some of his contemporaries, with his signature "Touchdown, Tech!" call simple and straightforward.

That's not to say he didn't get excited during some iconic calls. When the Hokies rallied for 22 points in the fourth quarter of a 36–29 win against Virginia in 1995, Roth famously declared, "Jim Druckenmiller has engineered the greatest comeback I've ever seen!"

When cornerback DeAngelo Hall ripped a fumble away from Miami receiver Roscoe Parrish and returned it for a touchdown in 2003 to jumpstart the Hokies in a 31–7 win against No. 2 Miami, which had won 39 straight regular season games, Roth said what everyone was thinking: "He said, 'Give it to me, Roscoe!'"

And voted No. 1 by a fan vote of Roth's list of iconic calls was the end of a 16–15 win against No. 19 Nebraska in 2009, when quarterback Tyrod Taylor scrambled around to buy time before finally finding Dyrell Roberts for an 11-yard game-winning touchdown pass with 21 seconds left. The broadcaster, like everyone in the stadium, could hardly contain his excitement. "Tyrod did it, Mikey! Tyrod did it!" he shouted to Burnop in the booth.

Roth was voted by his peers as the Virginia Sportscaster of the Year 11 times, earning induction into the Virginia Sports Hall of Fame in 2013.

Like all good things, Roth's time at Virginia Tech came to an end. In the spring of 2015, he left to become the play-by-play man for UCLA's football and basketball programs, a major career move to the country's No. 2 media market. He spent just one year there, however, quickly growing weary of the L.A. lifestyle and wanting to return to his Eastern roots.

"It's the best job in the country for what I do," Roth said. "It's just not the best job for me."

With successor Jon Laaser already in place as the new voice of Virginia Tech, Roth added TV to his vast portfolio, calling football games, basketball games, and other events on ESPN and CBS Sports Network, in addition to some radio duties.

He also returned to Virginia Tech itself. After creating the Student Broadcaster Program during his first stay in Blacksburg, he's come back as a professor of practice, teaching sports journalism classes, and helping launch the Sports Media Analytics program in the university's communications department. He's started what he hopes will be an annual tradition, with students using analytics to predict the Final Four during the NCAA basketball tournament.

"We want Virginia Tech to become the Quinnipiac of the Final Four," Roth said, a nod to Quinnipiac University's place in presidential polling.

Most importantly, though, after his sojourn out to Los Angeles, he's back "home" in Blacksburg.

"When you spend 27 years in one place," Roth said, "you develop such deep roots."

61 Kevin Jones

As a native of Chester, Pennsylvania, just outside of Philadelphia, the college football world fully expected running back Kevin Jones, the nation's top recruit, to stay close to home and choose Penn State as his college destination.

He threw a curveball during his commitment ceremony in January 2001, however, holding up a Nittany Lions jersey before declaring: "Penn State is not where I'm going." He finished the stunt by taking off his sweatshirt to reveal a Michael Vick Hokies jersey underneath, cementing his commitment to Virginia Tech.

It was a recruiting coup for the Hokies, who'd played in the Bowl Championship Series title game a little over a year earlier, and Jones remains the most highly-touted player they've ever landed in a signing class. He delivered too, turning out to be one of the most productive running backs in school history.

Ranked as the No. 1 prospect in the nation by SuperPrep after rushing for 5,878 yards and 84 touchdowns in four years at Cardinal O'Hara High in Springfield, Pennsylvania, Jones had a profound effect on the Virginia Tech running game.

Not lacking in confidence, he snagged Vick's No. 7 jersey upon enrolling, the first to wear it after the quarterback went pro. Jones was a rare blend of power and speed who arrived in Blacksburg as nearly the 6-foot-1, 210-pound specimen who'd slice and dice opposing defenses for the next three years.

"When Kevin Jones arrived here he looked like a man," running backs coach Billy Hite said. "When you watch his high

Kevin Jones running for 241 yards and four touchdowns in a 2003 game against Pitt. (Sean Brady / Getty Images)

school tape, he was a man playing with boys. Physically he was put together better than anyone I've ever seen in my coaching career."

Returning starter Lee Suggs, who rushed for 1,207 yards and 27 touchdowns in the 2000 regular season, suffered a season-ending injury in the 2001 opener, opening a door for Jones to get more carries. The freshman was electric, rushing for 957 yards and five touchdowns in his debut year and doing so despite not supplanting Keith Burnell as the starter until Week 8. Jones earned Big East Rookie of the Year honors, rushing for 496 yards in the final three games of the regular season.

Suggs returned in 2002 and the fear was that there wouldn't be enough carries to keep everyone happy. But the tailbacks got along famously, dubbed "The Untouchables" in a Tech-sponsored fan contest. Suggs led the team with 1,325 yards and 22 touchdowns, but Jones was no slouch, finishing with 871 yards and nine touchdowns in a complementary role. They both topped 100 yards in the same game three times that season.

Suggs was gone in 2003, which was Jones' time to shine as the featured back. The junior ran it 281 times that year for what was then a single-season school record 1,647 yards, scoring 21 touchdowns and earning near-unanimous first-team All-America honors. He ran for 241 yards and four touchdowns in Virginia Tech's 31–28 loss at Pitt, which was at the time the best single-game rushing effort by a Hokie.

With 3,475 yards in three years, Jones was only 292 yards shy of Cyrus Lawrence's Virginia Tech record for career rushing yards. His 15 career 100-yard games were also second on Tech's all-time list to Lawrence's 16.

But Jones decided to forego his final year of eligibility and enter the NFL Draft, where he went in the first round with the 30th pick to the Detroit Lions in 2004. He got off to a promising start, rushing for 1,133 yards as a rookie, only the third Lions player to do so in his debut season, joining Billy Sims and Barry Sanders.

Injuries took their toll, however. A Lisfranc sprain of his left foot ended his 2006 season early and sapped much of his explosiveness. Jones played only two more seasons after that, finishing with a brief stint with the Bears in 2008 when he rushed for 109 yards. Jones ran for 3,176 yards and 24 touchdowns in parts of five NFL seasons.

After his retirement, Jones returned to Virginia Tech to complete his degree in industrial design. He graduated in 2014 and later that year returned to the athletics department for two years as a special assistant to athletic director Whit Babcock. Jones was a 2016 inductee to the Virginia Tech Sports Hall of Fame.

62 Two No. 1 Overall Draft Picks

Only 17 schools in the history of college football have had more than one No. 1 overall pick in the NFL Draft. Virginia Tech is one of them, having seen defensive end Bruce Smith go first overall to the Buffalo Bills in 1985 and quarterback Michael Vick going to the Atlanta Falcons in 2001.

That recency makes Virginia Tech one of only nine schools to have done so twice since 1980, joined by USC, Oklahoma, Auburn, Stanford, Ohio State, Miami, Penn State, and South Carolina. Not bad company.

Smith, who'd go on to be the NFL's "Sack King," was the first to do it, rising to the top of the draft board after finishing his college career with 46 sacks, being a consensus All-American and winning the Outland Trophy for the Hokies 1984.

The Bills picked first that year after going 2–14 in 1984, their worst season since 1971. Looking for a cornerstone player to build around, they took the 6-foot-4, 280-pound physical specimen Smith, who ran a 4.71 in the 40-yard dash prior to the draft, an unheard-of time for a man that size. (He was also selected by the Baltimore Stars in the 1985 USFL Territorial Draft but opted to go to the NFL.)

Buffalo touted him as a future star. Owner Ralph Wilson said Smith reminded him of Pittsburgh Steelers stud lineman "Mean" Joe Greene. Player personnel vice president Norm Pollom said Smith was the best player he'd seen in 25 years, comparing him to Tampa Bay Buccaneers lineman Lee Roy Selmon. Smith signed a four-year, $2.6 million contract with the Bills.

He got off to a rocky start in Buffalo, getting up over 300 pounds, but he finally got his training habits down, working himself into a sleek pass-rushing force at 265 pounds who'd terrorize opposing offenses for nearly two decades. He was a 10-time All-Pro selection who was a two-time NFL Defensive Player of the Year and helped lead the Bills to four straight Super Bowl appearances. He was inducted into the Pro Football Hall of Fame in 2009, one of only 14 former No. 1 overall picks to earn that honor.

In a 2018 ranking of No. 1 overall picks in the 51 years since the NFL established a single college draft, NFL.com analyst Elliot Harrison ranked the Bills' selection of Smith in 1985 as the second-best player, ahead of John Elway, who the Colts took in 1983 and traded to the Broncos, and behind only Peyton Manning, who went No. 1 to the Colts in 1998.

Vick came in at No. 27 on that list. He entered the 2001 NFL Draft after his redshirt sophomore season at Virginia Tech, having led the Hokies to a 20–2 record as a starter, including an improbable appearance in the 2000 BCS title game against Florida State. Though his stats were modest by today's standards, he reinvented the quarterback position as a dynamic dual threat.

The lightning-quick lefty was a good bet to go No. 1 overall in the draft. It was just a matter of who was going to take him.

First Round Hokies Draft Picks

	Player	Overall Pick	Team	Year
DE	Bruce Smith	1	Buffalo Bills	1985
QB	Michael Vick	1	Atlanta Falcons	2001
CB	DeAngelo Hall	8	Atlanta Falcons	2004
OT	Eugene Chung	13	New England Patriots	1992
CB	Kyle Fuller	14	Chicago Bears	2014
LB	Tremaine Edmunds	16	Buffalo Bills	2018
LB	Mike Johnson	18 (supp.)	Cleveland Browns	1984
QB	Jim Druckenmiller	26	San Francisco 49ers	1997
OT	Duane Brown	26	Houston Texans	2008
S	Terrell Edmunds	28	Pittsburgh Steelers	2018
RB	Kevin Jones	30	Detroit Lions	2004
RB	David Wilson	32	New York Giants	2012

The San Diego Chargers, who'd gone 1–15 in 2000, picked first that year, but just three years removed from the Ryan Left debacle at quarterback, they balked at paying another up-front bonus that large and were unable to come to terms with Vick ahead of the draft.

Instead, they traded out of the top spot. The day before the draft, the Falcons, who picked fifth, acquired the No. 1 pick for their picks in the first and third round, a second-round pick in 2002, and wide receiver Tim Dwight. (The Chargers used the No. 5 pick on running back LaDainian Tomlinson and grabbed a quarterback at the top of round two by selecting Purdue's Drew Brees. Both will be Hall of Famers.)

Atlanta got Vick, who was the first black quarterback selected No. 1 overall in the league's history, signing him to a six-year, $62 million contract. Upon taking over for an injured Chris Chandler as the starter his rookie season, he became the Falcons' most electrifying sensation since Deion Sanders. In his second season, he ran for 173 yards against the Vikings, then a single-game NFL record for a quarterback. He guided the Falcons to the playoffs with a 9–6–1 record and led an upset of the Brett Favre-led Green Bay in Lambeau Field in the first round, the Packers' first home playoff loss in the franchise's history.

Though Vick was a three-time Pro Bowler with Atlanta, his association with dog-fighting and subsequent prison stretch that began in 2007 ended his time with the franchise. Vick and the Falcons have since mended fences, with the team honoring the quarterback with a ceremony following his retirement in 2017.

"Life is really all about learning from your mistakes, redemption, learning to be a better person, moving on and making a difference in the lives of other people," Falcons owner Arthur Blank said at the time. "There are many people I know in life who have done that and I would say none more than Michael Vick."

63 Dell Curry

Though Bimbo Coles holds Virginia Tech's records in scoring, guard Dell Curry probably has the better argument for being the best player in Hokies basketball history. And, oh, what could have been if his son would have followed suit.

That's playing the what-if game, however. The elder Curry's contributions to the Virginia Tech basketball program are undeniable.

He came to Blacksburg out of Harrisonburg, Virginia, a McDonald's All-American in 1982. Curry wasn't just a sharpshooter who was the all-time leading scorer at his high school. He was a standout pitcher in baseball (his favorite sport), who won a state championship and was taken by the Rangers in the 37th round of the '82 Major League Draft and by Orioles in the 14th round of the 1985 Draft.

He was simply too good at basketball not to pursue that path, however, and came to Virginia Tech to play for Charlie Moir's high-scoring teams.

Curry, a 6-foot-4 dead-eyed shooter, fit right into that, averaging 14.5 points as a freshman in 1982–83 as a young Hokies squad that started three freshmen and two sophomores made it to the NIT second round. That season included a 69–56 upset of No. 1-ranked Memphis, with Curry scoring 16 points.

As a sophomore, Curry earned first-team All-Metro Conference honors for the first of three times, averaging a team-high 19.3 points per game as the Hokies made it to the NIT semifinals.

Virginia Tech made the NCAA Tournament in Curry's junior year, though Curry's scoring average dipped a little to 18.1. (Showing his versatility, Curry also pitched for the baseball team his junior year, going 6–1 with a 3.81 ERA.)

As a senior, he improved his scoring average by six points to 24.1, leading the league and being named Metro Conference Player of the Year. He was named a first-team All-American by *Basketball Times* and got a second-team nod by the Associated Press and the Basketball Writers of America, having his No. 30 jersey retired prior to his final home game on March 1, 1986, the first player in school history bestowed with that honor.

The Hokies were again bounced in the first round of the NCAA Tournament, but Curry ended up making the postseason in all four of his years in college. He finished his Tech career having scored 2,389 points, all before the 3-point line was adopted in college basketball. That was a school record that was second all-time in the Metro Conference history, since surpassed by Coles. Curry is also Tech's all-time leader in steals with 295.

Curry was selected in the first round of the 1986 Draft by the Utah Jazz, still the only player in Hokies history to be taken in the first round until Nickeil Alexander-Walker joined him in 2019 when he was selected No. 17 overall.

He'd go on to be a great pro, someone who'd become one of the most prolific 3-point shooters in the league. In a 16-year NBA career, he made 1,245 3-pointers at a 40 percent clip, retiring with the ninth-best percentage in league history.

Though he had stints with the Jazz, Cavaliers, Bucks, and Raptors, he's most remembered for being the first player selected by the Charlotte Hornets in the 1988 Expansion Draft. He was an offensive force off the bench for the Hornets, averaging double digits in points in all but one of his 10 seasons with Charlotte. He won the NBA's Sixth Man of the Year Award in 1994.

Though Curry's revered forever at Virginia Tech, just think of what it'd be like if his sons, particularly Stephen Curry, had been able to come to Blacksburg, too.

How that situation played out will forever be debated and lamented in Virginia Tech circles. The short version is this: Stephen Curry, a 6-foot-2, 165-pound point guard in the 2006 class, wanted to come to Blacksburg and play where his dad was a legend in hoops and his mom played volleyball.

The Hokies were receptive. Coach Seth Greenberg just wanted him to spend one year as a non-scholarship, practice-only player. Tech had a senior backcourt of Zabian Dowdell and Jamon Gordon at the time, so playing time was going to be limited anyway.

Instead, Curry, who didn't have a scholarship offer from a major school, went to Davidson to play for Bob McKillop, who did give him a full ride.

The rest is, regrettably for Hokies fans, history. Stephen Curry, who had a shooting stroke just like his pops, blossomed with the Wildcats, starring in Davidson's magical run to the Elite Eight in 2008 and leading the nation in scoring in 2008–09 at 28.9 points per game. He's since led the 3-point shooting revolution in the

NBA, winning two MVPs and three NBA championships with the Golden State Warriors.

Compounding the Hokies' woes was Tech's similar snub to Dell Curry's younger son, Seth, who played for a year at Liberty and was Big South Freshman of the Year before transferring to Duke, where he averaged 17.5 points per game as a senior in 2012–13.

It's a great "What if?" of Virginia Tech basketball history, though Hokies hoops fans are still thankful they at least got the original Curry lighting up scoreboards in the mid-1980s.

64 1973 and 1995 NIT Titles

Virginia Tech doesn't have a deep history of NCAA Tournament success in basketball, having only made the field 11 times in its history. The furthest the Hokies have advanced is the Sweet 16.

But the program has a pretty strong history in the National Invitation Tournament, winning two titles a little more than two decades apart.

The Hokies first did it in 1973 under coach Don DeVoe in what was their third postseason trip in school history. Senior Allan Bristow, a 6-foot-7 forward who finished his career with the most points in Tech history (1,804) and had his jersey retired, led the team, averaging 23.9 points a game. Craig Lieder (16.5 ppg) and Charlie Thomas (12.2 ppg) also averaged in double figures. Tech, an independent at the time, was 18–5 that season.

It was a 16-team NIT field back then, though the tournament was still strong. The NCAA Tournament had 25 teams at the time, with only one team per conference.

"With the NCAA sweeping up conference champions plus the best of the independents, not too much remained," Pat Putnam wrote in a *Sports Illustrated* article about the tournament that centered a great deal on the attractiveness of Virginia Tech's cheerleaders. "But this year the NIT emerged with some legitimate muscle in Minnesota and Alabama and North Carolina, and there were those who wept for the Irish and the, ah, Gobblers. For goodness sakes, the Gobblers?"

Though not the favorites by any means, the Hokies managed to get through the four games (all in Madison Square Garden in New York), by the skin of their teeth, beating New Mexico 65–63, Fairfield 77–76, and Alabama 74–73 to reach the final against Notre Dame.

The Hokies had to rally to beat Notre Dame, too. They trailed 70–58 with seven minutes left but managed to force overtime on a 15-footer from Lieder with two seconds left.

The Irish took a four-point lead with 55 seconds left in the extra session, but guard Bobby Stevens wasn't about to let it slip away. He made a short jumper with 43 seconds left while being fouled, hitting the free throw to trim the lead to one. After Notre Dame missed the front end of a one-and-one, Stevens came down and missed a shot, but he grabbed a long rebound and swished a 20-footer at the buzzer to lift the Hokies to a 92–91 victory.

"It is *the* memory," Bristow told the *Roanoke Times* on the 40th anniversary of the win. "Even playing 10 years as a pro and even coaching for 15 years, it's a big, huge, monumental chapter in your life. It was a championship. I didn't win any championships in the NBA."

Virginia Tech did it again 22 years later in 1995. Forwards Shawn Smith (16.0 ppg) and Ace Custis (15.8 ppg) and guards Damon Watlington (13.8 ppg) and Shawn Good (12.9 ppg) led the way for the Hokies that season

The Henson Heave

You'd be hard-pressed to find a more unbelievable basketball shot that looked so casual than when Hokies forward Les Henson chucked the ball the length of the court with one hand and sank a basket at the buzzer to beat Florida State 79–77 in 1980.

Tech and FSU were tied at 77 coming down to the wire at Tully Gym in Tallahassee, Florida. Seminoles forward Pernell Tookes' jumper from the foul line glanced off the rim and to the left, where Henson gathered it nonchalantly with seconds left. He turned, switched the ball to his right hand and heaved it down the court like a baseball.

Incredibly, it went in, giving Tech the two-point win (this predated the 3-point line).

"At first I thought it was going to hit the lights, but it kept going," Henson told the *Wilmington Morning Star* in a story published January 23, 1980. "When it went through, I turned to a Florida State cheerleader and said, 'Can you believe that shot?'"

Henson's heave is officially measured at 89 feet, 3 inches, the longest documented basketball field goal at the time, according to the *Guinness Book of World Records.* It was broken five years later by Marshall's Bruce Morris, who hit a 92-foot shot.

"It was a hope shot, one in a million," Henson said. "I'll never make a shot like that again."

Bill Foster was in his fourth year as coach, having turned things around from a 10–18 mark in his first season. Tech went 20–9 in the regular season, but a first-round upset loss to Southern Miss in the conference tournament dashed its NCAA hopes. Still, even getting to the postseason was an accomplishment for a team that because of injuries sometimes only rotated six or seven players into the game.

"We had two practices in December when we came back after Christmas. We had eight guys that could get on the floor, an assistant coach and a student," Foster said. "And I was sitting in a hotel room wondering how we're going to get through the year. But somebody's looked out for us."

The Hokies hit their stride in the NIT, beating Clemson 62–54, Providence 91–78, and New Mexico State 64–61 to get to Madison Square Garden for the tournament semifinals. There Tech easily dispatched of Canisius 71–59 to reach the championship against Marquette.

Like the 1973 final, the Hokies had to come from behind (they trailed by 10 in the second half) and it went down to the wire. Smith, who scored 24 points and had 12 rebounds, and 176-pound freshman and seventh man Myron Guillory, who scored 10 points, kept the Hokies in it.

With 0.7 seconds left and Tech trailing 64–63, Smith was fouled. The 6-foot-6, 249-pound junior calmly stepped up to the line and sank both free throws to give the Hokies a 65–64 lead. Marquette guard Anthony Pieper's half-court heave at the other end drew front iron, giving the Hokies their second NIT championship.

"The biggest thing is, it's a big game on the line and I knew it was on my shoulders," Smith said afterward. "If I miss the free throw, the blame will probably be put on me. If I hit the free throw, then I'll be a hero. But it wasn't just me. It was the whole team."

65 Eugene Chung

Every coach needs an early recruit to help set the tone for his tenure by achieving a certain level of success. For Frank Beamer, that player was offensive lineman Eugene Chung, the first All-American for the Hall of Fame coach and an eventual first-round NFL Draft pick.

Chung came to the Hokies from Northern Virginia in Beamer's first recruiting class in 1987. In fact, he was the first recruit at Tech for a young assistant coach who followed Beamer from Murray State: Bud Foster.

Chung wasn't an obvious prospect on the recruiting trail, garnering just one college offer, but after Tech got a hold of the 6-foot-5, 260-pounder as a freshman, he developed into one of the best linemen in college football, a nice blend of power and agility. Eventually growing close to 300 pounds, he could bench press 225 pounds 25 times and had a 32-inch vertical leap, at a time when that was rare.

Virginia Tech drew up a specific pass play to take advantage of Chung's athleticism, one that called for him to release from his tackle spot, block a lineman on the way and run outside to clear the way for a receiver down the field after a quick screen pass. Cornerbacks weren't prepared for the freight train coming full speed at them.

"What that says is here is this big old 290-pound guy coming out and blocking corners in the open field," Beamer said. "And he's running very well. I mean there just aren't many linemen who can do that. That put Eugene above the rest of the pack."

By Chung's senior season in 1991, he was a first-team All-America choice by the Football Writers Association of America, having only allowed one sack in his final two seasons. That selection put him in elite company. He was only the sixth Tech player ever to earn first-team All-America honors at the time and just the second in the last 20 years, joining No. 1 overall draft pick Bruce Smith.

As the 1992 NFL Draft drew closer, more of a big deal was made about how Chung, the son of a Korean immigrant, was paving the way for Asian-Americans in football. When he got to the NFL, Chung became only the third Asian and second Korean-American to play professional football.

And he did it at a position (offensive line) that was new. The first Korean-American to play pro football was St. Louis Cardinals kicker John Lee, who spent one year in the NFL.

"You always have your stereotypes about Asians," Chung told the *Washington Post* ahead of the draft. "People say they're always small, they can't play sports, and if they do it's tennis or golf or something like that. I think by having a chance to play in the NFL it's going to do a lot for the Korean community. I'd like to be somewhat of a spokesperson for that. Playing in the NFL, you're going to be in the limelight.

"This whole thing could do a lot for the confidence of the Korean community. I think a lot of Koreans still have memories of the Korean War and the Vietnam War and even the bombing of Japan. I think by doing this it will let the people know back in Korea and in the United States to be aware that we are able to do this. We're not a meek people. The Korean-American kids should know that Asians can do more than play ping-pong."

The New England Patriots selected Chung with the 13th pick in the 1992 Draft, the highest a Virginia Tech player had gone since Smith went No. 1 to the Bills in 1985 and the highest a Hokie would be selected until Michael Vick went with the top pick overall to the Falcons in 2002.

His NFL career wasn't a lengthy one. He played three unremarkable seasons with the Patriots before the Jacksonville Jaguars selected him in the 1995 expansion draft, making him an inaugural member of the team. He played a year there and one with the Colts before retiring.

After a brief hiatus following retirement, he got back into football, interning with the Jaguars before catching on with the Eagles as an assistant offensive line coach under Andy Reid. He followed Reid to Kansas City, then came back to the Eagles with Reid protégé Doug Pederson in 2016, winning a Super Bowl with Philadelphia in 2018.

Chung's connection to Virginia Tech remains strong. He was a 2008 inductee into the Virginia Tech Sports Hall of Fame and his son Kyle played offensive line for the Hokies from 2014 to

'18, starting his final two seasons and becoming an indispensable member of the line as a jack-of-all-trades.

"Playing football is something I've always wanted to do my whole life," the younger Chung said. "And to follow in his footsteps here, it's kind of cool how it all worked out."

66 Lee Suggs

On the same day that running back Lee Suggs committed to Virginia Tech, quarterback Michael Vick did, too. And in the same backfield that Suggs would star over the years with the Hokies, Kevin Jones did as well. So, Suggs was used to sharing the spotlight in his career.

He took a backseat to nobody, however, when it came to finding the end zone.

Suggs, one 6-foot, 201-pound half of the running back duo "The Untouchables," was exactly that when it came to scoring at Virginia Tech. The two-time Dudley Award winner as the top Division I player in the state scored more touchdowns than anybody in Hokies history, both for a single season (28 in 2000) and a career (56 from 1999–2002), and ranks third on Virginia Tech's all-time scoring list with 336 points, the only non-kicker in the top nine. In fact, he set a Division I-A record by scoring a touchdown in 27 straight games at one point.

That was nothing out of the ordinary for the local product. He ran for more than 5,000 yards at Roanoke's William Fleming High, finishing with 2,918 yards and 30 touchdowns as a senior.

After a redshirt year that allowed him to pack on 20 pounds, Suggs hit the ground running—and scoring—in 2000. As if Vick

Virginia Tech All-Time Scoring Leaders

	Player (Years)	Total points
1.	K Joey Slye (2014–17)	403
2.	K Shayne Graham (1996–99)	371
3.	RB Lee Suggs (1999–2002)	336
4.	K Brandon Pace (2003–06)	310
5.	K Carter Warley (2000–03)	307
6.	K Ryan J. Williams (1991–94)	254
7.	K Chris Kinzer (1985–88)	234
8.	K Cody Journell (2010–13)	233
9.	K Don Wade (1981–84)	224
10.	RB Kevin Jones (2001–03)	210

wasn't enough of a headache for opposing defenses to deal with, Suggs rushed for 1,207 yards and scored an unfathomable 27 touchdowns on the ground and one in the air in 11 regular season games, earning Big East Co-Offensive Player of the Year honors. (He ran for 73 yards and three more touchdowns in Tech's 41–20 Gator Bowl win against Clemson, though the NCAA doesn't recognize postseason stats prior to 2002.)

The closest anyone else in Tech history has come to 27 rushing touchdowns in a single season, other than Suggs himself later in his career, were Jones and later Ryan Williams, who peaked at 21. Or, put another way, from 2011 to '18, only once did the Hokies even run for 27 as a team, hitting that number exactly in a 14-game season in 2016.

When Vick entered the draft in 2001, Suggs and the new kid on the block, Jones, were expected to soften the blow. Instead, Suggs tore his ACL in the season opener that year against UConn. He'd miss the rest of the season, a major setback for someone who'd never suffered a major injury before.

"It was hard," Suggs said years later. "I didn't want to watch football after that, wanted nothing to do with it anymore. But [trainers] Mike Goforth and Keith Doolan worked with me. They kept me going every day at 8:00 AM, rehabbing and coming back. I lost a little speed, but the knee was stronger than ever."

Jones held down the fort in 2001, rushing for 957 yards. When Suggs came back, they became one of the most unstoppable running back duos in the country, dubbed "The Untouchables" after the school opened a naming contest to the public.

Though Jones was perceived as the one with the higher ceiling, it was Suggs who the Hokies leaned on the most that year. Showing no ill effects from his knee injury, he carried it 257 times (35 more than two years prior) for 1,325 yards and 22 touchdowns. Jones

Lee Suggs drives past Miami's Sean Taylor to score a touchdown in a December 2002 game at the Orange Bowl. (Jed Jacobsohn / Getty Images)

provided the counterpunch, adding another 871 yards and nine scores on the ground. On three occasions, they both went over 100 yards in the same game.

"It's hard to get one back like one of those guys. When you get two, it's really unbelievable," coach Frank Beamer said. "They're really just two quality players. If one gets tired, you just put the other one in."

Suggs was taken by the Cleveland Browns in the fourth round of the 2003 NFL Draft, though injuries, particularly his suspect knee, limited him to four seasons and scuttled a potential trade one year to the New York Jets. In three years with the Browns and one with the Dolphins, he ran for 1,074 yards and four touchdowns.

In 2014, Suggs was inducted into the Virginia Tech Sports Hall of Fame.

"For me, to be from Roanoke and to go to school just up the street at Tech, it's a very special honor," Suggs said.

67 Maurice DeShazo and Tech's Preference for Mobile Quarterbacks

Though Cornell Brown is often referenced as Frank Beamer's first big-time in-state recruit and Jim Druckenmiller gets a lot of credit at quarterback for helping guide Tech to its first two Big East titles, there was a player who preceded both of them who did a lot of the heavy lifting in both of those categories.

Maurice DeShazo was both a well-regarded in-state prospect and a highly-productive quarterback in the early '90s who got the Hokies into their first bowl game under Beamer and was a forerunner to of the dual-threat quarterbacks who'd help Tech rise to national prominence over the next two decades.

"I don't think there is any question that he had an impact on our program's recruiting in Virginia," Beamer said. "A highly recruited in-state guy, and then he comes to Virginia Tech. I think a lot of people took notice of that. I think he went a long ways to helping us establish this program at Virginia Tech."

DeShazo was an option quarterback from nearby Bassett High, just an hour and a half south of Blacksburg. He was the No. 3 recruit in the state, according to the *Roanoke Times*, and a member of Tom Lemming's 1990 All-America team, so landing him that year was no small feat for the up-and-coming Hokies, who were coming out of NCAA probation. Tech beat out Nebraska, Tennessee, Virginia, and North Carolina for his services.

DeShazo didn't disappoint, turning into a three-year starter during Tech's initial rise under Beamer. Though he was an athletic quarterback who ran the option well, the 6-foot-1, 200-pounder was far more than just a runner, dispelling negative stereotypes about black quarterbacks.

"They say, 'He's not smart enough. All he does is drop back and roll.' That's bull," DeShazo told the *Washington Post* in a 1994 profile. "They say, 'He's a good option quarterback or he's a good sprinter.' But, hell, it takes more than that to be a quarterback.

"People look to you for leadership. When the team is down, you've got to be able to make that play. I say there are three things about being a quarterback. One is the responsibility, two is the blame, three is the glory."

DeShazo threw for 1,504 yards and 12 touchdowns with 11 interceptions in the Hokies' hard-luck 1992 season, when they went 2–8–1 with a series of close losses.

But that was just a warmup for the team's and DeShazo's breakout 1993 campaign. The quarterback improved dramatically that season, throwing for 2,080 yards and a school-record 22 touchdowns with only seven interceptions. That put him tops in the Big East in passing efficiency. He added another 97 yards and three scores on the ground.

DeShazo capped the year by earning offensive MVP honors in the Independence Bowl win against Indiana, throwing for 193 yards and two touchdowns, one to his favorite target Antonio Freeman.

His senior season didn't go as well, with his numbers dropping dramatically. He threw for more yards than he ever had (2,110) but was far less efficient, with 13 touchdowns and 13 picks, including five in a 42–23 loss to UVa to finish the season. He still led the Hokies to back-to-back bowl appearances for the first time.

"Going to back-to-back bowls, to know where we came from to where we are at now as a university, you know, it's an honor," said DeShazo, a 2009 inductee into the Virginia Tech Sports Hall of Fame. "We went 2–8–1, then we went 9–3. I think it was one of biggest turnarounds at that time in NCAA history. We were pretty proud."

Overall, he finished his Hokies career with more passing touchdowns than anyone in school history, with 47. Technically, he had 5,720 passing yards, third at the time behind Don Strock and Will Furrer, but that's only because the NCAA didn't account for bowl stats at the time. Add in the 333 yards he threw for in two bowl games, and his 6,053 career passing yards would have stood as a school record until Bryan Randall came along.

But most important in his legacy was that Beamer figured out he liked having a quarterback who could make a play with his feet if things broke down, ushering in an era in Blacksburg with Al Clark, Michael and Marcus Vick, Bryan Randall, Tyrod Taylor, and Logan Thomas.

DeShazo might not have had as gaudy of rushing stats as many of those players, but he set the stage for a run of quarterbacks who had the ability to make something out of nothing.

68 Buzz Williams

It was a bold move but a needed one. Virginia Tech basketball had languished for years, with three last-place finishes in the ACC obscuring what had actually been a fairly successful run for the Hokies in their early years in the league.

When athletic director Whit Babcock pried Buzz Williams away from Marquette in March of 2014, the hope was that the peculiar bundle of energy would invigorate a basketball program that had long played second fiddle to the football team at Virginia Tech.

In five years, Williams did just that, taking the Hokies from the ACC's basement to three straight NCAA Tournament appearances for the first time in school history, a No. 9 ranking in 2019 that was one spot shy of the highest Virginia Tech has ever reached in the polls, and a Sweet 16 run.

Not bad for a football school.

Brent Langdon "Buzz" Williams had a winding path to Blacksburg, growing up in Van Alstyne, Texas, and earning his degree from Oklahoma City University in 1994, but not before going to Navarro Junior College, where he was a student assistant coach/team manager whose boundless energy earned him the nickname "Buzz."

He started to ascend the coaching ranks, an assistant at five different stops before getting a head coaching job at New Orleans for one year. He joined Tom Crean's staff as an assistant at Marquette in 2007 and became the Golden Eagles' head coach the next season when Crean left for Indiana.

Williams went to five NCAA Tournaments in six seasons with Marquette, twice making the Sweet 16 and getting to the Elite

Eight in 2013. So why leave that for a program in need of a complete overhaul like Virginia Tech? He's never really said, though he was thankful to have the opportunity to lead an ACC program.

"You can't imagine or think or come up with a story where you would say, 'A kid from a graduating class of 45 in northeast Texas, who attended a junior college, who attended an NAIA school in Oklahoma, that in his 20th year of coaching would be the head coach of an ACC program,'" Williams said at his introductory press conference at Tech. "No way that I can take credit for that. I've been unbelievably blessed, way more than I deserve."

Williams' quirky ways were a hit for Hokies fans. He was as high energy as they come, a one-man show while standing courtside, whether it's donning a maroon-and-orange argyle sweater he pulled out one game or seizing the public address microphone to address fans with a straightforward message after they got a little too worked up by the officiating. "Quit cussin'," he said sternly before getting back to coaching the game.

He's a one-of-a-kind personality off the court too, a voracious reader who draws inspiration from whatever source he can. He keeps in regular touch with hundreds of people from his past and spends hours with his charitable foundation for special needs children, Buzz's Bunch.

Williams also engineered one heck of a turnaround. Tech went 11–22 and had another last-place finish in the ACC in his first year, but he overhauled the roster. Soon, his roster rejiggering, preseason "boot-camp" style training sessions, and X's and O's acumen started to pay off. The Hokies jumped to 20 wins in Year 2 and a return to the postseason for the first time in five years, making the NIT's second round.

The 2016–17 season saw a significant jump, with Tech upsetting No. 5 Duke in Cassell Coliseum and making it back to the NCAA Tournament for the first time since 2007, where it would lose to Wisconsin in an 8-9 matchup.

All-Time Basketball Coaching Victories

1. Charlie Moir, 213–119 (1976–87)
2. Seth Greenberg, 170–123 (2003–12)
3. Chuck Noe, 109–51 (1955–62)
4. Howie Shannon, 104–68 (1964–71)
5. Bill C. Foster, 101–78 (1991–97)
6. Buzz Williams, 100–69, (2014–2019)
7. Don DeVoe, 88–45 (1971–76)
8. Red Laird, 77–120 (1947–55)
9. Monk Younger, 66–85 (1920–23, 32–37)
10. Branch Bocock, 57–13 (1909–11, 13–16)

The 2017–18 Hokies had even more highs, knocking off No. 10 North Carolina, No. 2 Virginia and No. 5 Duke on their way to a second straight NCAA Tournament appearance. Led by Justin Robinson, Justin Bibbs, Kerry Blackshear and Nickeil Alexander-Walker, Tech very nearly pulled out its first NCAA Tournament win in over a decade, losing a tight game to Alabama in yet another 8-9 matchup.

Robinson, Blackshear and Alexander-Walker all returned for the 2018–19 team which took Hokies basketball to heights never reached before. Despite losing Robinson for a stretch with a foot injury, Virginia Tech won a school-record 26 games and qualified for a third straight NCAA Tournament. The Hokies made some waves in the postseason too, beating Saint Louis and Liberty to make it to the Sweet 16, the first Tech team since the 1967 regional finals squad to win two NCAA Tournament games in the same year.

The end of the run came in excruciating fashion, with the Hokies coming oh-so-close to taking top overall seed Duke—which was led by Zion Williamson—to overtime. A brilliantly designed inbounds play in the final seconds got Ahmed Hill open on a lob pass inside the circle, but his shot drew iron and bounced away for a heartbreaking 75–73 loss.

That also marked the end of the Williams era. He left for the Texas A&M job less than a week later, with the Hokies replacing him by hiring Wofford's Mike Young. While it disappointed Tech fans to see their coach up and leave after a run of success, this much is undeniable of the Buzz era in Blacksburg: he made Hokies fans care about basketball again.

69 Jerod Evans

His time in Blacksburg lasted a little less than a calendar year, from the time he enrolled out of junior college to the time he entered the NFL Draft a year early, but quarterback Jerod Evans made quite an impact in his single season at Virginia Tech, one of the most prolific offensive efforts in Virginia Tech history.

Evans was the first signature recruit of the Justin Fuente era. Originally recruited by Fuente when he was at Memphis, Evans followed the coach when he took over at Virginia Tech ahead of the 2016 season, ranked as the No. 1 junior college quarterback in the country.

The 6-foot-4, 235-pound Evans had taken a circuitous path to get to Blacksburg. An underutilized quarterback in high school in Mansfield, Texas, he wasn't a sought-after recruit, eventually choosing to go to the Air Force Academy in 2013. He tore his ACL there and decided the military life wasn't for him, transferring back to Texas to attend Trinity Valley Community College.

There, he blossomed into a dual-threat star, throwing for 3,164 yards and 38 touchdowns in only eight games in his final year and drawing comparisons to another Texas community college legend who took the league by storm a few years earlier at Blinn College: Cam Newton.

"[Jerod] is the closest this league has had since that guy came out of here and went to Auburn," Trinity coach Brad Smiley said. "The fact is when they stepped on the field you knew who, quote-unquote, 'The Dude' is that's standing on the field. You know who that guy is. It was that feeling in this league. Everybody knew who the best player on the field was before the game, during the game and after the game. And it was that same type of feeling with Jerod."

Though Evans wasn't officially named Virginia Tech's starter until a few weeks before the 2016 season in August, it quickly became clear he had star potential from the get-go. He threw for 221 yards and four touchdowns in a little over three quarters against Liberty in his debut, adding another 46 yards on the ground.

That'd be a familiar stat line the rest of the season. Evans was a do-everything threat for the Hokies. He tied a single-game school record by throwing for five touchdowns in a 49–0 win in Week 3 against Boston College. In Week 4 against East Carolina, he ran for 97 yards, including a weaving 55-yarder that he stretched just over the goal line for a highlight-reel touchdown in a 54–17 win.

"I saw someone who was determined to get it into the end zone," receiver Isaiah Ford said. "You could see it in his eyes after the play that he was determined to score and make it happen. And it was an amazing play. I kind of caught myself watching a little bit. I should have been blocking, but I was a little bit in awe."

Evans accounted for three or more touchdowns in 10 of Virginia Tech's 14 games that season, helping the Hokies win the ACC's Coastal Division for the first time in five years.

Evans shattered Logan Thomas' school mark for total offense in a season, racking up 4,392 yards. He threw for 3,546 yards and 29 touchdowns, both of which broke Virginia Tech records, a sign that the Fuente era was the dawn of a new day for the Hokies' offense, which was often thought to be outdated under Frank Beamer's watch.

At 235 pounds, Evans also shouldered a great deal of the rushing load, leading Tech in carries (204), rushing yards (846), and rushing touchdowns (12).

Despite his standout season, he was an All-ACC snub, left off the first three teams in a loaded quarterback class that included Heisman Trophy winner Lamar Jackson out of Louisville, Heisman runner-up Deshaun Watson out of Clemson, and soon-to-be No. 2 pick in the NFL Draft Mitch Trubisky of North Carolina.

Unflustered, Evans nearly led the Hokies to an upset of No. 3 Clemson in the ACC title game, accounting for 310 yards and three touchdowns in Tech's 42–35 loss in Orlando.

He helped spearhead the Hokies' comeback from 24–0 down in the Belk Bowl to finish the year against Arkansas, throwing for 243 yards and two touchdowns and running for 87 yards and two more scores in a 35–24 victory.

As it turns out, that was his final game in a Tech uniform. Despite receiving advice to stay in college for another year, Evans went pro after the season. He was not drafted and bounced around a few NFL practice squads before showing up in The Spring League, a semi-professional showcase event in Texas, in 2018 and the Arena League in 2019.

Regardless of how his pro career has turned out, his one-year stop in Blacksburg was a memorable one, helping return the Hokies to their historic place atop the ACC Coastal Division.

"I came here for the goals I want to accomplish with this team and this coach," Evans told the *Washington Post* midway through the season. "Fuente doesn't let me get away with things. He's always going to stay on me, and my whole journey's been that. High school, junior college, here, there's always been somebody that never let me take it easy on myself. That's kind of why I picked this place, I know he's always going to be yappin', 'Jerod fix this, Jerod fix that.' It's never easy. But my journey's never been easy, so it kind of fits."

70 Antonio Freeman

Virginia Tech has never been known much as a passing school. In fact, it took until 2015 for the Hokies to officially have a 1,000-yard receiver.

But in the early Frank Beamer days, Tech produced Antonio Freeman, a great receiver who'd go on to be a top target on a Packers team that won a Super Bowl and made it to another.

Freeman came to Virginia Tech in 1990, Beamer's fourth signing class, choosing to play football instead of basketball after starring in both at Baltimore Polytechnic Institute. After a redshirt year, he began on the JV team in 1991 but was so good the coaches bumped him up to the varsity squad.

He caught 19 passes that year, then broke out in 1992, a tough year for the 2–8–1 Hokies, but a productive one for Freeman, who, despite not being the biggest or the fastest, caught 32 passes for 703 yards and six touchdowns.

Freeman continued that success in Tech's first bowl season under Beamer in 1993, catching 32 passes again for 644 yards and nine touchdowns. He put an exclamation mark on the season by hauling in a 42-yard pass from Maurice DeShazo in the Hokies' groundbreaking 45–20 win against Indiana in the Independence Bowl.

As a senior, he caught 38 passes for 586 yards and five touchdowns as Tech went back to a bowl game, qualifying for the Gator Bowl against Tennessee.

When his Hokies career was all done, he'd set school records in receptions (120) and receiving touchdowns (22), marks that wouldn't be broken for more than a decade and made him a Virginia Tech Sports Hall of Fame inductee in 2006. Eleven of his touchdowns covered 45 yards or longer. His 2,200 receiving yards ranked second all-time at Tech upon his graduation, 65 behind Tech's first great deep threat Ricky Scales, and still ranks eighth as of 2018.

"If I was defending against us," Frank Beamer said years ago of Freeman, "I know I'd try to get a couple of guys on him."

He was also a standout punt returner who had a 10.2-yard average for his career and returned one for a touchdown in 1994, when he led the Big East in return yards.

For as much of a weapon as Freeman was in college, however, he'd be an even more lethal threat in the pros. He found a perfect situation with the Packers as one of Brett Favre's go-to targets along with Robert Brooks, though Freeman had a chip on his shoulder after falling to the third round before Green Bay took him in the 1995 NFL Draft.

"I think I should have been one of the Top 5 receivers taken," Freeman said. "I was a third-rounder. I felt like I got cheated in the draft. I felt like I had to prove some people wrong. I had to show people what I could do. And that's how I approached it. I was extremely hungry."

He proved his doubters wrong. After a quiet rookie season in which his biggest highlight was a 76-yard punt return for a touchdown against the Falcons in the playoffs, the 6-foot-1, 198-pound Freeman became a star in Green Bay. He caught over 50 passes for six straight seasons starting in 1996, eclipsing the 1,000-yard mark on three occasions and earning first-team All-Pro honors in

1998 after catching 84 passes for a league-high 1,424 yards and 14 touchdowns.

He went to back-to-back Super Bowls with the Packers in 1997 and '98, winning a ring in the former when Green Bay beat New England 35–21 in New Orleans. He caught three passes for 105 yards in that game, including an 81-yard touchdown that was the longest reception in Super Bowl history at the time.

He'll forever have a place in NFL highlight history for his Monday Night Football catch in overtime against the Vikings in 2000. Favre appeared to throw an incompletion on a fade pattern that Vikings corner Cris Dishman knocked down. But it didn't hit the ground, resting on Freeman's back and left shoulder as he laid on the ground, then bouncing up just high enough for him to slide his hands under it for a catch. Untouched, Freeman got up, dodged a tackle and ran into the end zone for a wild 43-yard touchdown to give the Packers a 26–20 win.

Years before he'd shout the same for Odell Beckham Jr.'s one-handed catch, broadcaster Al Michaels exclaimed, "He did WHAT?!"

Freeman spent eight of his nine NFL seasons with the Packers, spending one year in Philadelphia. All told, he had 477 catches for 7,251 yards and 61 touchdowns.

71 The Commonwealth Cup

Created in 1996, the Commonwealth Cup is the rivalry trophy that goes to the team that wins Virginia Tech and Virginia's annual football showdown.

It hasn't spent very much time in Charlottesville.

Since it was created, the Cup has resided in Blacksburg for 20 of its 23 years of existence, including, as of 2018, the last 15 years, a streak of more than 5,000 days and counting.

The marble and cherry wood trophy, which has a detachable silver cup on top, has the scores of every game between the schools since 1996 listed on the base. A map of the Commonwealth of Virginia is etched onto the front of the cup itself, with Blacksburg and Charlottesville marked with stars.

The postgame tradition is for the victorious team to drink water out of the Cup on the field in celebration, with more adult beverages always on tap during a night on the town by the players after the game.

You'll often see a senior clutching the Cup after wins, be it on the field, during interviews or in the locker room.

"This grip right here? Whoever can pry this kung-fu grip away from this cup can have it," Hokies senior linebacker Bruce Taylor said while clutching the Cup following a 17–14 win in 2012. "And I don't see that happening."

Taking the Cup out for a night on the town has been a long-held tradition.

"Bringing that downtown was pretty cool," said Ken Ekanem, a Hokies defensive end from 2012 to '16. "Bringing it bar to bar and hearing everyone yelling and screaming and always wanting to take pictures with it or drink out of it. So, it was a pretty cool moment to be a senior and we'll remember it for a lifetime."

Even players who admittedly are not big nightlife guys come out for the occasion.

"I promised myself that I would at least go see them downtown," fullback Sam Rogers said after Tech's 52–10 win in 2016. "I'm not a huge guy for crowds anyway, so I literally went down, saw the Cup and left, because I don't really like being around there. Yeah, it was fun for those guys and fun for all the seniors."

Virginia Tech's dominance in the series has rendered the Cup but a fable for a generation of UVa players. The incoming class of freshmen in 2019 were preschoolers the last time the Cavaliers held the Cup, back in 2003. The streak has stretched so long that a Twitter account, @CommonwlthCup, keeps a daily count of how many days Virginia Tech has been in possession of the Cup. (Twitter did not exist the last time UVa held the Cup.)

It's why Cavaliers coach Bronco Mendenhall put so much focus on winning the game for the Cup ahead of the 2018 season, which ended, as it usually does, in a 34–31 overtime Hokies win in Blacksburg.

"It's not just another game," he said. "Virginia hasn't won the game in a significant amount of time. It's an in-state rival game. It's hard to take over a conference until you take over your own state, and certainly then your side of the division. So, to say it's just another game, I think we all realize the implications aren't just normal implications. They're at a higher level. So, again, my approach has always been just to state the brutal facts."

The battle for the Commonwealth Cup is just one part of the Commonwealth Clash, an all-sports competition between Virginia Tech and Virginia that was a rebirth in 2015 of the Commonwealth Challenge that existed for a couple years starting back in 2005. The football contest between the schools counts for only one point out of 21 or 22 available.

Virginia, which has always been strong in the Olympic sports, won the Clash those first two years, though the Hokies bounced back with victories in 2016–17 and 2017–18 before UVa won again in 2018–19. Football and wrestling are the only sports Virginia Tech has won every year of the competition.

72 Mike Gentry and the Evolution of the Hokies' Strength and Conditioning Program

For nearly three decades when football players got to Virginia Tech, they found out quickly that their best path to the field was through the team's strength and conditioning program.

You needed to get bigger, faster and stronger and strength coach Mike Gentry was the guy to get you there. The term, over the years, came to be "Gentry-fied," and it became as integral a part of Virginia Tech's success as anything in his 29 years with the school on Frank Beamer's staff.

"I'll say this: Mike Gentry has had as big an impact on this program as anybody that has been in this building," longtime defensive coordinator Bud Foster said. "What he means as far as his toughness—obviously everybody understands the physical part of what he does in the weight room—but the mental part of it, the mental toughness, the mental strength, the attitude, the demeanor, that's all Mike Gentry. That was our foundation. And that's back to him."

Gentry graduated from Western Carolina University and got his first college gig as a GA at North Carolina, then went on to get a full-time strength coach job from 1982 to '87 at East Carolina. He was one of Beamer's first hires at Virginia Tech when the coach took over the program ahead of the 1987 season.

The Hokies weren't a recruiting powerhouse by any means in those days. They had to rely on finding under-the-radar guys they could develop into good players, which is where Gentry stepped in, helping transform their bodies by emphasizing speed and explosion.

The Hokies' walk-on success over the years? Much of it is because Gentry helped undersized players bulk up enough to compete at the college level. John Engelberger might be the classic example. He arrived in Blacksburg as a 209-pound walk-on tight end and transformed himself into a 6-foot-4, 262-pound All-American by the time he left, someone who'd get drafted and play nine years in the NFL. Tech's history is littered with such players.

"Guy after guy after guy after guy," Foster said. "You could go through every class and if I started naming them, we don't have enough time and I'd be leaving some guys out."

Long snapper Shane Beamer remembers a good example: himself.

"I came in as a 168-pound little receiver from Blacksburg High School and walked out of here 4½ years later, had put on 30 pounds," he said. "And I'm not going to say I was one of his best performers in the weight room, but I certainly made some gains and gave myself the ability to play out there on Saturdays, and that's directly because of Coach Gentry and the way we worked in the weight room, the mental toughness that he instilled, the physical toughness that he instilled."

Over time, Tech's facilities got an overhaul, from humble beginnings in a 2,700-square foot facility to a weight room more than five times that size now. Gentry started the Super Iron Hokie designation to signify standouts in the program and had a serious approach to strength and conditioning. One of his famous mottos was "Sweat Blood."

"When I get around with former players, they still talk about Coach Gentry and horror stories, whether it be 6:00 AM workouts in the two back practice gyms or the summer conditioning out there running," Shane Beamer said.

Gentry was more than just someone who pushed players to lift weights and run sprints, however. He finished his time at Tech with the official title of Associate Athletics Director for Athletic Performance for all of Virginia Tech's varsity sports and had a hand in everything the Hokies were doing to prepare their teams for competition.

He was ahead of the curve on the holistic approach of college athletics, initiating the sports nutrition and psychology wings of the Virginia Tech athletic department when those weren't commonplace. Now, every major athletic department has them.

Several former players have cycled through his strength staff over the years, including Jarrett Ferguson, Keith Short, Ryan Shuman, and Nick Acree, and Gentry had a very personal connection to the program when his son, Bo, played offensive line for the Hokies from 2008 to '11.

His work over the years has been nationally-recognized, with Gentry inducted into the USA Strength and Conditioning Coaches Hall of Fame in 2010. Upon Gentry's retirement, Virginia Tech athletics created an endowed scholarship in his name.

"He's nationally recognized anywhere that I've coached over my career," Shane Beamer said. "Every strength coach that I've been around, they always want to talk about Mike Gentry and what he does."

73 The Night Virginia Tech Ended Miami's Streak

In the early 2000s, there wasn't a better football program in America than Miami, which had a loaded roster that won a national championship in the 2001 season by crushing Nebraska and would have had another the following year if not for a late pass interference flag that kept Ohio State alive.

By 2003, the Hurricanes weren't showing any signs of slowing down. Ranked No. 2, they started the year 7–0, running their regular season winning streak to 39 games and their Big East run to 27 games. With a roster that included safety Sean Taylor, cornerback Antrel Rolle, defensive tackle Vince Wilfork, linebackers Jonathan Vilma, tight end Kellen Winslow, and more, it didn't look like Miami would hit a wall anytime soon.

That was until the 'Canes made a trip to Blacksburg on November 1.

The Hokies were no slouches at that point of the season, though they were coming off a tough 28–7 loss at West Virginia only 10 days earlier, their only black mark in a 7–1 season, but one that dropped them from No. 3 in the polls to No. 10.

They were playing with revenge on their minds, too. The Hokies played No. 1 Miami tough the previous two years, nearly derailing the Hurricanes' national title runs. In 2001, they almost pulled off a furious comeback in Lane Stadium, though Ernest Wilford's dropped two-point conversion took the air of the stadium in a 26–24 loss. Tech scored more points against Miami than anyone in 2002 but lost a shootout 56–45 in South Florida.

There'd be no such heartbreak in 2003. The Hokies humbled the 'Canes 31–7 in front of a rabid, sellout Lane Stadium crowd, Virginia Tech's first victory in 34 tries against a team ranked No. 8 or higher.

"We wanted to come out tonight and show people we were for real," cornerback DeAngelo Hall said afterward.

It was Hall who provided the game's most memorable moment, starting the scoring in the second quarter. Miami receiver Roscoe Parrish got the ball on an end around and was stood up after a moderate gain by Hall. As he was, Hall stripped loose the ball, which popped up into his arms. He raced down the field for a 28-yard touchdown return as the crowd went nuts.

Bill Roth's famous radio call of, "He said, 'Give it to me, Roscoe!'" was one for the ages.

It was the start of a very "Beamer Ball" night. The Hokies never got much going offensively, finishing with 219 yards and only passing for 44, using a rotation of Bryan Randall and Marcus Vick.

Highest-Ranked Teams Virginia Tech Has Beaten

No. 2 Miami, 2003: 31–7 in Blacksburg

No. 6 West Virginia, 2004: 19–13 in Blacksburg

No. 8 Ohio State, 2014: 35–21 in Columbus, Ohio

No. 9 Miami, 2009: 31–7 in Blacksburg

No. 9 Miami, 2004: 16–10 in Miami

No. 9 Texas, 1995: 28–10 win in the Sugar Bowl in New Orleans

No. 9 West Virginia, 1989: 12–10 in Morgantown, W.Va.

No. 10 Clemson, 2006: 24–7 in Blacksburg

No. 10 Florida State, 1964: 20–11 in Blacksburg

No. 11 Boston College, 2007: 30–16 in the ACC title game in Jacksonville

No. 12 Cincinnati, 2009: 20–7 in the Orange Bowl in Miami

No. 12 N.C. State, 1946: 14–6 in Blacksburg

No. 13 Virginia, 1995: 36–29 in Charlottesville

No. 13 Boston College, 2005: 30–10 in Blacksburg

No. 14 LSU, 2002: 26–8 in Blacksburg

No. 14 Wake Forest, 2006: 27–6 in Winston-Salem, N.C.

No. 14 Miami, 2013: 42–14 in Miami

No. 15 Georgia Tech, 2005: 51–7 in Blacksburg

No. 15 Louisville, 2006: 35–24 in the Gator Bowl in Jacksonville

But the Hokies' defense was too tough, forcing four turnovers. After a field goal, Bud Foster's group scored again in the third quarter when cornerback Eric Green, who earlier had blocked a field goal, intercepted Brock Berlin and returned it 51 yards for a touchdown to make the score 17–0.

"It showed a lot of character," Foster said. "I'm really proud of our guys. We knew this was going to be a big game. I told them after the West Virginia game that they shouldn't come to practice expecting to win. I told them to come to practice knowing they were going to win."

A 44-yard interception return by linebacker Michael Crawford on a ball Berlin was trying to throw away later in the third quarter set up a 2-yard touchdown run by Kevin Jones, who ran for 124 yards. Vick hit Ernest Wilford for a 46-yard touchdown, one of only two completions for the Hokies on the night, to make it 31–0 before the fourth quarter even began.

That'd be the high mark of the season for Tech, which shot back up to No. 5 in the polls but lost four of five down the stretch for a forgettable end to a strange season. But the Hokies always have the Miami game to look back on, to date still the only win against a Top 5 team in program history.

"From the fans to the players to the coaches, it was a great win for our football program," coach Frank Beamer said after the game. "I'm very, very proud of this one. We beat a great football team that is very talented and extremely well-coached. It was just our night."

74 Jim Druckenmiller

They don't make quarterbacks bigger or stronger than Jim Druckenmiller, who stood 6-foot-4, 225 pounds and could lift weights like a lineman, someone Tech quarterbacks coach Rickey Bustle called a "freak of nature."

He was also the quarterback who helped the Hokies during their initial rise to prominence, someone who went 20–4 as a starter, won two Big East titles, led the offensive attack in the groundbreaking 1995 Sugar Bowl and would be selected in the first round of the NFL Draft.

Like a lot of players early in Frank Beamer's run as the Hokies' coach, Druckenmiller wasn't necessarily a player everyone was clamoring to get. He was lightly recruited out of Northampton High in Pennsylvania, getting some QB offers from lower-division schools. Penn State wanted him to walk-on as a linebacker.

So, he headed to Fork Union Military Academy to try to raise his profile. He eventually signed with Virginia Tech, where he'd wait his turn behind Maurice DeShazo, who got the Hokies to their first bowl game under Beamer.

""I prayed just to get a scholarship to a Division I school," Druckenmiller said. "Once you get here, you set goals higher. You don't go through life with things happening to you. You go through life making things happen. Nothing is given to you."

A 215-pound signee, Druckenmiller, packed on the size and set all sorts of records in Mike Gentry's weight room at Tech—and not just at his position. Before he'd ever started a game, he could bench press 335 pounds, squat 500, hang clean 376 and overhead push 321, impressive numbers for anyone but particularly for a quarterback.

After DeShazo wrapped up his career in 1994, Druckenmiller, who teammates simply called "Druck," got his turn under center in 1995. He was a big-armed pocket passer who threw for 2,103 yards and 14 touchdowns in the regular season, capping it off with a come-from-behind win at UVa when he hit Jermaine Holmes for a 32-yard touchdown in the final minute of a 36–29 victory.

That was a breakout year for the Hokies, who went 10–2 and won the Big East for the first time. The season culminated with the program's watershed Sugar Bowl victory against Texas, a 28–10 final in which Druckenmiller threw for 266 yards, including a 54-yard touchdown strike to Bryan Still.

He was even better statistically in 1996, earning first-team All-Big East honors after throwing for 2,071 yards and 17 touchdowns and cutting his interceptions from 11 to five. Tech again shared the Big East title and went to the Orange Bowl to play Nebraska.

Though never the most efficient thrower, particularly by today's standards, Druckenmiller was especially sharp down the stretch that year, throwing for 11 touchdowns in his final five games. Although the Hokies lost to the Cornhuskers in his final game, he threw for 214 yards and three touchdowns.

Druckenmiller ended up throwing for 4,174 yards and 31 touchdowns in his two years as a starter with the Hokies, and because he had such great size and strength, NFL scouts loved his upside in the leadup to the 1997 NFL Draft.

The San Francisco 49ers took the plunge, taking Druckenmiller in the first round with the 26th overall pick. He was the first quarterback off the board, selected ahead of Jake Plummer and Heisman Trophy winner Danny Wuerffel.

Expected to be groomed as Steve Young's successor, his NFL career can't be classified as anything other than a bust. He played six games in two years in San Francisco, throwing one touchdown and four interceptions. When Bill Walsh returned as the team's general manager, the 49ers traded him to Miami, where he was cut ahead of the 1999 season.

"I just felt like I was never in the right place at the right time," he told the *Morning Call* in Pennsylvania years later. "I think it comes down to getting an opportunity to play. The only thing that bugs me is whether I could have done it. I never got to prove that. I wish I would have gotten a year to play, or even half a season."

He had a stint in the Arena League and later the XFL for the Memphis Maniax in 2001, but he was out of football by 2003.

Nevertheless, his time at Virginia Tech coincided with one of the best stretches in school history.

"His competitiveness, when he gets in the game and handles situations," Beamer said, "that's what's great about him."

75 The Walk-On Tradition

As the story goes, Frank Beamer was one of the guests of honor at the All-Metro Banquet in Richmond late in 2012. The get-together celebrated all the city's best high school players, with one of the top honors of the night going to a sturdily-built quarterback from Hanover High named Sam Rogers.

Frank leaned over to his son, Shane Beamer, a Hokies assistant who recruited the Richmond area, and asked why Virginia Tech hadn't recruited Rogers. The younger Beamer wondered exactly what position Rogers would play at the next level but made a note that if the head man wanted to give the kid a look, so should he.

"I'd like to say that I saw him and that he was a diamond in the rough, but you can really thank my dad for a lot of that stuff," Shane Beamer said. "I remember when we were driving back to the airport and he was telling me, 'You need to call him, and you need to get him an official visit right now because I like what that kid's about.'"

Rogers, as it turned out, would become one of the most beloved players and consummate leaders in Virginia Tech history during his four-year run as the Hokies' starting fullback from 2013 to '16, beginning his career like plenty of successful players have at Tech—as a walk-on.

Virginia Tech's had a strong legacy of walk-ons, particularly under Frank Beamer, a fact the coach was able to sell hard during his time in Blacksburg, able to convince some players who'd slipped through the recruiting cracks to come play for the Hokies, with a possibility that a scholarship could be in the works down the line.

"We tell them, we've had a great walk-on program for a long time," Beamer said. "A lot of kids who have walked on here have turned out to be really good players. And I think that's one thing that we really talk about and emphasize, is really evaluate walk-on guys. You want to get a guy walking on that you think is going to have a chance to earn a scholarship if he got a little stronger or got a little faster or got a little heavier or whatever it is, would have a chance to earn a scholarship.

"But then the second part of it is I think you've got to reward those guys when they do. We tell them when they figure into playing, we're going to get them on scholarship as soon as we possibly can, at the next opportunity when we have one."

Some of the most famous walk-ons from Beamer's time include:

- John Burke: A tight end who joined the Hokies in 1989, he worked his way into a starting role and was a key member of Tech's first bowl team, catching 10 passes for 142 yards and two touchdowns as a senior. A fourth-round pick by the Patriots in 1995, the 6-foot-3, 248-pounder played in a Super Bowl with New England in 1997.
- William Yarborough: Out of Newport News, Yarborough walked on in 1991, eventually getting on scholarship and making 29 starts in his career. His 11 interceptions are tied for 10th all-time at Virginia Tech and he was a two-time All-Big East selection, earning first-team honors as a senior on the 1995 Sugar Bowl team.
- John Engelberger: The other defensive end on the 1999 national title game team, he walked on to the Hokies in 1995 (along with a local long-snapper who had a good connection, the aforementioned Shane Beamer). He came to Tech as a 209-pound tight end. He left as a 262-pound defensive end who was a three-time All-Big East pick and a second-team All-American as a senior. He had 26½ sacks in his four years and went in the second round of the 2000 NFL Draft to the 49ers.

Engelberger played nine NFL seasons, making 262 tackles and 20½ sacks.

- Will Montgomery: Originally joining the team as a defensive tackle, he ended up on the offensive line, succeeding Jake Grove at center in 2004. He was a first-team All-ACC pick in 2005. A seventh-round NFL pick, he carved out quite a pro career for himself, starting 75 games in a nine-year career, with his most success coming with the Redskins.
- Cody Grimm: The son of NFL Hall of Fame offensive lineman Russ Grimm, Cody came to Tech out of the Northern Virginia area in 2005. He bided his time before making a splash as a senior in 2009 at the whip linebacker spot, leading Tech with 106 tackles and 12½ tackles for a loss and forcing seven fumbles to earn third-team All-America honors. A seventh-round draft pick, he played three years for the Buccaneers from 2010 to '12.
- Jack Tyler: From the same high school as Grimm (Oakton High), Tyler followed a similar path, walking on in 2009 and turning in one of the most productive careers in Tech's linebacker history. Tyler started 2½ years and made 286 tackles and 32½ tackles for a loss in his career, twice earning All-ACC honors, including a first-team nod in 2012.
- Joey Slye: A long list of kickers and punters have had successful careers at Tech after walking on. In the Beamer era, in fact, the following earned All-Conference honors: Ryan Williams (1994), Carter Warley (2000), Brandon Pace (2004–06), Dustin Keys (2008), Matt Waldron (2009), Brian Saunders (2010), Chris Hazley (2010), and A.J. Hughes (2013). None quite had the longevity of Slye, who was a four-year starter and became Tech's all-time leading scorer as a senior, finishing his career with 403 points and 78 made field goals.

76 Mike Johnson

If it weren't for Bruce Smith, linebacker Mike Johnson might have been the most famous defensive player from Virginia Tech in the early 1980s.

The 6-foot-1, 230-pounder was a tackling machine in the middle of the Hokies' defenses under Bill Dooley from 1980 to '83, pairing with Smith to give Tech a terrorizing duo on the defensive side.

One of the first recruits longtime Virginia Tech assistant Billy Hite pulled out of DeMatha Catholic High in Hyattsville, Maryland, Johnson fit in well with the Hokies, who went 31–14 during his time there. He averaged 13 tackles a game in his final two seasons, finishing with 148 and 135 total stops in 1982 and '83.

Tech was especially good on defense in Johnson's senior year, when the Hokies went 9–2. They allowed only 8.3 points per game and finished with four shutouts, including a 48–0 blanking of rival Virginia. That team allowed more than 14 points just once, and that was in a 59–21 rout of William & Mary.

Johnson also embodied what a student-athlete was all about. He was an architecture major who took extra interest in his studies.

"I was a nerd who could play football, and that's been me for my entire life," Johnson told TheACC.com when he was honored as an ACC Legend in 2011, despite never playing in the league.

How far did he take his architecture infatuation? Enough to break the team-imposed curfew over it.

"Used to sneak out every day to go back to the architecture building," Johnson said. "I thought I was being surreptitious, but

Notable Virginia Tech Tackling Records

Most tackles in a game: Rick Razzano, 30 (at Kentucky in 1977)

Most tackles in a season: Scott Hill, 177 (1987), Rick Razzano, 177 (1975)

Most tackles in a career: Rick Razzano, 634 (1974–77)

Most quarterback sacks in a game: J.C. Price, 4 (against Miami in 1995), Morgan Roane, 4 (against William & Mary in 1985), Bruce Smith, 4 (against Duke in 1983 and against William & Mary in 1984)

Most quarterback sacks in a season: Bruce Smith, 22 (1983)

Most quarterback sacks in a career: Bruce Smith, 46 (1981–84)

Most tackles for a loss in a season: Bruce Smith, 31 (1983)

Most tackles for a loss in a career: Bruce Smith, 71 (1981–84)

(Hite) knew about it all the time. He knew I wasn't going to a party."

Johnson's devotion to his studies made him an Academic All-American in 1982, one of only 11 Virginia Tech's had in football in its entire history. His senior thesis involved a project seeking to integrate commercial real estate and residential space in a down-trodden area of Washington D.C.

He went on to have one of the better professional careers for a Virginia Tech alum, doing it in a couple different leagues. He was a first-round pick by the Cleveland Browns in the supplemental NFL Draft in 1984, though he chose to play for the Philadelphia Stars in the upstart USFL, moving with the team to Baltimore when it relocated in 1985.

His coach was Jim Mora and he played next to linebacker Sam Mills, two people who'd have notable NFL careers, helping the Stars win titles in '84 and '85.

When the USFL folded in 1986, Johnson joined the Browns. The team employed a 3–4 scheme for Johnson's first few years, but when it switched up to a 4–3, with Johnson manning the middle, he thrived. He made the Pro Bowl in 1988 and '89, years when he racked up 133 and 161 tackles, respectively. He was a first-team All-AFC in 1989.

Johnson led the Browns in tackles in six of seven years from 1987 to '93, only failing to do so in 1991, when he played in just five games because of a broken foot. He played his last three years in Cleveland for Bill Belichick, who was then a first-time head coach. The *Cleveland Plain-Dealer* voted Johnson at No. 69 in its 2012 countdown of the Top 100 Browns of all-time.

Johnson left Cleveland in 1994 to play for the Detroit Lions, finishing with 250 tackles in two seasons.

"I'm happier than a pig in mud right now and I'm having a great time playing football," Johnson said at the time. "It's nice to be having fun again."

He retired at age 33 after a 10-year NFL career in which he made 125 starts and finished with 1,224 tackles, 14½ sacks, 13 interceptions, and three touchdowns. He's one of only nine former Hokies to have started at least eight seasons in the NFL and in 1994 was chosen for the Virginia Tech Sports Hall of Fame.

77 Have a Rail at TOTS

Virginia Tech's a campus that likes to have a good time, especially on football weekends. Part of that involves imbibing a few spirits to help get in the mood to cheer on the Hokies.

There's no way to ingratiate yourself to the Virginia Tech football fan base than to partake in one of the town's signature drinks—a Rail at Top of The Stairs, an aptly named second-story bar on College Avenue not far from the campus' student center.

Don't go into this one on feebly. The Rail's robust $9 price tag might be off-putting, but it packs a punch. One will give the average bar-going fan all the extra spirit they need. Two might make the walk to Lane Stadium a little troublesome. Three and you'll probably need help up off the floor.

What's in a Rail, you ask? Well, just about everything on the rail at the bar, hence the name. It's a little bit of vodka, rum, gin, triple sec, bourbon, whiskey, cranberry juice, grenadine, sours mix and Sprite—a fruity finish that hits you with quite a wallop.

It's no wonder Tech fans fondly remember (or maybe don't remember so much, come to think of it) all the times they've spent their nights with Blacksburg's signature mixed drink.

The *Collegiate Times*' Andrew Reilly summed up the Rail experience in 2011 when he wrote:

> What more can be said about this monument to excess? Rails are for nights when the morning after doesn't matter, when the need for liquid courage supersedes any concern for body or mind. Rails are an H-Bomb of alcoholic fury determined to bring you to your knees. But not before you parade your foolishness around the wide-open TOTS patio. Here's to you, rail—the cause of and solution to all of life's problems.

TOTS, with its prime location right on the edge of campus and its distinctive staircase to the bar area upstairs, is probably Blacksburg's most well-known bar, one ranked 11th by *USA Today* in 2013 and 18th by Buzzfeed in 2015 among the best college bars in the country.

But a football Saturday in Blacksburg comes with all sorts of partying options downtown, and Hokies fans usually hit it hard. PK's Bar and Grill, London Underground Pub, Rivermill, Big Al's, Champs, Hokie House, Sharkey's, The Cellar, and Frank's Bar at

622 North are just some of the town's options where Tech fans gather in bunches before and after games.

Head downtown the weekend Virginia Tech plays rival Virginia and there's a good chance you'll catch a glimpse of the Commonwealth Cup making the rounds during Blacksburg's bar hours. It's become a tradition for the Hokies' seniors to take the Cup out for a night on the town for a few drinks whenever Tech wins the game, which occurs, well, pretty much every year.

It is a cup, after all. And beer sure pours in and out of it just fine.

Has a Rail ever made it into the Cup? Considering the number of times it's hit the Blacksburg nightlife, it seems like a good possibility.

You might want to leave that much of a Rail for the 300-pound football players to consume. For the average person, a single one will usually do the trick.

78 The 2014 Upset of Eventual National Champion Ohio State

Virginia Tech's history against top-tier opponents left a lot to be desired under Frank Beamer, and really through its entire history, so few gave the Hokies much of a chance heading up to play Ohio State in the Horseshoe in the second week of 2014.

Yet Virginia Tech pulled off one of the biggest victories in school history, winning 35–21 and knocking off an Urban Meyer–coached squad that would eventually turn things around and win the national championship.

You could perhaps see the faint glimmers of an upset when the Buckeyes, who were No. 5 in the preseason rankings, dropped down to No. 8 in Week 2 after a less-than-dominant Week 1 win against Navy, on the heels of August news that quarterback Braxton Miller would miss the year with a shoulder injury.

The unranked Hokies, who were coming off an 8–5 season, at least had a puncher's chance with OSU redshirt freshman J.T. Barrett only making his second career start, though they still went off as 10-point underdogs.

Ohio Stadium was a scene that night, the Buckeyes' home opener with over 107,000 in attendance, including NBA star LeBron James. The result left a lot of the home crowd disappointed.

Virginia Tech took the fight to Ohio State right away. A pair of freshman running backs, Marshawn Williams and Shai McKenzie, scored first-quarter touchdown runs to give the Hokies a 14–7 lead.

Though he didn't have eye-popping stats, quarterback Michael Brewer, who was making his second start as a grad transfer from Texas Tech, made all sorts of big throws running Scot Loeffler's offense. Tech moved him around and out of the pocket all night to keep him away from Ohio State's pass rush and Brewer, despite still taking some monster hits, responded by making plays when the Hokies needed them.

His 10-yard touchdown strike on a checkdown pass to fullback Sam Rogers gave the Hokies a 21–7 lead at halftime.

Ohio State, as you'd expect, came back, with future NFL stars leading the way. Barrett connected to Michael Thomas on a 53-yard touchdown pass and Ezekiel Elliott ripped off a 15-yard touchdown run to tie things up at 21 early in the fourth quarter.

But the Hokies had a response, going 65 yards in six plays before Brewer hit tight end Bucky Hodges for a 10-yard touchdown pass and a 28–21 lead with 8:44 left, a play commemorated by Hodges' penalty-flag inducing "Shmoney Dance."

Bud Foster's defense made sure that would hold up. Employing his "Bear" front—essentially a 3–3–5 look with three down

Michael Brewer stands in against the Ohio State pass rush as Ohio Stadium goes mad all around him. Brewer's two touchdowns and the late play of the defense would lead the 35–21 upset. (Jamie Sabau / Getty Images)

linemen and standup defenders blitzing on each side of the line—the Hokies stymied the Buckeyes for much of the night.

"A lot of people, when they get up, they kind of want to play prevent or play zone, keep people in front of you," Beamer said. "But we don't do that. We try to keep getting after you and keep the heat on. And I thought our defense did a good job of that."

Tech made Ohio State one-dimensional, holding the Buckeyes to 108 rushing yards and just 2.7 yards per rush.

"Once we shut down the run game and had these guys behind the sticks trying to catch up, now it's fun," defensive end Dadi Nicolas said. "I mean, the whole game was fun, but it gets better."

Able to crank up the pass rush, the Hokies brought pressure from all angles, sacking Barrett seven times and confounding him into a 9-for-29 night, with three interceptions. The coup de grace came on Ohio State's last-gasp drive, when cornerback Donovan Riley picked off an errant Barrett pass up the sideline and took it back 63 yards for a touchdown, sending the Hokies' bench into pandemonium.

"This win puts everyone on notice," cornerback Brandon Facyson said. "Like I said, no one believed in us.... This definitely opened up everyone's eyes. I hope it does, because we're tired of people saying that we're not the same Virginia Tech."

Though many thought the result meant Ohio State was simply overrated and Barrett not ready for primetime, that narrative changed as Barrett went on to finish fifth in the Heisman voting after accounting for 3,772 yards and 45 touchdowns. The Buckeyes became the hottest team in the country down the stretch and, as a No. 4 seed in the inaugural College Football Playoff, beat Alabama then Oregon to claim the national championship.

Virginia Tech, meanwhile, went in a different direction, losing to East Carolina at home the next week. Beset by mounting injuries, youth, and offensive dysfunction, they finished the season 7–6 after barely getting to a bowl game.

But on that September night in Columbus, they gave a sound beating to the eventual national champion, with the benefit of hindsight one of the best teams the Hokies have ever beaten.

"It may have been a shock to the world," safety Kyshoen Jarrett said, "but it wasn't a shock to us."

79 André Davis

Virginia Tech's had its share of speedsters over the years, though nobody quite embodied that football and track combination quite as well as receiver André Davis, one of the fastest players to ever put on a Hokies uniform, who was also one of the school's most feared punt returners and deep threats.

That Davis even played major college football was sort of a happy accident. He was a track star in high school in Niskayuna, New York, who initially only drew interest from some I-AA football programs.

The Hokies needed speed at receiver, however, so they offered him a scholarship and let him run track as well. That success came quickly. Davis won the 100- and 200-meter titles at the Atlantic 10 Conference outdoor championships his first two years.

Football success soon followed. With his speed, he became the best deep threat on the 1999 team that went to the national championship game, catching 35 passes for 962 yards and nine touchdowns in the regular season. His 27.5 yards per catch that year remains a single-season school record.

His big-play potential was on full display in the Boston College regular season finale. He had touchdown catches of 69 and 59 yards from Michael Vick in the first half of a 38–14 win that locked up a national title berth.

Davis proved to be a home run threat in the national title game too, hauling in a 49-yard touchdown toss from Vick for the Hokies' first points. He caught seven passes for 108 yards that night. That gave him 1,070 yards for the season, the first Hokie to top the 1,000-yard mark, though an NCAA statistical quirk that didn't

Football Players/Coaches in the Virginia Tech Sports Hall of Fame

1982	Frank Loria, Carroll Dale, Hunter Carpenter, C.P. Miles (coach), Frank Moseley (coach)
1983	H.M. McEver (coach), Frank Peake, George Preas, Bob Schweickert
1984	William "Monk" Younger (coach)
1985	Leo Burke, Madison "Buzz" Nutter, Don Strock
1986	Mel Henry, George Parrish, Henry Redd (coach), Howie Wright
1987	Dickie Beard, Hank Crisp, Sonny Utz
1988	Tom Beasley, Mike Widger
1989	George Foussekis, Herb Thomas
1990	Dick Esleeck (coach), Ken Whitley
1991	Al Casey, Joe Moran
1992	William Grinus Jr., H.V. "Byrd" Hooper, James Franklin Powell
1993	Jack Prater (coach)
1994	Mike Johnson
1995	Waddey Harvey, Tony Paige, Bruce Smith
1997	Frank Beamer (coach), Cyrus Lawrence, Rick Razzano, Sterling Wingo
1998	Robert Brown, Don Divers, Kenny Lewis
1999	Ken Barefoot
2000	Mike Burnop, Ken Edwards, Ki Luczak, Bobby Smith
2001	Don Oakes, Ricky Scales
2002	Gene Breen, Mickey Fitzgerald
2003	Jerry Claiborne (coach), Ron Davidson, Dennis Scott
2004	Jim Pyne, Dick Redding (coach)
2005	Billy Hardee, Terry Strock
2006	Antonio Freeman
2007	Cornell Brown
2008	Eugene Chung
2009	Maurice DeShazo
2010	Gene Bunn, Corey Moore
2011	Shayne Graham, John Moody (administrator), Phil Rogers
2012	André Davis
2013	John Engelberger
2014	Jake Grove, Lee Suggs
2015	Roscoe Coles, Will Furrer, Bryan Randall
2016	DeAngelo Hall, Kevin Jones, Ashley Lee
2017	Ben Taylor, Michael Vick
2018	Billy Holsclaw, Eddie Royal, Darryl Tapp

recognize bowl stats until the 2002 season means Tech's first official 1,000-yard receiver is Isaiah Ford in 2015.

Davis' receiving production waned a bit the next two years, partially due to injury, though he still finished his career with 103 catches for 1,986 yards and 18 touchdowns. But in 2000 and 2001 he also turned himself into a feared punt returner.

In 2000 alone, Davis returned three punts for touchdowns, the first Hokie to do that in a single season since Frank Loria back in 1966. He was second nationally to Kansas State's Aaron Lockett with a 22.0-yard average on 18 returns and earned first-team All-America honors.

Though his touchdown against West Virginia is his most well-known return—primarily because of Wayne Ward's bone-rattling block—Davis remembers fondly the 71-yarder he had in the first quarter against Boston College that year.

"I got hit when I caught the ball, made a guy miss and then kind of reversed field and out-ran everybody," Davis said.

By the end of his college career, Davis had four punt returns for touchdowns, a figure that today trails only DeAngelo Hall's five. He's third on Tech's all-time punt return yardage list (872), despite having half as many attempts as the two players ahead of him, Eddie Royal and Greg Stroman. Hall's career average of 15.9 yards per return is tops in school history.

Davis was a second-round pick by Cleveland in 2002, and he would go on to spend nine years in the NFL with the Browns, Patriots, Bills, and Texans. He had 2,470 receiving yards and 17 touchdowns, including a 99-yarder with the Browns that tied an NFL record. But he really made his mark as a return man, one of only 10 players in NFL history to return two kickoffs for touchdowns in the same game, doing it for the Texans against Jacksonville in 2007.

A 2012 Virginia Tech Sports Hall of Fame inductee, Davis has worked closely with Tech's athletics department, returning as a director of student-athlete support and community engagement. He also pledged a philanthropic gift to support the Hokies' Leadership Institute.

80 The Battle at Bristol

For the better part of two decades, it was nothing more than a pipe dream: Play a football game at a NASCAR track? How would it even work?

But persistence paid off for administrators at Virginia Tech and Tennessee, and the dream of visionary NASCAR Hall of Famer and Speedway Motorsports, Inc. owner Bruton Smith finally came into fruition in 2016, when the Hokies and Volunteers played a regular season game at Bristol Motor Speedway in front of a crowd of 156,990, a record for a college football game.

It wasn't the first time a football game was held in BMS. That honor belongs to an NFL exhibition game played between the Eagles and Redskins in 1961, though that had only an estimated 8,500 people in attendance.

This idea was far more grandiose than that, first floated as far back as 1997. Bristol, Tennessee, the approximate halfway point between Virginia Tech and the University of Tennessee, was a logical location if it was ever going to happen. Logistically, it was a nightmare to coordinate, however, and several efforts to make the game happen—including a 2005 offer from Smith to pay each school $20 million that may have been more bluster than anything—fell by the wayside.

That changed in 2013, when the game was formally announced, agreed to by Jim Weaver and Dave Hart, then the athletic directors at Tech and Tennessee.

"Dave and I said, 'Why not?' instead of, 'We can't,'" said Weaver, who called it "a reality that's as big as has happened in the world of football."

"It's just a great idea," said Marcus Smith, Bruton's son and the president and COO of Speedway Motorsports. "So many fans over the years have said, 'We'd love to see a football game at Bristol. Can you do that?' And we finally have been able to pull it all together. All the people that needed to be on board, got on board. And really the stars aligned to be able to get the game on the schedule and make it a reality."

The transformation of the half-mile track dubbed "The Last Great Colosseum" was substantial. The track removed the scoring pylon and videoboard in the infield, turning the existing concrete slab into a playable football field.

The turf field that was installed was done so in the eight days after Bristol's fall race in 2016, with approximately 8,500 tons of rock used as the base of the field, brought in by 400 truckloads. Temporary seats were installed along the sidelines to get some fans closer to the action.

Above, a new four-sided videoboard called "Colossus" was suspended from the four corners of the stadium, with four 30'x63' high-definition screens. The track called it the largest outdoor-hung display of its kind in the world.

By the time the setup was complete, close to 160,000 fans could fit to watch the game, a capacity that would shatter the college football single-game attendance record. Since official attendance records were tracked starting in 1948, the largest crowd for a college football game was 115,109 fans for Notre Dame at Michigan in 2013. An estimated 120,000 fans attended a Notre

Dame–USC game at Soldier Field in 1927, though that was an unofficial count.

The game itself was every bit the spectacle that you'd expect from a NASCAR race, with a supercharged national anthem by country singer Jennifer Nettles, complete with a giant American flag on the field and a choreographed card stunt in the crowd to simulate more flags in both grandstands. A bomber did a flyover after the anthem and, as if day wasn't red, white, and blue enough, Lee Greenwood performed his trademark song "God Bless the U.S.A." at halftime.

Dignitaries from both schools were on hand. In his first year of retirement, former Virginia Tech coach Frank Beamer joined the pregame coin toss for the Hokies along with Hall of Fame defensive end Bruce Smith. Tennessee had some sideline firepower of its own, with quarterback Peyton Manning on hand, as well as Tennessee governor Bill Haslam.

The game itself didn't go Virginia Tech's way. Wearing special black-and-gray Hokie Stone uniforms, Tech got off to a great start in what was Justin Fuente's second game as head coach, taking a 14–0 lead after running back Travon McMillian ripped off a 69-yard touchdown run late in the first quarter.

The No. 17 Volunteers, who were coached by Butch Jones, scored 31 straight points, however, getting five touchdowns (three passing, two rushing) from quarterback Joshua Dobbs and taking advantage of five Virginia Tech fumbles in a 45–24 victory.

"It was an incredible atmosphere," Hokies fullback Sam Rogers said. "This was so fun to play in, it's something that I'm going to remember for a long time. It's something you get to tell your kids about and your grandkids about."

81 Cyrus Lawrence

Virginia Tech's never quite had a workhorse back like Cyrus Lawrence, who remains the school's all-time leading rusher nearly 40 years after the conclusion of his college career.

He wasn't the biggest back, standing 5-foot-9, 210 pounds, but he was a powerful runner and Tech fed him repeatedly in his career—843 times. That's 187 more than anybody else in Hokies history, though the fact that he never played a down in the NFL because of injuries suffered in college serves as a cautionary tale about overusing backs.

Lawrence came to Virginia Tech from Southampton High in Courtland, Virginia, where he played in three state championship games and won two, setting a school record with 4,424 rushing yards in his career.

He kept churning out yards when he got to Virginia Tech in 1979 to play for Bill Dooley. On the second carry of his career, he burst free for a 59-yard touchdown, though that was unusual. In his career, he had only 14 runs that went for more than 20 yards and three that went for more than 40.

Instead, he churned out yards in short but effective chunks, helping Dooley's ground-based offense get going.

After a 791-yard freshman season during which he scored nine touchdowns, the most in his career, Lawrence became just the fourth back for the Hokies to top 1,000 yards in a season, doing so as a sophomore in 1980 when he ran for a school-record 1,221. That came on 271 carries, which was also the heaviest workload ever by a Hokies runner. Lawrence ran for 134 yards and scored Virginia Tech's only touchdown in a 20–10 Peach Bowl loss to Miami that year.

Roscoe Coles

Right before Lawrence became known as the Hokies' biggest workhorse back, that distinction belonged to Roscoe Coles.

Coles was the first Tech running back to go over 1,000 yards in back-to-back seasons, doing so in 1975 and '76 in Jimmy Sharpe's wishbone offenses. He set school records with 1,045 and 1,119 yards those years.

He had an 89-yard touchdown run that lifted the Hokies to a 23–16 win at Auburn in 1975, part of an 8–3 season that was the high-water mark of the Sharpe era. He ran for 214 yards against Tulsa in 1976, a modern-era school record at the time.

Coles finished his career with 3,459 yards, a number that still ranks third on Virginia Tech's all-time list behind Cyrus Lawrence and Kevin Jones.

"You couldn't give me the ball 15 times a game, because if I only got it 15 times a game, I wouldn't even warm up," Lawrence told the *Daily Press*. "I think I averaged about 30 carries a game in high school, so it was nothing unusual for me to carry the ball 25, 30, 35, or 40 times a game. It was whatever it took to win a game. To be honest with you, it never fazed me. I never thought once in any game I played that I carried the ball too much. I enjoyed it."

Dooley and Tech dwarfed that when 1981 came around. The Hokies fed Lawrence 325 times that season and he broke his own school record with 1,403 yards, a single-season mark that would stand until Kevin Jones broke it in 2003. He averaged 30 carries a game that year and ran for 202 yards against Virginia.

The workload might have taken its toll on Lawrence, however. He injured his knee only four games into his senior season in 1982, prematurely ending his college career. He still finished his 35 games at Virginia Tech with a record 3,767 rushing yards, a mark that still stands today, even with great backs like Kevin Jones, Lee Suggs, Ryan Williams, David Wilson, and others carrying the ball in Blacksburg.

His 16 100-yard rushing games are top in school history, too, one ahead of Kevin Jones, and Lawrence averaged 107.6 yards per game over the course of his career. He ran for 30 career touchdowns.

With his knees beat up, Lawrence never had a carry after his Virginia Tech career. He wasn't drafted and never carried the ball in the NFL.

Lawrence's pro career that wasn't marked a shift in Hokies running backs coach Billy Hite's philosophy on using tailbacks. From that point on, Hite always strived to have more than one back to rely on.

"I felt like I cost Cyrus Lawrence his pro career by running him that many times," Hite said.

Indeed, Hite split the workload immediately after Lawrence's departure. From 1983 to '86, Tech had the famed "Stallions" backfield of Maurice Williams and Eddie Hunter, who had 550 and 466 carries in their careers, respectively. Williams ranks fourth on Tech's all-time rushing list with 2,981 yards and Hunter 10th with 2,523. They were the forerunners to Hite's most famous running back duo, "The Untouchables," Lee Suggs and Kevin Jones just after the turn of the century.

Since Lawrence's 325-carry season, the closest a Tech tailback has come to 300 carries in a season was Ryan Williams in 2009 with 293.

82 Bimbo Coles

In his four years on the Virginia Tech basketball team, there was no more decorated player than Bimbo Coles, the school's all-time leading scorer and the Hokies' first Olympian in any sport, a standout who'd go on to have one of the most successful NBA careers of any Tech alum.

Contrary to his name, Vernell Eufaye Coles is not ditsy. He's been known as "Bimbo" since he was three months old, getting the nickname from an older cousin who couldn't pronounce Vernell and enjoyed Faron Young's country song, "Bimbo."

Growing up in Lewisburg, West Virginia, Coles was a four-sport star in high school—an All-American safety in football, a shortstop/outfielder/pitcher who was drafted by the Angels, a track runner, and, of course, a standout basketball player. Though he was more recruited heavily to play football in college, he opted for the basketball path after averaging 27 points a game as a senior. He chose wisely.

Coles was interested in going to West Virginia but felt too much pressure from the coaches there to sign during his official visit. He visited Virginia Tech, where coach Charlie Moir didn't press him. He liked that approach and ended up becoming a Hokie.

Virginia Tech is thankful that he was, even though the Hokies struggled during his four years in Blacksburg from 1986 to '90, going 53–63 while dealing with the weight of sanctions for NCAA violations.

Still, Coles, a point guard, became a scoring machine for the Hokies, leading the Metro Conference in scoring his final three seasons, the only player in league history to do so.

That started with his sophomore season in 1987–88 when he averaged 24.2 points a game in Frankie Allen's first year as coach, earning league Player of the Year honors and helping the Hokies finish 19–10 and tie for third in the Metro. Tech couldn't play in the postseason because of sanctions, however.

Coles certainly had his highlights, though. He scored a Metro Conference-record 51 points, coming up one shy of Allan Bristow's school record, in the Hokies' 141–133 double-overtime win against Southern Mississippi at Cassell Coliseum.

That summer, he was selected to play for the 1988 U.S. Olympic basketball team in Seoul, South Korea, making him the first Olympian from any sport in Virginia Tech history. That team, the last before NBA players were allowed to participate, won the bronze medal. On a team that included David Robinson, Danny Manning, Dan Majerle, and Mitch Richmond, Coles played in eight games and averaged 7.1 points.

Coles came back to Tech as a junior the next fall and had his best season statistically in 1988–89, averaging 26.6 points and making 37 percent of his 3-point attempts, though the Hokies fell back to an 11–17 mark.

He returned for his senior season and, despite garnering all the attention you'd expect of the Metro Conference's all-time leading scorer, averaged 25.3 points a game. Tech went 13–18, failing to make the postseason in any of Coles' seasons.

"I'd love to leave here with a winning record," Coles said as his career concluded. "I've had a great career here and I've had fun at Virginia Tech, and I'm not going to let the losing take anything away from that.

"It's definitely been frustrating. But I haven't been frustrated with any of the players or anything like that, it's just been frustrating that we have the talent and haven't been able to put it all together and play well every game."

Nevertheless, he had quite a career, scoring 2,484 points to become the leading scorer at Virginia Tech, in the Metro Conference and in state Division I history. Coles topped 40 points in four games during his career. He's still atop the Hokies records books in points and just saw his assists record broken by Justin Robinson.

The Hokies retired his No. 12 jersey before his final home game in 1990 and he was later inducted into the Virginia Tech Sports Hall of Fame in 2000.

Coles was a second-round pick by the Sacramento Kings in the 1990 NBA Draft, though he was traded immediately to the

Miami Heat. There, he started a 14-year NBA career that included stops with the Golden State Warriors, Atlanta Hawks, Cleveland Cavaliers, and Boston Celtics.

In 852 career games, he scored 6,628 points and had 3,313 assists, averaging 7.8 points and 3.9 assists per game, primarily as a backup point guard.

He'd later spend some time as a scout for Miami but eventually moved back to his native West Virginia. Coles stays connected to the Hokies' basketball program today, hired in 2017 as an ambassador for Virginia Tech focusing on student-athlete support and community engagement.

83 *College GameDay*

ESPN's wildly popular Saturday morning pregame show *College GameDay* has broadcast on location at campuses across the country since 1993, growing from humble beginnings to the traveling rock show it is now, its destination a big deal in the college football world every week.

The Hokies played a part in making the show that way. Virginia Tech hasn't hosted the show the most—16 other schools have welcomed the *GameDay* crew more often that Tech's six times—but the Hokies helped put the show on the map back before it became the carnival that it is today.

Chris Fowler, who hosted the show from 1990 to 2014, remembered the *GameDay* visit to Lane Stadium during the Hokies' 1999 national championship game run as a turning point. The show set up in Lane Stadium and coach Frank Beamer, who had gotten his program on the map in part by his willingness to play on ESPN's Thursday night games starting in the '90s, urged Hokies fans to pack into a corner of the stadium.

They did, with an estimated 13,000 rowdy fans showing up for the taping of the show.

"For us, it was a mind-boggling display," Fowler later wrote on ESPN.com. "Sure, we knew they hadn't necessarily shown up to hear three guys on a set many yards away talk football. They came to show the nation how strongly they felt about their team and their school. And I can't tell you how much it meant to us to share the day with them."

GameDay came back to Blacksburg a few weeks later when the No. 2 Hokies hosted No. 19 Miami. Fowler figured the novelty had worn off since the first time, but no, an even bigger, louder crowd showed up for the 90-minute program.

"After that, our little traveling circus was never the same," Fowler wrote. "The ante had been upped for every other school. Virginia Tech set the standard. We really have savored each visit since."

The show has been in Blacksburg for some highs (Tech walloped Syracuse and Miami in '99 and did the same with a 51–7 pasting of Georgia Tech in 2005) and some lows (later in 2005, No. 5 Miami upended No. 3 Virginia Tech 27–7).

Tech's 4–7 all-time when *GameDay* has done its game, though it has a 4–2 mark at home. When Lee Corso makes his pick at the end, you might want to listen. The lovable analyst is 11–0 when picking games involving the Hokies.

No appearance ever had more gravity than the season opener in 2007, however, Virginia Tech's first home football game after the shooting tragedy the previous spring. It wasn't a blockbuster game, with East Carolina coming to Blacksburg, but that wasn't the point.

Hokies from all over had tried to return to normalcy after the heinous act. A *GameDay* appearance, which had more somber notes than its usual joyful tone, played a part in helping the campus heal 4½ months later, with fans packing the lacrosse fields across from the stadium to take in the show before Virginia Tech beat East Carolina 17–7.

"It strikes me: The many Tech students I have seen interviewed were so thoughtful and reasonable, even in moments fresh with confused fear," Fowler wrote. "A strong sense of humanity shines through."

"I feel a strength here that it's just better than ever," Beamer said during the broadcast.

That was the last *GameDay* show in Blacksburg while Beamer was the coach, though not without a lack of trying from the fans. They mounted a "GameDay4Frank" campaign after the longtime coach announced he would retire following the 2015 season, attempting to get the show to come to his home finale against North Carolina.

Alas, with the Hokies 5–5 at that point of the year and bigger games on the schedule, the show opted to go to a more high-profile game that day, choosing to set up in Columbus, Ohio, for No. 9 Michigan State's game at No. 2 Ohio State.

But Fowler, Kirk Herbstreit, and Corso taped a message for Beamer, congratulating him on his career and thanking him for helping make the show what it became.

Still, the show continues to have Virginia Tech as one of its favorites stops. After attending the Battle at Bristol in 2016, *GameDay* came back to Blacksburg for the first time since that 2007 opener in 2017 when No. 2 Clemson came to town, setting up shop in front of the recognizable pedestrian bridge on Alumni Mall. The Hokies might have lost that game, 31–17, but they made an impression.

In 2018, Rece Davis, who succeeded Fowler as the show's host in 2015, listed his Top 5 locations for *GameDay.* At No. 1, ahead of Penn State, James Madison, TCU and LSU, was Virginia Tech.

84 Bruce Arians

Through his time in college and the NFL, first as a player and later as a coach, Bruce Arians lived his football life with one philosophy: "No risk it, no biscuit."

It's an approach that's served him well as a two-time Super Bowl champion and two-time NFL Coach of the Year who has been the head man at Indianapolis, Arizona, and Tampa Bay.

He got his start at Virginia Tech, however, a native of Paterson, New Jersey, who was recruited by Hokies assistant John Devlin to come to Blacksburg to play quarterback. Arians spent years on the scout team and wouldn't start until he was a senior, though that came under new coach Jimmy Sharpe, a veteran of Paul "Bear" Bryant's Alabama staff who ran a more conservative, run-based offense than the wide-open, pass-happy scheme under Charlie Coffey.

It didn't curtail Arians' gusto, however. He recalled his time at Virginia Tech in his book, *The Quarterback Whisperer: How to Build an Elite NFL Quarterback*:

> I bartended my way through college at Virginia Tech—sometimes I had to hustle from football practice to be on time for my shift—and I loved working late nights so I could listen to boozy old-timers share their stories. They all told me variations of a single theme, a lesson I carried with me long after I quit slinging cocktails. "In life," the old-timers said time and again, "you must take chances."
>
> You do in football as well. During my senior season at Virginia Tech, I was a wishbone quarterback, one with hair that fell below my shoulders and a mustache that would

> have made Jimmy Buffett jealous. I looked like a rebel. And I sure as hell tried to play like one.
>
> If we had the ball at the one-yard line and the defensive backs were playing at the line of scrimmage in press coverage, our coach, Jimmy Sharpe, would tell me, "We're calling the 'Go' route." And sure enough, I was going to take my shot—even though we might have 99 yards to go for a score. You can't play or coach in fear, ever, and if there's one word that's not in my vocabulary, it starts with the letters c-o-n-s-e-r and ends with v-a-t-i-v-e.

As a starter in '74, Arians threw for 952 yards and three touchdowns with seven interceptions. He ran for 243 yards and 11 scores, a school record for a quarterback, though Tech finished with a 4–7 record.

That rushing touchdown mark would hold even through Michael Vick's brilliance, with Vick never rushing for more than nine touchdowns in a season. Logan Thomas equaled it in 2012 before Jerod Evans finally broke it with 12 rushing touchdowns in 2016.

When Arians enrolled at Tech in 1970, his roommate was fellow freshman James Barber, a running back who'd later become the father of NFLers Ronde and Tiki Barber. It was the first time in Tech history a white player roomed with a black player. They hung a sign on their dorm room door that read "Salt and Pepper, Inc."

"I didn't think twice about breaking this segregation barrier; my closest friends in my old neighborhood in York were black," Arians wrote in his autobiography.

After graduating, Arians got his coaching start with the Hokies as a graduate assistant from 1975 to '77. He became the youngest head coach in the country when he was hired at Temple at age 30 in 1983 and was a candidate for the vacant Virginia Tech job late in 1986 when Frank Beamer was hired.

Eventually, he made his way into the NFL, where he was known as a renowned quarterbacks coach and offensive coordinator. He was Peyton Manning's first quarterbacks coach with the Colts in 1998.

From 2004 to '11, he coached for the Steelers, first as receivers coach and later as offensive coordinator with quarterback Ben Roethlisberger. He won a pair of Super Bowls there in 2006 and '09.

His shot as an NFL head coach appeared to have already passed when, as offensive coordinator, he took over on an interim basis with the Colts in 2012 after Chuck Pagano was diagnosed with leukemia. Arians led rookie quarterback Andrew Luck and the Colts to a 9–3 record and a trip to the playoffs in Pagano's stead, the most victories by an interim coach in NFL history and a complete turnaround from a 2011 season in which Indianapolis only won two games. He earned his first NFL Coach of the Year honor for his efforts.

That earned him his first full-time head coaching gig in Arizona, where he went 49–30 in five years and took the Cardinals to a 13–3 record and NFC title game appearance in 2015. After retiring following the 2017 season, Arians got back in the game in January 2019 when he was hired at age 66 to be the head coach in Tampa Bay.

Wearing what's become his trademark look, black-rimmed glasses and a Kangol cap, he spoke at his introductory press conference about how he couldn't stay away from the game.

"There's something about growing up in the locker room, the bonds and relationships you build in building a football team""
said Arians, who's been a regular visitor in Blacksburg over the years. "The ups the downs, and all the things that go in between, is probably what I love most about the game. I missed the arena."

85 The Corps of Cadets

Virginia Tech was founded as a college made up entirely of cadets, so the history of the university is interwoven with military principles and core values. It's no surprise then that today, as one of six remaining senior military colleges in the country, Virginia Tech's Corps of Cadets holds a special place at the university and has a unique bond with the football team.

The Corps, a military component of Tech's student body that's about 1,100 strong and receives leadership training on a number of tracks, has been there since the start.

The first football team assembled at what was then called Virginia Agricultural and Mechanical College in 1892 was made up entirely of cadets, with coaches pulling players from barracks to participate. Though the student body's grown significantly more diverse than that in the 125-plus years since, the Corps is still ubiquitous on gamedays in Blacksburg.

The cadets are easy to spot at football games, seated in the south end zone just off the field, usually wearing their blue and white uniforms.

The Hokies run onto the Lane Stadium field to "Enter Sandman" through two phalanxes of freshman cadets and Highty-Tighties, the school's regimental band made up entirely of cadets, which then breaks into a rendition of the school's fight song, "Tech Triumph." The players sprint all the way to the end zone, jumping up into the edge of the crowd to be greeted by the Corps.

Three players are selected as flag-bearers for each game, passing the American flag, the Virginia flag and the team's spirit flag to cadets at the south end of the stadium once they take the field. The Color Guard that bears the flags, the Gregory Guard that's Tech's

He Played in More Games Than Anyone in Virginia Tech History

There are more games these days, so players have more opportunities to suit up in a Virginia Tech uniform. But nobody did it more often than defensive tackle Luther Maddy from 2011 to '15.

Maddy played in 56 games in his college career, breaking by one the record of 55 set by long-snapper Collin Carroll from 2007 to '11.

"It's crazy for an interior lineman to be getting that record," Maddy said. "In the trenches, it's tough in there."

It took a weird circumstance to get there. Maddy, who was a two-star recruit and was the last member to join the 2011 signing class out of Delray Beach, Florida, got thrust into action right away because of Tech's dire defensive tackle depth. He quickly turned into a factor, starting seven games that year and playing in 13.

Maddy played in all 13 games in 2012, too, starting nine, and started all 13 games in 2013. He figured to be a senior leader in 2014, but a knee injury forced him to cut short his season after four games. He got a medical hardship waiver and came back for 2015, where he started all 13 games and earned first-team All-Conference honors.

For his career, Maddy had 175 tackles, 29½ tackles for a loss, and 14 sacks. Not bad for a two-star prospect.

military drill team, and the Esprit de Corps that's the group's yell team (the ones who do pushups to match the Hokies' point total after Tech scores) are all fixtures at football games.

After Virginia Tech scores, a 17-person crew of cadets fires "Skipper," a 1,000-pound Civil War-style cannon first used during the VMI game in 1963. It was named to honor slain president John F. Kennedy, a former naval officer.

A presence at football games since 2016 has been Growley II, a Labrador retriever who is the canine ambassador for the Corps. It's common to see him with a stuffed Cavaliers doll in his mouth.

Though membership on both the football team and the Corps has dwindled over time, it still happens occasionally. Danny Wheel came to Tech to be a member of the Air Force ROTC in 1993 before walking on with the football team as a defensive end. He ended up being a three-year letterman and two-year starter for the Hokies. Late-1990s long snapper Cliff Anders was a member of the Army ROTC.

In 2014, tight end Kalvin Cline, who got a late scholarship offer from the Hokies in 2013 and had a surprisingly effective freshman year considering his lack of football experience, enrolled in the Army ROTC and was part of the Corps.

Pulling off that double dip is not for the feeble or weak-willed. Wakeup call is at 5 AM for physical training, with daily formation scheduled for 7:30. After that, it's off to class like a regular student, with football practice, meetings and weight-lifting in the afternoon typically from 2:00 to 6:00 and a mandatory study period with the Corps from 7:00 until lights out at 11:00.

"You're definitely sacrificing the normal experience," Cline said. "Even as an athlete, your off time you're sacrificing. But I'm more futuristic. I like looking down the road and seeing where I'll be in a few years. That's more important to me than enjoying college and going out and partying and stuff like that."

There's plenty of crossover between the two groups. Getting yelled at by coaches isn't all too different from higher-ranked members of the Corps barking out orders.

"They're trying to get in your face to teach you that no matter how much chaos is going on, you still have to be able to do what you're asked and carry out the command," Cline said.

"And that kind of translates to football. When there's a lot of things going wrong and a lot of hectic things going on, you've got to know your assignment, know what you need to do."

86 Schweickert, Utz, and the 1963 Southern Conference Champions

When 14 teams in the Southeast joined together in 1921 to form the Southern Conference, a forerunner to the modern-day SEC and ACC, Virginia Tech was one of the charter member institutions.

For 44 years the Gobblers played in the league before becoming an independent again, but they won one outright football conference championship before they left—in 1963.

Jerry Claiborne, a future College Football Hall of Famer, was the coach, in his third year at VPI after going 9–10 in his first two seasons, but he found the right touch in 1963, riding the all-star running combination of quarterback Bob Schweickert and fullback Sonny Utz.

Together, Utz, a bruiser, and Schweickert, who had speed, were known as "Mr. Inside" and "Mr. Outside," combining for more than 5,000 yards of offense during their three varsity seasons.

It all came together in 1963, with Schweickert setting conference records with 839 rushing yards and 1,526 yards of total offense, scoring seven touchdowns to earn Southern Conference Player of the Year honors. Utz chipped in with 10 rushing touchdowns, giving the Hokies a powerful one-two punch.

The season actually didn't start out great. The Gobblers lost the opener to a Kentucky team that would finish 3–6–1. VPI won eight of its next nine games, however, to finish 8–2.

The Gobblers blanked Wake Forest and Virginia 27–0 and 10–0 before beating George Washington and William & Mary to run their record to 4–1.

A trip to Florida State ended in a 31–23 VPI win. Utz scored two touchdowns in that game, and Newt Green, a two-time

Southern Conference Award Winners

Coach of the Year: Frank Moseley, 1956; Jerry Claiborne, 1963

Player of the Year: SE Carroll Dale, 1958; QB Bob Schweickert, 1963, 1964

Outstanding Blocker (Jacobs Award): FB George Smith, 1933, 1934; C John Hall, 1956; SE Carroll Dale, 1958; FB Sonny Utz, 1964

All-Conference player during his Tech career, blocked a punt that Jake Adams picked out of the air and returned 38 yards for a touchdown.

Tech won at Richmond 14–13 the next week, sealing the game when senior Mike Cahill picked off a two-point conversion attempt to preserve the win.

The team's lone blemish the rest of the way was a 13–7 loss at N.C. State against a team that went 8–3 and was co-ACC champions. Down the stretch, Tech beat West Virginia 28–3 and VMI 35–20, the latter thanks to running back Tommy Walker, who caught a 26-yard touchdown pass and returned a kickoff 99 yards for a score in Roanoke.

Virginia Tech's eight wins were its most since the Gobblers went 8–0–1 in 1954 under coach Frank Moseley. (VPI was 3–0–1 in the Southern Conference that year, but West Virginia, which it didn't play, went 3–0 to claim the league title.) VPI went 5–0 in the Southern Conference in 1963.

"I think we didn't have as much talent as some people, but we had a bigger heart than anyone we played," Schweickert said in the book, *Always a Hokie: Players, Coaches, and Fans Share Their Passion for Virginia Tech.*

"I think Coach Claiborne was a coach we believed in, and when you believe in one another and believe in your coach, good things seem to happen."

Schweickert, Utz, Green, and lineman Gene Breen were all named to the All-Conference first team, while end Tommy Marvin was a second-team pick. Schweickert was named a third-team All-America by the *Associated Press*, joining end Carroll Dale as only the second All-American in school history.

Claiborne was named Southern Conference Coach of the Year, but his Gobblers didn't get a postseason invitation. He'd later guide Virginia Tech teams to the Liberty Bowl in 1966 and '68.

Schweickert and Utz returned in 1964 and ran for 1,353 yards and 19 touchdowns, though Schweickert battled injuries. Despite a 20–11 win against unbeaten and nationally-ranked Florida State, the Gobblers finished 6–4 and 3–1 in the Southern Conference, second in the league to West Virginia, which beat them 23–10.

VPI split from the Southern Conference before the 1965 season, choosing to go the independent route until joining the Big East in 1991, with its next league title coming in 1995.

87 Chuck Hartman

If there's a hall of fame out there, chances are former longtime Virginia Tech baseball coach Chuck Hartman is in it.

His 47-year coaching career, which started during the Eisenhower administration, concluded 10 presidents later and included 28 seasons in Blacksburg, certainly warrants it.

Hartman won 1,444 games in his career, retiring in 2006 as the fourth-winningest coach in Division I history. He still ranks seventh on that list today.

That included 961 wins at Virginia Tech, nearly three times as many victories as the next closest Hokies coach on the list, G.F. "Red" Laird, who coached Tech for 30 years.

A native of Gastonia, North Carolina, Hartman was a 1957 graduate of the University of North Carolina, where he was a second baseman who hit .224 in 107 at-bats. He began his coaching career at High Point College (now University) in 1960. He spent 19 years there, won 483 games and was named the Carolinas Conference Coach of the Year five times before taking over the Hokies' program.

He'd guide Virginia Tech to some of its most successful seasons in school history. Teams in 1982 and '85 set school marks with 50 wins in a season and six of his squads won 40 or more games. Going back to his High Point days, from 1969 to 2004, 35 of his 36 teams posted a record of .500 or better.

From 1994 to 2000, the Hokies made the NCAA regionals four times, equaling their total in the program's history prior to that. (Amazingly, those 50-win teams in the '80s were tournament snubs.)

During his time at Tech, his teams won conference championships in three different leagues—the Metro, Atlantic 10, and Big East. His squads won two Metro Conference regular season titles (1981, '95) and a tournament crown in 1994. The Hokies won the Atlantic 10 West in 1996 and claimed the conference tournament title in '97, '98, and 2000. After moving to the Big East, Tech shared a regular season title with Notre Dame in 2002.

Hartman was generally considered a player's coach, one who let his guys do their thing as long as they played hard.

"He lets you play," former All-American first baseman George Canale told the *Daily Press* back in 1992, when Hartman reached win No. 500 with the Hokies. "He doesn't try to overcoach like a lot of the others try to do. He lets you perform to your capabilities. He's the one guy I've seen who could take 25 personalities and have 20 of them liking each other. In pro ball, you don't have that."

Hartman's approach was simple but effective.

"I wanted to pat them on the butt," Hartman told the *Roanoke Times* ahead of his induction into the Virginia Sports Hall of Fame in 2018. "But sometimes that doesn't work because you've got some kid that's not doing what you want him to do or he's been in a little trouble."

Hartman coached 13 All-Americans and saw 56 of his players at Tech go on to sign with pro teams, with four going in the first round of the draft—first baseman Franklin Stubbs (19th overall to the Dodgers in 1982), pitcher Brad DuVall (Orioles, 15th overall in 1987 and 23rd overall to the Cardinals in 1988), pitcher Denny Wagner (42nd overall to the Athletics in 1997) and pitcher Joe Saunders (12th overall to the Angels in 2002).

Two of his players, Pirates reliever Mike Williams and Saunders, made all-star teams in the majors. He also served on the coaching staff of the U.S. All-Star teams that competed internationally in 1984 and '85.

His familiar No. 1 jersey was the first retired by the Hokies baseball team in 2006, and he's been a member of the Virginia Tech Sports Hall of Fame since 2002. In 2004, he was inducted into the American Baseball Coaches Association Hall of Fame.

By the time he finished his college coaching career, the 47 years he'd done it were tied for the most ever by a Division I coach. He summed up the nature of that kind of life thusly:

"A coach is a manic depressive. Also schizophrenic, because you have to be three different people at times," he said. "But it's been interesting. And I've enjoyed it, I can say that. If I had it to do over again, I'd do it the same way.'"

88 Visit the Pylons above War Memorial Chapel

As one of six senior military colleges in the country, the very fabric of Virginia Tech is tied closely to military service, and the school pays tribute to those who have made the ultimate sacrifice for their country.

Nowhere on campus is that more evident than at the Pylons above War Memorial Chapel on the northeast side of the campus' Drillfield. There stand eight sculpted Indiana limestone pylons that represent the core values of Virginia Tech—Brotherhood, Honor, Leadership, Sacrifice, Service, Loyalty, Duty, and Ut Prosim (the Latin phrase, "That I may serve," which is the school's motto).

The Pylons are etched with the names of every Virginia Tech student and graduate who died defending our country, starting in World War I. Over 400 names are etched into the memorial.

Each name is added with a special dedication ceremony conducted by the school's Corps of Cadets. The Corps' regiment gets in formation on the roads facing the War Memorial, with the precision rifle drill team performing a rifle salute, firing three volleys. The Color Guard presents the flag, and the Highty-Tighties—the school's regimental band—play and a bugler performs "Echo Taps."

In the center of the War Memorial is a cenotaph that displays the names of Virginia Tech's seven recipients of the Medal of Honor, America's highest award for valor. The honored are Antoine August Michel Gaujot, Julien Edmund Victor Gaujot, Earle Davis Gregory, Herbert Joseph Thomas, Jimmie Watters Monteith Jr., Robert Edward Femoyer, and Richard Thomas Shea Jr.

Football coach Frank Beamer aimed to instill the values of the Pylons in his football team, too. In 2013, before move-in day for students in August, he brought his team to War Memorial Court to get a closer look and better understanding of what it means.

The football team incorporated a lot of that into their daily routine under Beamer, with the coach rattling off the first letter of each of the pylons (B.L.L.U.S.S.H.D) and the players responding with the corresponding word.

"Everything that's a core value of Virginia Tech should be the core value of a good football team," Beamer said. "It's one and the same. That's why we remind each other each and every day what our core values should be."

During a game at Georgia Tech in 2013, the Hokies wore maroon jerseys and pants with a special helmet that had a Hokie Stone design. Instead of the customary "VT" on the side of the helmet, Virginia Tech had a logo featuring the War Memorial Pylons, with the date of the school's founding underneath it.

The athletic department dipped into the terminology of the memorial when launching its response to NCAA reforms in 2015, calling its pact with student-athletes, which included among many things paying for a full cost of attendance, the "Pylons of Promise."

How woven into the fabric of the team are those values? When the football team's $21.3 million indoor practice facility was built in 2015 on the north side of Lane Stadium, the eight core beliefs found on the Pylons were etched along the base of Hokie Stone columns on the exterior.

"It turned out even better than any of us really envisioned it looking," then-assistant coach Shane Beamer said. "It's a beautiful building, and it really just encompasses so much of the tradition of Virginia Tech with the Hokie Stone and the Pylons from the War Memorial."

Make sure to check out the indoor facility for sure, but in order to get a true sense about what Virginia Tech's all about, a trip to the Pylons at the War Memorial is a must on your itinerary.

89 Seth Greenberg

Turn on ESPN anytime and if there's a college basketball conversation going on, it usually involves Seth Greenberg in some capacity, especially when the basketball version of *College GameDay* travels around the country each winter.

Though Greenberg has been in television since 2012, taking to the medium seamlessly, he spent 34 years before that as a basketball coach, 22 of them as a head coach and the last nine of his career at Virginia Tech, where he helped transition the Hokies from the Big East to the ACC.

Greenberg came to Blacksburg in 2003 after coaching at Long Beach State and South Florida and helped legitimize a basketball program that hadn't gone to the postseason since a 1996 NCAA Tournament appearance.

By his second season, he had Virginia Tech back in the postseason, with the Hokies making a run to the second round of the NIT. For leading a team picked to finish 10th in the ACC in the preseason to a fourth-place finish and into the postseason, he won the ACC Coach of the Year for the first time.

With the backcourt duo of Zabian Dowdell and Jamon Gordon, energetic wing Deron Washington, and sharp-shooter A.D. Vassallo, the Hokies got back to the Big Dance for the first time in over a decade in 2007, earning a No. 5 seed and beating Illinois in Columbus, Ohio, before falling to fourth-seeded Southern Illinois in Round 2. Still, the first-round win was only the Hokies' fourth NCAA tournament victory in the previous 40 years.

Greenberg's time in Blacksburg would come to be known for its big-time performances against highly-ranked teams and the Hokies' perpetual life on the wrong side of the NCAA Tournament bubble. (And, perhaps unfairly, since no other major basketball school offered him a scholarship, letting Hokies legacy Stephen Curry slip through Tech's fingers.)

Virginia Tech beat the No. 1–ranked team in the country three times under Greenberg, first doing so in its NCAA Tournament season in 2007, when in a little over a week the Hokies topped No. 5 Duke in overtime at Cameron Indoor Stadium before returning home and beating No. 1 North Carolina 94–88.

Greenberg won his second ACC Coach of the Year award in 2008, though the 21–14 Hokies were an NCAA Tournament snub, despite finishing fourth in the conference and taking North Carolina to the last second in the ACC Tournament semifinals before Tyler Hansbrough hit a baseline jumper for a 68–66 win.

The Hokies knocked off No. 1 Wake Forest 78–71 in 2009, though again they faltered down the stretch and were relegated to the NIT. Malcolm Delaney and Jeff Allen led a 2011 team that knocked off No. 1 Duke 64–60, leading to a court storming in Cassell Coliseum. ESPN commentator Dick Vitale declared to Greenberg in a postgame interview, "Go get your dancing shoes, 'cause it's locked. You're in. There's no way in the world they can deny you now, my friend."

Au contraire. The Hokies lost to Boston College and Clemson down the stretch and couldn't pull off another upset of Duke in the ACC Tournament, leaving them on the outside looking in on Selection Sunday for the fourth straight year.

The often-cantankerous Greenberg, whose frequent half-serious back-and-forths with *Roanoke Times* beat writer Mark Berman were legendary, openly questioned whether the tournament selection committee had an agenda

"I feel for these kids," said Greenberg, the patron saint of tournament snubs. "You would hate to think that politics would be involved, but it makes you wonder."

After Virginia Tech cratered to a last-place tie in the ACC the following season, Greenberg was fired by athletic director Jim Weaver, more than a month after Tech's season ended. Greenberg was "completely blindsided and shocked" by Weaver's decision.

Despite his unceremonious exit, Greenberg still finished his Virginia Tech career with a 170–123 record, making him the second-winningest coach in Hokies history behind Charlie Moir, who went 213–119 from 1976 to '87.

Greenberg had a second act in life, however, becoming a popular TV commentator on ESPN, someone who has blossomed in the role as an outspoken former coach, bringing his hoops acumen and courtside mindset to the broadcast and generally telling it like it is. Despite his name popping up for coaching vacancies a couple times over the years, he's stuck with TV.

"We're not curing cancer, and this is not rocket science," Greenberg told the *Times-Dispatch* in 2016. "We're talking about basketball. It's something I've done my whole life, and I'm very comfortable doing. I didn't expect to be doing it at this juncture of my career, but I think the transition has been smooth. And it's been fun. When you can trust the people you're working with, it's a great environment."

90 Virginia Tech's Evolving Set of Uniforms

The original colors of Virginia Tech were a bit drab—black and gray—and when appearing in stripes on the school's athletic uniforms, they looked like prison clothes.

An 1896 committee was formed to remedy that. It chose Chicago maroon and burnt orange because it was a unique combination not worn by any other college at the time, and on October 20, 1896, Virginia Tech debuted its maroon-and-orange look in a football game against Roanoke College.

Those colors have since come to define the Hokies' athletic teams, with the school exhibiting no shortage of experimentation with its apparel partner of two decades, Nike.

For much of its existence, like most football programs, Virginia Tech's uniforms weren't anything too fancy. White pants with either a maroon or white jersey was the standard look for a long time, with the school's "VT" logo on maroon or white helmets nearly every year from the mid-1960s to the early '80s.

Tech adopted the interlocking VT logo that's the standard look today in 1985, wearing it on a maroon helmet and eventually removing the stripes down the middle in 1998, when Nike began providing uniforms for the team.

Before Nike's arrival, there wasn't too much variety in Virginia Tech's look from week to week, though a big moment came in the 1990 UVa game, when Tech's seniors voted to wear maroon pants and jerseys for the first time since 1984—an all-maroon everything ensemble that's among the program's most popular uniform combinations today.

To complete the more menacing look, Virginia Tech's players spray-painted their white Converse shoes black just hours before they played the Cavaliers. The Hokies rolled to a 38–13 win, Frank Beamer's first against UVa.

Tech had as plain of a look as possible during its national title game season in 1999, with a maroon helmet that had a maroon facemask and no stripes on it. The Hokies had plain white pants and either a maroon or white jersey depending on if they were the home team or road.

That plain look started to change when Nike came on the scene. The school's rise to prominence in football made it a longtime target of the Swoosh, which eventually signed a long-term apparel deal with Virginia Tech for all its sports that began in 2007. The apparel distributor was so tied to Beamer that when his statue was unveiled outside the stadium in 2018, it's of him wearing a Nike jacket.

In their early ACC days, the Hokies became one of Nike's lab rats with new and often off-the-wall uniforms designs, following in the footsteps of Oregon. Maroon and orange piping was on the

The "Incredible Hulk" Mickey Fitzgerald

His career's been somewhat forgotten, both because of his position (fullback) and the time period he played (in the late '70s originally for Jimmy Sharpe), but Mickey Fitzgerald, a 6-foot-2, 250-pounder nicknamed the "Incredible Hulk," was one of Tech's finest ballcarriers, even though he only finished with 1,449 yards in his career.

A highly-touted tight end out of E.C. Glass High in Lynchburg who the *Roanoke Times* ranked as the top prospect in the state, he moved to fullback in Sharpe's wishbone offense midway through a rough 1977 season for the Hokies. He took off. Fitzgerald became the first modern-era player in Tech history to rush for more than 100 yards in each of his first four starts, scoring seven touchdowns in those games.

Sharpe was gone the next year and Bill Dooley felt the fullback existed to block, though Fitzgerald still scored 10 touchdowns in his career and topped 400 yards in each season. A nasty knee injury suffered on West Virginia's turf field in 1979 cut short his college career.

He was briefly on a few NFL rosters, injuring his other knee, and played for the USFL's Memphis Showboats before getting out of the game and pursuing an array of interests. He worked in real estate and was even a professional Sumo wrestler in Japan before coming back to the U.S. and launching his own medical company in Atlanta, Dynamic Orthotics & Prosthetics.

He's also taken on charitable causes. Raised in a Lynchburg orphanage, he established Mickey's Rascals for underprivileged kids in rural areas and Calvary Children's Home, a residential facility in Powder Springs, Georgia, for abandoned children.

jerseys and pants from 2004 to '07. Tech was one of a handful of teams that wore Nike's mostly-panned mismatched sleeve design (one orange and one maroon) a couple times in 2005.

Nike had its hits, though. Virginia Tech unveiled its all-white Pro Combat uniforms that featured a gradient fade pattern on the helmet, numbers and pants in 2009 against Maryland and UVa. The Hokies beat the Cavaliers 42–13 that year.

Tech unveiled a black version of the duds to open the 2010 season against Boise State, which countered with all-blue uniforms, making it an interesting TV viewing experience. Though the uniforms were fondly remembered by all the players of that era, ranked near the top by everyone who wore them, they've been left behind in the dustbin of history because the game resulted in a heartbreaking 33–30 loss at FedEx Field.

The Hokies went retro from 2010 to '17, adopting an old-school shoulder stripes look that hearkened back to Frank Beamer's playing days in the late '60s.

Tech and Nike have had no shortage of experiments in the last decade, however, with some hits (several military appreciation ensembles, a retro orange pants/white jersey/maroon helmet look in Beamer's final season, and the Fighting Gobbler logo's swan song in the 2012 Russell Athletic Bowl), some misses (the turkey tracks helmet, the gray jerseys vs. Alabama to open 2013, and the orange camouflage look), and some abominations (the flexing HokieBird helmet logo that resembles Foghorn Leghorn and debuted in 2012 should be burned with fire).

Perhaps the boldest design came for the 2016 Battle at Bristol against Tennessee, when the Hokies went back to their roots with a black-and-gray design that incorporated Hokie Stone for the jerseys and as trim on black pants. Tech has since worn the Hokie Stone jerseys with white helmets and pants.

It's not all just about being fashion-forward. Virginia Tech's put its many one-off looks to good use, auctioning off helmets afterward and donating some of that money to charities like Herma's Readers, an organization Beamer founded to honor his late mother that distributes books to children and encourages reading.

A 2018 refresh of the uniforms brought sleeker shoulder stripes at a more diagonal angle, which were hit-or-miss with fans but will probably gain acceptance over time. The Hokies typically wear a different uniform combination for every game, with its reveal by the equipment staff on Twitter a popular weekly feature.

Though every combination of white, orange, and maroon exists for the helmets, jerseys, and pants, nothing quite gets Hokie Nation going like a good ol' all-maroon everything look, which pops when Tech plays under the lights in Lane Stadium.

Though superstition will persist among the fans, the uniforms have never had any impact on the outcome of the game. Beamer never cared much what the Hokies wore on the field.

"I just want them ready to play," he said. "I don't care what they're playing in. If they like it, I like it. So, let's just go play with them."

91 Isaiah Ford and Cam Phillips

Virginia Tech was never known as a program that passed the ball a lot. For the longest time, the Hokies held a stigma usually reserved for option teams, having never had a 1,000-yard receiver in a single-season. (Even though André Davis technically did it when factoring in bowl stats in the 1999–2000 season, which the NCAA didn't count at the time.)

That perception around Virginia Tech started to change with the arrival of Isaiah Ford and Cam Phillips, who began their careers in the latter Frank Beamer years and helped Justin Fuente achieve success in his first few seasons.

They weren't the only dynamic receiving duo in Virginia Tech history. Jarrett Boykin and Danny Coale were the standard bearers before them, wrapping up their Hokies careers in 2011 first and second on Tech's all-time receiving list, with 2,884 and 2,658 yards, respectively. But Ford and Phillips raised the bar statistically.

They both arrived in Blacksburg in the 2014 signing class, recruited heavily by then–first-year receivers coach Aaron Moorehead. They weren't sure things, both ranked as high three-star recruits—Phillips hailed from Hyattsville, Maryland, while Ford, a late recruiting flip from Louisville, was from Jacksonville—but they both showed up ready to contribute.

Both played as true freshmen, with Ford starting from the get-go and Phillips working his way into the starting lineup later in the year. Despite joining a receiver group that had three players returning who'd caught more than 40 passes and racked up at least 600 yards each the year before, Ford became the go-to guy in the offense, setting freshman receiving records at Tech by leading the team with 56 catches for 709 yards and six touchdowns. Phillips added 40 catches for 498 yards and three scores.

They hit their stride the next season. Ford became Virginia Tech's first 1,000-yard receiver and the first player in program history to catch double-digit touchdown passes in a season. A 12-catch, 227-yard showing in an Independence Bowl win against Tulsa in Beamer's final game gave Ford 75 catches for 1,164 yards and 11 touchdowns, earning him first-team All-ACC honors. Phillips, again, was no slouch, with 49 catches for 582 yards and two touchdowns.

They both thrived when Fuente brought his wide-open offense to Blacksburg, filling two of the three receiver spots, with tight end Bucky Hodges converting to a receiver to round out the lineup.

With Jerod Evans throwing them the ball, they put up big numbers again. Ford repeated his 2015 numbers, catching 79 passes for 1,094 yards and seven touchdowns. Phillips saw an uptick in production, too, shifting to the slot late in the year and nearly getting to the 1,000-yard mark himself. He caught six passes for 115 yards to earn Belk Bowl MVP honors in a comeback win against Arkansas, getting him to 76 catches for 983 yards and five touchdowns on the season.

If ever there was a game that signified Virginia Tech's shift from a ground-and-pound offense to one capable of airing it out, it was a 39–36 win at Pittsburgh in 2016. Ford, Phillips, and Hodges beat Panthers defensive backs on jump balls down the field all night long, much to Pitt coach Pat Narduzzi's chagrin, with all three going over the 100-yard mark in the same game. The trio combined for 22 catches for 397 yards in the victory.

Ford parlayed his three years of success into entering the NFL Draft a year early, going in the seventh round of the 2017 Draft to the Miami Dolphins. Hodges also left early and was picked by the Vikings in Round 6.

That opened up an opportunity for Phillips to emerge from Ford's shadow and be Tech's go-to receiver in 2017. The senior obliged, getting off to a roaring start with a nation's-best 523 receiving yards in the first four weeks, including a program-record 14-catch performance that included 189 yards and three touchdowns against East Carolina.

A sports hernia injury limited Phillips' effectiveness for part of the year, and he had to miss the Hokies' bowl game after needing surgery, but he still caught 71 passes for 964 yards and seven touchdowns.

Notable Virginia Tech Receiving Records

Most passes caught in a game: Cam Phillips, 14 (at East Carolina in 2017)
Most passes caught in a season: Isaiah Ford, 79 (2016)
Most passes caught in a career: Cam Phillips, 236 (2014–17)
Most yards in a game: Ernest Wilford, 279 (at Syracuse in 2002)
Most yards in a season: Isaiah Ford, 1,164 (2016)
Most yards in a career: Cam Phillips, 3,027 (2014–17)
Most touchdowns in a game: Ernest Wilford, 4 (at Syracuse in 2002)
Most touchdowns in a season: Isaiah Ford, 11 (2015)
Most touchdowns in a career: Isaiah Ford, 24 (2014–16)
Best average per catch in a season (min. 20 catches): André Davis, 27.5 (1999)
Best average per catch in a career: Ricky Scales, 20.1 (1972–74)

All in all, Ford and Phillips' names are etched in Virginia Tech's record books. Although Ford out-paced Phillips his first three years, Phillips' longevity put him atop the Hokies' all-time receiving list, with 236 receptions and 3,027 yards. Ford is No. 2 with 210 catches for 2,967 yards, though his 24 touchdowns are still the most in Virginia Tech history. Phillips' 17 receiving touchdowns rank seventh. Hodges, meanwhile, had 1,747 yards and 20 touchdowns in his career, numbers that rank 12th and third all-time.

Even though Phillips chased down Ford's records, Ford was supportive the whole time.

"Our relationship is still the same as it's ever been," Phillips said. "We're brothers, really. He already knew it wouldn't be much to break the records. He's saying, 'It should be easy for you to get them.' But no hostility. Nothing like that. Records are made to be broken anyway, so I'm glad I'm the one to do it."

92 The Hokies Finally Beat Bobby Bowden and Florida State

Frank Beamer had accomplished nearly everything in his coaching career by 2007, but one team was an ever-present burr in his saddle. He simply could not get over the hump against Bobby Bowden and Florida State.

That was no great shame. The Seminoles were *the* program of the late '80s and '90s, with an incredible run of 14 consecutive Top 5 finishes. They victimized Virginia Tech repeatedly, understandably so while Beamer was building up the Hokies into a national power early in his run, but more excruciatingly once Tech got really good.

FSU beat Virginia Tech in the 2000 Bowl Championship Series title game in the Sugar Bowl, though the Hokies, led by Michael Vick, actually took a 29–28 lead into the fourth quarter of that contest. The 'Noles beat the Hokies in the 2002 Gator Bowl and again in the inaugural ACC title game in 2005, when No. 5 Virginia Tech was two-touchdown favorites against four-loss FSU. That loss dropped Beamer to 0–7 all-time against Bowden.

That all changed in 2007. Both coaches were well on their way to the Hall of Fame by then, but this matchup felt different—nearly everyone agreed that the Hokies were a better team than a far-from-vintage FSU squad that would go on to lose five games that season.

"Everyone understood if the Hokies didn't win that game, when was Coach Beamer ever going to beat Coach Bowden?" longtime Hokies broadcaster Bill Roth said.

Virginia Tech dished out some payback with a hard-hitting defensive performance and one of the first breakout performances by a freshman quarterback named Tyrod Taylor.

Taylor had split duties with Sean Glennon that year, thrust into action after the Hokies' offensive line was exposed in a 48–7 loss to LSU in Week 2, but he hadn't really starred in any game to that point. He showed his playmaking abilities early on a third-and-31. Tech called a simple QB draw play, hoping to recoup some yards in field position. Instead, Taylor juked his way for 38 yards and a first down, giving birth to a legend.

Glennon got knocked woozy on a quarterback keeper a few plays later, making it Taylor's show. He didn't disappoint, throwing for 204 yards and two touchdowns and running for 92 more yards and another score.

Tyrod Taylor runs away from Florida State's Emmanuel Dunbar on a scramble during Virginia Tech's 40–21 win over Florida State. (AP Photo / Don Petersen, File)

"I didn't expect to see the second coming of Vick," Bowden said afterward. "We couldn't tackle that guy. We'd get in a position—on that third-and-a-million, he ran. Couldn't tackle him."

Virginia Tech's defenders came primed to tackle and with some oomph behind it. Cornerback Brandon Flowers knocked out starting FSU quarterback Drew Weatherford with a double forearm shiver early on. Safety Kam Chancellor de-cleated running back Russell Ball on a hard hit on the sideline after a long gain on a screen pass.

"When Florida State had the football, it was a really violent game," Roth said. "Because our guys were like missiles."

Florida State being Florida State, however, things weren't going to come easy. Like a horror-film villain, the Seminoles wouldn't die, rallying from a 20–6 halftime deficit to take a 21–20 lead after linebacker Dekoda Watson intercepted a ball on a tipped pass and returned it for a touchdown and backup quarterback Christian Ponder hit De'Cody Fagg with a touchdown pass.

The Hokies didn't wilt. Taylor provided a response, rolling to his left away from pressure early in the fourth quarter and, with the flick of a wrist, delivering a perfectly-placed pass on the run to Justin Harper up the sideline for a 45-yard gain. Taylor scored on a touchdown run a few plays later to make it 28–21 Hokies.

They added a field goal before defensive end Chris Ellis put the game away. With Florida State backed up near its own goal line, Ellis halted his pass rush after recognizing that the Seminoles were going to throw a screen to a receiver, baiting Ponder into throwing an interception that the senior returned five yards for a touchdown, keeping his balance despite stumbling and barrel-rolling into the end zone as Lane Stadium erupted.

"It was unreal," Harper said. "Because it was kind of like you knew. You knew it was over and you knew that Coach Beamer kind of got the monkey off his back against Coach Bowden. It was special."

The Hokies ended up winning 40–21, with TV cameras catching an emotional Beamer giving a big exhale on the sideline in the final minutes as players and coaches came up one-by-one go hug him and offer congratulations. Even though it wasn't a great Seminoles squad, the win still meant a lot.

"We had gotten over the hump with Miami a little bit, but we had never gotten over the hump with Florida State," defensive coordinator Bud Foster said. "And I think that made a statement for us as a program at that time, that maybe we were for real in the ACC. And we can compete with the top programs, the elite programs in the ACC."

Bowden would beat Beamer one more time before he retired, winning 30–20 in Tallahassee the following year to run his record against Beamer to 8–1. But Beamer still has the 2007 game to point to.

"That win meant a lot," Roth said, "not only to the guys on the '07 team, but the '99 team and the '89 team and '88 team, and all those other guys that came so close to beating Florida State but didn't. Because there were sometimes where Tech had a chance to beat Bowden but never did until that day."

93 The No. 25 Jersey

Seeking a way to honor his predecessor—Hall of Fame coach Frank Beamer—Justin Fuente huddled with Beamer's longtime right-hand man John Ballein to come up with a worthy tribute before he ever coached a game in Blacksburg.

One of Beamer's greatest legacies as a football coach was his contributions to special teams, so the two of them came up with an idea that was a nod to that: each week, the Hokies would honor Beamer by awarding his old No. 25 to a standout special teams player from the week of practice. Beamer wore that number while he was a defensive back at Virginia Tech from 1966 to '68.

"It is something that I think shows we take great pride in the past and want to continue to pay tribute to the way ball has been played here for quite some time," Fuente said.

"Someone wearing that jersey, I think it makes a big statement to kind of tie in the old with the new and thus keeping with the tradition of being dynamic on special teams," said defensive coordinator Bud Foster, who coached with Beamer for more than three decades. "I think that's a pretty neat deal."

The tradition quickly caught on, with Fuente and his staff making a big deal about announcing it each Thursday in front of the entire team, building up to the reveal with some complimentary words about whoever is about to get it. The players, particularly those who played for Beamer in his later years, are always eager to receive the honor.

"You stand out when you wear No. 25," said defensive tackle Tim Settle, who wore it in Week 3 in 2016 against Boston College. "Everyone knows what it means—that you're a big part of the team when you wear No. 25."

The first year the Hokies rolled out the new tradition, whoever wore the jersey seemed to play especially well in it.

Greg Stroman wore it in Week 4 against East Carolina and turned in a star performance, returning a punt 87 yards for a touchdown to jumpstart a 54–17 rout. The Hokies also blocked two kicks that day, as "Beamer Ball" of an effort as you could have asked for, showing that Fuente and special teams coordinator James Shibest's commitment to special teams isn't just lip service.

"(Fuente's) trying to keep 'Beamer Ball' alive, and that's a big part of the game anyway," Stroman said. "He emphasizes going hard like Coach Beamer did."

There were several other notable performances by players wearing the number in the first year of the tradition, with safety Divine Deablo recovering a fumble on a kickoff in a 39–36 win at Pitt and receiver C.J. Carroll jumpstarting a second-half comeback at Notre Dame with a 62-yard catch in the third quarter of a 34–31 win.

But the pièce de résistance came in the regular season finale when fullback Sam Rogers, who Beamer brought in as a walk-on in 2013 and was someone who thrived on special teams his entire career, suited up in the No. 25 on Senior Day in Lane Stadium against rival Virginia.

Rogers, who spent nearly his entire career primarily as a blocker or pass-catcher out of the backfield, served as the team's primary ballcarrier that day, running for a career-high 105 yards and two touchdowns as the Hokies routed the Cavaliers 52–10. (Hours later, he proposed to his girlfriend in a nearly empty Lane Stadium.)

"Coach Beamer means so much to me, my family, and the guys in this locker room," Rogers said afterward. "So, it's a huge honor wearing that number."

Though the tradition had extra meaning for players who had a connection to Beamer, whether through their recruitment or actually playing for him, Fuente hopes it serves a larger purpose going forward, educating players who were never linked to the Beamer era about why special teams is held in such high regard in Blacksburg.

It's not a one-time deal, nor is it only for skill players. Stroman wore it three times in his career, as did defensive tackle Ricky Walker. (The only players who can't, because of number restrictions, are offensive linemen.)

Though not a steadfast rule, the Hokies have given the number to a senior leader for their final home game of each season. Rogers wore it in 2016, linebacker Andrew Motuapuaka in 2017, and Walker in 2018. Each one turned in a standout performance to help the Hokies win.

"When we decided to do this, I felt like the fans and the people who love Virginia Tech would appreciate it," Fuente said. "But I really wanted the kids to get excited about it and take great pride in it, and they certainly have. And the way that those guys have played, wearing that jersey has just contributed to that, which has been a neat thing."

94 Don Strock and Logan Thomas

Though they played 40 years apart, Don Strock and Logan Thomas have plenty in common. They both played quarterback at Virginia Tech. They both put up volume numbers that are still all over the Hokies' record books today. And they both carved out pretty good NFL careers for themselves, though in vastly different ways.

Strock, who played for the Hokies from 1970 to '72, was an outlier in his time at Tech, a school whose offensive history is almost entirely predicated on running the ball. As the quarterback in Charlie Coffey's wide-open offense, he threw for 6,009 yards in three years, tops in school history at the time.

During his senior season, Strock threw for 3,243 yards and 16 touchdowns, leading the nation in passing and total offense. He also threw 40 more passes than anyone in college football that year, finishing ninth in the Heisman Trophy voting and taking home the Sammy Baugh Trophy as the nation's top passer.

Some bad came with the good, throwing that much. Though Strock threw for a school record in yards and touchdowns (29), he also threw 47 career interceptions, including a 27 during his senior year, an unfathomable figure by today's standards.

Even with today's more wide-open offenses, Strock remains fourth on the Hokies' all-time passing list and still holds the record for passing yards per game for a season (294.8). He had one of the most memorable single-game performances in Tech history, completing 34 passes for 527 yards, both school marks, in a 27-all tie against Houston in 1972.

Strock wasn't a superstar in the NFL after being selected in the fifth round of the 1973 Draft by the Miami Dolphins, but he carved out a nice pro career as a backup, first to Bob Griese and later to Dan Marino. He won a Super Bowl ring with the Dolphins in 1974.

He had his moments, most famously for coming off the bench in the 1982 AFC Divisional Playoff Game against the San Diego Chargers (also known as the "Epic in Miami" or the Kellen Winslow game), throwing for 403 yards and four touchdowns in a 41–38 overtime loss. It's widely considered one of the best games in NFL history.

In his 15-year NFL career, Strock played in 167 games, starting 22, and threw for 5,349 yards, 45 touchdowns, and 42 interceptions. He later coached at Florida International for five years.

Thomas had a similar high-volume career at Virginia Tech, though his path there was a little more winding to get there. The eventual 6-foot-6, 250-pounder was a standout quarterback at Brookville High in Lynchburg but was recruited as a tight end—one of the top recruits in the state in the 2009 class.

When he got to Blacksburg, the Hokies pulled the ol' switcheroo, trying him out at quarterback, liking the way he threw the ball and setting him up to be the heir apparent to Tyrod Taylor.

That time came after Taylor exhausted his eligibility after the 2010 season, and Thomas had a breakout redshirt sophomore season in 2011, throwing for 3,013 yards to go with 19 touchdowns and adding another 469 yards and 11 scores on the ground for a team that went 11–3 and played in the Sugar Bowl.

The hype train got a hold of Thomas, who was mentioned as a possible future Top 5 draft pick that off-season, though with a dwindling supporting cast and ongoing accuracy issues, he had a tough time living up to it.

With record-setting running back David Wilson off to the NFL and no clear successor in backfield, Thomas had to shoulder much of the Hokies' rushing load, too. He led the team in passing and rushing in 2012, a year in which he broke his own school record for total offense (3,500), a mark that stood until Jerod Evans broke it in 2016.

Thomas ended up finishing with 10,362 total yards in his career, topping Taylor's school mark by over 1,000. He also threw

Charlie Coffey's Aerial Attack

Virginia Tech's offense has been grounded, quite literally, for most of its football history, but the Hokies briefly departed from a line of Bear Bryant-inspired coaches who loved the wishbone when it hired Charlie Coffey to replace Jerry Claiborne in 1971.

What occurred the next three years was an aerial attack, with quarterback Don Strock throwing the ball at will in Dan Henning's offense.

Hokies pass-catchers thrived. Mike Burnop, now a beloved radio analyst, caught a team-record 46 passes as a tight end in 1971. Donnie Reel led the team in receiving yards with 705, at a time when no Tech player had topped 500 before that.

While Strock led the nation in total offense in 1972, one of the Hokies' first real deep threats emerged in Ricky Scales, who'd lead Tech in receiving yards from 1972 to '74. By the time Scales finished his career, he was the school's all-time leader in receptions (113), receiving yards (2,272), and receiving touchdowns (18), marks that would last one to three decades before being broken.

Tech peaked under Coffey with a 6–4–1 record in 1972, upsetting No. 19 Oklahoma State in Blacksburg. After a 2–9 record in 1973, Coffey was out, replaced by another Bryant protégé in Jimmy Sharpe who'd return to Tech's more conservative offenses.

more completions (693), touchdowns (53), and for more yards (9,003) than anybody in Hokies history, though Tech struggled to a 15–11 record in his final two seasons, dealing with an overhaul to the offensive coaching staff between 2012 and '13.

"Logan's been a really positive player for Virginia Tech," coach Frank Beamer said. "We haven't always had consistent people around Logan, but I think he's got a great ability."

Thomas was picked in the fourth round of the 2014 NFL Draft by the Arizona Cardinals and coach Bruce Arians, a former Hokie, though his quarterback career never took off. After bouncing around the league for three years, he latched on with Buffalo, which had him play the position he was supposed to in college—tight end. He's found his niche there, sticking on the Bills' roster in 2017 and '18 and catching 19 passes for 144 yards and a touchdown. He signed with Detroit in 2019.

95 Miracle on Dirt

Angela Tincher is a pitching legend in Blacksburg, raised locally in Botetourt County outside of Roanoke, starring at James River High School and doing the same at Virginia Tech from 2005 to '08.

Tincher holds 57 school records and led the Hokies to the program's only Women's College World Series appearance in 2008, when she was the USA Softball National Player of the Year. And she's still the ACC's career leader in wins (123), strikeouts (2,149), shutouts (54), innings pitched (1,116.1), and no-hitters (14).

Her biggest moment of national fame, however, will be in 2008, when she pitched a 10-strikeout no-hitter in a 1–0 victory against the U.S. women's national team, snapping the squad's 185-game winning streak.

It's since been dubbed the "Miracle on Dirt" in Blacksburg circles, memorialized with a 2017 school-produced documentary by that name.

The game took place on March 26, 2008, in Oklahoma City, Oklahoma, a mid-week exhibition between ACC series for the Hokies. For Team USA, it was a tune-up for the Beijing Olympics. The squad was a three-time defending Olympic gold medalists, having won it all in Atlanta in 2004.

The exhibition circuit hadn't been particularly daunting for Team USA. Just before it played Virginia Tech, the U.S. walloped a ranked DePaul team 23–0, running its "Bound 4 Beijing" tour record to 17–0. Since its last loss in pre-Olympic exhibitions back in 1996, Team USA had outscored its opponents 1,475–24.

"It was such an experience no matter what happened," Tincher said years later in the documentary. "It was going to be something that we remember forever."

Jennie Finch, the face of USA Softball who pitched the U.S. to gold in Atlanta in 2004, was Tincher's opposition in the circle, but it was the Virginia Tech right-hander who stole the show.

Tincher might have foreshadowed her performance years earlier, before she was even at Virginia Tech. As a member of a Salem (Va.), All-Star team in 2004, she pitched in an exhibition game against Team USA. She ended up giving up two runs in an inning of work, but the 18-year-old struck out the first batter she faced, slugger Stacey Nuveman, on three pitches.

Tincher had Olympic hopes in 2008 but didn't make the team, with Team USA already having a stacked pitching rotation. But she showed them what they were missing out on that March night.

"She had nothing to lose, but she had everything to prove, that, 'Hey, I deserve to be in that uniform too,'" Hokies coach Scot Thomas said.

Tincher struck out the first two batters she faced, then got Jessica Mendoza, arguably the top hitter in the world at the time, to ground out to second to get through the first.

Virginia Tech gave her a 1–0 lead in the top of the second, getting a leadoff double from Kelsey Hoffman. Pinch runner Anna Zitt moved to third on an illegal pitch and scored on Caroline Stolle's two-out bloop single.

Incredibly, that was all the offense Tincher needed. She pitched around a one-out walk in the second—the only Team USA runner to reach base all night—repeating her 2004 feat by striking out Nuveman on three pitches to strand a runner at second.

Tincher was only supposed to pitch three innings in the exhibition, but after she got through the third with ease, having faced 10 batters, striking out five of them and allowing no hits, Thomas kept her in.

She continued to keep the world's best offense at bay. Tincher fanned Team USA's first two batters, Caitlin Lowe and Natasha Watley, twice in the game. She cruised through the sixth, getting a strikeout, a ground out, and a pop-up to head into the seventh and final inning up 1–0 with the no-hitter intact. She'd retired 14 straight at that point.

"Every inning that went by was such a blur," Tincher said. "But it was just so much fun, too."

The speedy Watley tapped a ball to third to lead off the ninth, with third baseman Charisse Mariconda throwing her out by a hair at first. Mendoza was next, striking out looking on a 3–2 pitch.

That brought up slugger Crystl Bustos, who had 21 home runs in her international career to that point, capable of tying the game with one swing. On a 2–1 pitch, Tincher got her to pop out to short, completing the no-hitter. The Hokies ran onto the field to mob Tincher, who was smiling ear to ear.

"It was like, 'Did it really happen?'" Tincher said. "You hoped that it could happen and the closer you got the final out, you felt like we had a shot. But just to see it pop up in the infield and that be it, I don't think it ever sunk in."

Tincher's final line was impressive, doubly so considering the lineup she shut down: seven innings, no hits, one walk, and 10 strikeouts. Team USA, which would go on to win silver in Beijing, never got the ball out of the infield.

"I felt good. I felt confident, at least in the sense that I was prepared," said Tincher, who described it as the game of a lifetime. "But I definitely didn't expect to do that well."

96 Do the Run in Remembrance

April 16 is a solemn day in Blacksburg, a day of remembrance for the 32 lives lost in the tragic shooting on campus in 2007. And while the Virginia Tech community mourns the victims in an annual ceremony on a weekend around the date, it also tries to create something positive out of the tragedy and aid the healing process.

The annual Run in Remembrance, which started two years after the shooting in 2009, is one of the university's signature events every April. It's a 3.2-mile run through campus, slightly longer than a 5K, to honor the 32 victims from the shooting.

The race is for runners, joggers, and walkers of any skill level. The point isn't to win but rather foster a sense of community by bringing Hokies together to celebrate the vibrant lives of friends and family members lost.

The rain-or-shine event, which is hosted by the school's Department of Recreational Sports, has had several routes but recently has started on the Drillfield near War Memorial Gym. Runners gather rows deep with orange and maroon balloon arches overhead, standing behind a "3.2 for 32" banner that participants get to sign with a Sharpie.

The start of the run in the mid-morning isn't signified with a starting pistol or other loud noise, like typical races. Instead, after a moment of silence lasting 32 seconds is observed to honor the lives lost, the first wave of racers are signaled to start. The organizers have released 32 white balloons into the air to signify the start of the event in the past.

The participants then head out in waves, with faster runners leading the way, though everyone enjoys the route at their own pace. Some people jog. Some walk. Parents will push their kids in strollers for the three-plus miles. Members of the school's Corps of Cadets sometimes try to make it more of a challenge. In 2017, seven of them did the route while carrying a giant log on their shoulders.

The run always includes a portion through Lane Stadium, down the famed tunnel where the football team lines up for its iconic "Enter Sandman" entrance before home games. It allows all the participants to slap the Hokie Stone slab as they exit the tunnel and head out to run alongside Wes Worsham field for a stretch.

The 2018 event finished at the April 16 Memorial back near the Drillfield across from Burruss Hall, where 32 Hokie Stones weighing 300 pounds each are arranged in a semi-circle with the names of each of the victims. A large group photo of all the participants is taken at the conclusion of the event.

The event's planners have also arranged in recent years for runners to gather in formations on the Drillfield, lining up in the shape of a giant VT logo one year and in a remembrance ribbon in another, something that's been captured in a time-lapse video.

The run has grown in popularity over the years. An estimated 4,000 runners participated in the first one in 2009. In 2019, the school put the number up around 14,500, all of them there as a reminder that neither Virginia Tech nor Blacksburg will ever forget.

97 Wayne Ward's Block

Wayne Ward was a running back for Virginia Tech around the turn of the century, though almost all of his playing time came on special teams. It's there that his legacy lives on to this day for one particular crushing block.

His famous moment came in the 2000 West Virginia game. The unbeaten Hokies, as was their trademark, had already made a big special teams play earlier in the game, when Lee Suggs came up the middle to block a punt in the first quarter that Ward picked up and almost returned for a touchdown.

Tech would find the end zone on a punt later in the game. The Hokies led 27–14 late in the third quarter when West Virginia lined up to punt from its own 37. Lane Stadium was already buzzing after the block earlier in the game, clamoring for another.

Instead, Virginia Tech set up the return. André Davis, a burner who was one of the most feared punt returners in school history, camped under a 39-yard punt from WVU's Mark Fazzolari at his own 24 with room to run.

He took off laterally from the middle of the field to his right toward the West Virginia sideline. Mountaineers linebacker Kyle Kayden tracked him, a couple steps behind. Just as he closed in and Davis started upfield, Ward leveled Kayden with a perfectly clean, textbook, jaw-rattling decleater of a block that sprung Davis free for what would be a 76-yard return for a touchdown.

The hit was so good, you could hear the Lane Stadium crowd audibly gasp as Ward hit Kayden, then explode in noise as Davis raced free up the sideline.

"Virginia Tech sets up for the return, trying to go for the knockout punch with Davis returning," was broadcaster Mike

Tirico's call, just before Ward did just that. "Got an unbelievable block! Davis is gone!"

While some teammates ran after Davis to celebrate in the end zone, many more mobbed Ward on the sideline, fully understanding who made the play happen.

"Did you get the number of that truck?" Tirico asked analyst Kirk Herbstreit after letting the celebration play out for a while.

"Put your seatbelt on at home, because this one's going to get a little bit scary," Herbstreit said as the replay showed. "Davis moves over to the right. Now keep an eye on No. 45, because he's going to get knocked into next week by Wayne Ward. He got leveled. Kayden's a linebacker, but I don't think he's gotten hit that hard in his entire life."

Davis, whose 15.9-yard return average for a career is still tops in Virginia Tech history and who had four punt returns for touchdowns with the Hokies, remembers that one distinctly.

"I tell people all the time I can literally remember the audible change in tone as I'm sitting there trying to make my moves," he said. "I remember coming around a guy, I heard the hit, but I remember specifically hearing the crowd change, and I was just like, 'I really wish I could turn around and watch and see what just happened.' But I'm like, 'Man, I'm still running. I need to keep this going and take this to the house right now.'

"When you see the video, you see me run into the end zone, run all the way across the end zone, all the way back to our sideline trying to figure out what happened, who was the one who made that hit. And then you see everyone smacking Wayne's head on the sideline. I think there were more people congratulating Wayne on the hit than they were for me on the touchdown."

If you could encapsulate Beamer Ball into one play, that might be it—an unheralded player doing the grunt work that led to a big play, with everyone on the sideline recognizing who made it happen.

Ward ended up blocking four punts in his career, putting him in a tie for the fourth-most blocked kicks under Frank Beamer, but he'll be forever remembered and will live on in YouTube glory for a play in which he never even touched the ball.

98 Eat a Smoked Turkey Leg at Lane Stadium

It's a philosophical question that's flummoxed Hokies football fans for more than a decade and a half when smokey turkey legs started to take off in popularity at concession stands around Lane Stadium.

It is really okay to eat your mascot?

Perhaps Virginia Tech fans can take solace in the fact that no HokieBirds have been harmed in the preparation of the giant smoked turkey legs served in the stadium over the years.

One whiff of the smoke emanating from the grills in the corner of the stadium or a taste of the juicy meat might be enough to make you forget about the cannibalistic conundrum altogether, however.

The unique gameday delicacy started to be served in Blacksburg in the early 2000s, at first spread out to several stands around Lane Stadium until they were considered a fire hazard and consolidated down to one giant, can't-miss grill in an open corner between the east stands and south end zone. Look for the sign that says "Smokin' Hokie Legs" or simply let your nose help you follow the wafts of smoke that smell so good.

With one grill, it was initially hard for the supply of meat to meet demand, though the workers operating the stand—who, according to a 2013 *Collegiate Times* article, are from God's House in Pembroke, Virginia, and get a small percentage of the profits to go toward the church's youth group—have a system down.

The legs arrive already cooked and frozen. They're thawed in a refrigerator two days before the game and on gameday are cooked at 165 degrees for 45 minutes in giant smokers. Workers wrap them in aluminum foil when they're done and place them on warmers or hand them out directly to waiting customers.

For 10 dollars, you get a substantial amount of bird—it's a 1½- to two-pound hunk of meat that looks like it's straight out of the caveman's cookbook—and there doesn't seem to be any shortage of demand. The stand sells around 1,000 succulent legs a game.

It's become part of the tradition of going to Lane Stadium for many fans. It even appears on the Hokie Bucket List, a collaboration of things every student should do in their college days put together by the alumni association and student alumni associates.

If you're skittish about chowing down on something that a little too closely resembles the school's mascot, consider all the turkeys Virginia Tech goes to great lengths to protect.

You know the fortunate fowls the president "pardons" every year around Thanksgiving? Since 2016 the lucky birds have been housed at Gobblers Rest, a home created for them at Virginia Tech's College of Agriculture and Life Sciences. "Peas" and its wingman "Carrots" were the two contestants to come on down in 2018 to Blacksburg, where they get around-the-clock care.

So don't feel guilty in the slightest about gnawing on a foil-wrapped hunk of meat when watching the Hokies play football. Just be sure to grab a few extra napkins and bring a healthy appetite.

99 The 1947 Sun Bowl Team

Long before Virginia Tech and Frank Beamer made going to a bowl game a birthright for its fans—heck, long before Beamer even went to a bowl game as a player for the Hokies—a VPI team that went 3–3–3 during the regular season was the first ever at the school to play in the postseason.

"I think it's probably the most unique team in Tech history," said Ross Orr, a tackle and place-kicker on the team who recounted the team's journey when the Hokies went back to the Sun Bowl in 2013 to play UCLA.

It was a different era of sports in America, with Virginia Tech shuttering its football program, which was populated primarily by the Corps of Cadets, in the 1943 and '44 seasons as the United States got pulled into World War II. The Gobblers returned to the field with a fresh-faced group of 17- and 18-year-olds dubbed the "Beardless Wonders" who went 2–6 in 1945. (Their claim to fame was that they beat a "Bear" Bryant coached Maryland team 21–13, Tech's only win against Bryant.)

As soldiers returned from war, the roster got a major makeover in 1946. Thirty-five veterans, many of them decorated soldiers of war, were on the team, with only 10 holdovers from the previous year.

Led by team captain William Elmer Wilson, the team wasn't overwhelming, going 3–3–3 in the regular season, but the Gobblers tied a North Carolina team that would finish No. 9 in the country and upset No. 12 N.C. State 14–6 in late October, the program's first win against a ranked team. The team finished the year with a 20–7 win against rival VMI in Roanoke.

"We didn't have the greatest record in the world, but we beat the good teams, we tied the great teams, and we barely got beat by a couple other teams," said Ray Beasley, a halfback. "It was a funny season."

As it turned out, that wasn't the team's last game. The Sun Bowl, which was one of only 11 postseason games at the time, needed an opponent to play 8–2 Cincinnati after Hardin-Simmons and Texas Tech declined. A Virginia Tech alum named Marion Adams was on the Sun Bowl committee and suggested the Gobblers. The school received $9,438 (the equivalent of over $100,000 in today's money) to play in the January 1 game.

Not only was it the first bowl game for VPI, but it was also the first bowl game ever for a team from the Commonwealth of Virginia.

The weather could have been better. Winter weather hit Blacksburg before the team left and once the team got to El Paso, even though it hadn't snowed in the city in decades. Travel wasn't a piece of cake either. The Gobblers loaded up two American DC-3s on a flight plan that included stops in Knoxville, Memphis, and Fort Worth before arriving in Big Spring, Texas, where the team bused the final 350 miles to El Paso because of storms.

The bowl, as it did today, rolled out the red carpets. The Gobblers stayed at the Hotel Cortez, one of the city's best establishments, went to two Texas ranch breakfast parties and made a trip across the border to Juarez to see the world renown Spanish bullfighter Manolete, months before he'd be gored to death.

The game didn't have a Hollywood ending. Kidd Field was already covered in frozen rain when three inches of snow fell on top of it the night before the game, making it tough to play football.

"It was the worst weather I think I've ever seen a football game played in," Beasley said.

In front of a crowd of 10,000, Cincinnati easily handled Virginia Tech, which was playing without injured star halfback and punter Bobby Smith. The Bearcats rolled up 463 yards, getting 369 on the ground, in an 18–6 win.

VPI blocked three extra points and a punt and got a 3-yard touchdown run by Ralph Beard in the fourth quarter, but the Gobblers never got much going offensively, finishing with only 119 yards.

"I don't know if we would have done better on a dry field or not," Orr said. "But you never know."

It'd mark the school's last bowl game for 20 years, until Tech went to the 1966 Liberty Bowl under coach Jerry Claiborne. As such, that 1946 team that extended its season into 1947 for the Sun Bowl holds a special place in school history.

Showing how much different of a time it was, Orr turned down a chance at a professional football career to become a vascular surgeon, developing the program at St. Luke's Hospital in Bethlehem, Pennsylvania, before he retired. He died in 2015.

Of the 46 members on the team, it's believed 45 of them graduated from Virginia Tech.

"They were students, in addition to football," Orr said. "And football was just not the overwhelming thing on campus like it is today. And I'm proud of that more than anything else."

100 Danny Coale Caught the Ball!

No. 17 Virginia Tech had not played perfectly in the 2012 Sugar Bowl against No. 13 Michigan, squandering several chances in regulation to win a game it had dominated in yardage. But the Hokies appeared as though they'd cap the 2011 season with an overtime

Bowl Championship Game victory, only the second under Frank Beamer in the 14-year history of the postseason format.

On third-and-5 from the 20-yard line on the Hokies' overtime possession, quarterback Logan Thomas looked in the direction of senior Danny Coale, the school's second all-time leading receiver at the time, who had eight catches for 117 yards to that point in his final college game.

Coale made a diving, one-handed snag on a pass in the end zone right near the Virginia Tech sideline, reeling it in and securing the ball with two hands as his elbow hit the ground in bounds before he bounced and slid toward a row of photographers.

The officials on the field immediately ruled it a touchdown, one that appeared to give the Hokies a 26–20 lead, with the extra point pending.

That's when a name entered the picture that'll live in infamy in Virginia Tech circles: Jim Fogltance. After several minutes of review in the booth, the replay official on the Pac-12 crew overturned the call and ruled the pass incomplete, saying that Coale did not maintain control of the ball as he went out of bounds, despite no clear evidence to support it.

Virginia Tech had to settle for a 37-yard field goal attempt that Justin Myer pushed wide to the right. Needing only a field goal to win on its ensuing possession, the Wolverines ran three times to set up a 37-yard field goal by Brendan Gibbons that won the game for Michigan 23–20.

The loss dropped Beamer to 1–5 in BCS games in his career and ended a strong season on a sour note. The Hokies, who began the year 11–1 and rose as high as No. 3 in the coaches poll, finished the season 11–3 and on a two-game losing streak, ranked 21st and 17th in the final polls.

The fan base quickly directed its ire at Fogltance. ACC supervisor of officials Doug Rhoads said publicly that there wasn't indisputable evidence necessary to overturn the call on the field, which was a touchdown. Virginia Tech athletic director Jim Weaver proposed adding a second replay official to conference championship and BCS games.

"Indisputable is a high standard," Rhoads told the *Daily Press*. "If you don't know, then you don't know, and you stay with the call on the field. The philosophy of replay is, it's right on the field. That's where the heart of the game is still played. Had they ruled it incomplete, it should have stayed incomplete. I saw nothing that rose to the level of indisputable."

The play unwittingly served as a line of demarcation in the latter Beamer years. The Hokies never got back to a BCS game after that and didn't again approach the program's lofty but consistent standard of 10 wins under the legendary coach, going 7–6, 8–5, 7–6, and 7–6 in his final four seasons.

After the controversial finish, Virginia Tech and Michigan agreed the following year to play a home-and-home series in 2020 and '21, a chance, many Hokies fans thought, to settle the score for the perceived Coale robbery. The Wolverines backed out of the agreement in March 2018, however.

Still, the memory of the play lives on. Bring up Michigan or that Sugar Bowl to any true Virginia Tech fan and you're bound to get the exact same fiery response: "Danny Coale caught the ball!"